M000094503

The keyword is CLUBS
Nearly there.
Now which letter is the odd one out?
CLAVMIX

KING OF CLUBS

KING
OF
CLUBS

PETER STRINGFELLOW
with
FIONA LAFFERTY

LITTLE, BROWN AND COMPANY

A *Little, Brown* Book

First published in Great Britain in 1996
by Little, Brown and Company

Copyright © 1996 by Peter Stringfellow and Fiona Lafferty

Picture credits

Every effort has been made to trace original copyright holders of
uncredited photographs not from private collections. Should anyone consider
his or her work to have been reproduced without proper authority then he or
she is invited to contact the publisher.

16. Sheffield Newspapers; 18. Richard Young; 21. Keith Butcher;
22. *News of the World*; 23. Keith Butcher; 28. Robin Kaplan;
29. Lance Jeffrey; 30. Lance Jeffrey; 31. Robin Kaplan; 32. People in
Pictures Ltd; 33. Alexander Sibaja; 34. Doug McKenzie;
40. Richard Young/Rex Features

A CIP catalogue record for this book
is available from the British Library.

ISBN: 0 316 87933 9

Typeset by Solidus (Bristol) Limited
Printed and bound in Great Britain
by Clays Ltd, St Ives plc

Little, Brown and Company (UK)
Brettenham House
Lancaster Place
London WC2E 7EN

To my mum and dad, James and Elsie;
my two children, Scott and Karen;
and my grandson, Taylor

CONTENTS

PREFACE

I've been asked for my life-story many times over the years, yet I never thought the time was right. Since opening Stringfellow's in London, I've always had a new project on the go. First it was the Hippodrome, then Stringfellow's in New York, Miami and Los Angeles, and then back to London. When I first started this project with Fiona Lafferty in May 1995, my life was more settled. I wasn't travelling as much and I knew that I had at least a year before the Cabaret of Angels opened.

I'm always amazed at the number of people who want to write their autobiographies before they've lived their lives. I've waited until my mid-fifties, and I know that I've got a great story to tell. In many ways it's been an astonishing experience. I'm not at all a retrospective person, so this is probably the first time I've sat down and indulged in a bit of nostalgia. At times it's been quite painful, especially reliving some of my experiences with the critical eye of hindsight, yet having said that there's nothing in my life I regret. On balance, the good times have outweighed the bad. People sometimes refer to my 'failed' marriages, but that's not how I look at them. My marriage to Coral was a great success. Sure, it ended, but then all good stories come to an end.

I'm amazed at how many stories I've had to cut – not for reasons of censorship, but through lack of space. I'd like to thank all the people I've mentioned in the book; they've all enriched my life in some way and I hope they enjoy the stories – especially Roger Howe, my brother Geoffrey, and Pat Jay.

I'd like to thank Fiona for her patience. I don't want anyone to think that I sat down and wrote this book myself – I'm a story-teller, but without her help I'd probably still be on the first paragraph of chapter one. From meeting her as a journalist she has now become one of my closest friends. I never thought I'd enjoy having a platonic relationship with a beautiful girl, but it happened.

Perhaps the most difficult part was knowing when to stop. The curtain is about to go up on the Cabaret of Angels, so I know, once again, that my life is going to change dramatically.

Peter Stringfellow
June 1996

1

JAILHOUSE ROCK

The smell of prison has stayed with me always. That peculiar mixture of fear, sweat and excrement has left an indelible mark on my memory. The tears I'd feigned in the Sheffield courtroom finally fell for real and I knew that this was going to be the beginning or the end of Peter Stringfellow.

June 1962 was the month I was detained at Her Majesty's pleasure in Armley Prison, Leeds. Only a month earlier I'd been hailed as a superstar salesman, and now, through a mixture of naïveté and greed, I was surrounded by burglars and fraudsters.

The events which led to this sorry state of affairs began in 1961, after I went to work for a large retail company in Sheffield called Dobson's. Dobson's sold goods door-to-door and allowed its customers to pay on a weekly basis. As one debt was paid off, the collector, or tallyman, as he was known, would sell them something new. I remember the tallyman from my childhood. When Mum didn't have the money to pay we'd all hide behind the sofa.

I had been at Dobson's only a few weeks when they promoted me to sales manager. I was ecstatic at the time, but looking back, it was a big mistake. I was twenty-one years old, but mentally and physically I could have been sixteen. The first thing I did was to buy two new suits on credit and try to grow a moustache.

My first job had been to go out with the salesmen and introduce new goods to the customers. I'd be selling washing machines, carpets and cutlery sets, and all these guys wanted to do was go home. I was notorious for ruining their day. After a couple of weeks, the general manager called me into his office and told me it wasn't working. Based on my previous experience, I thought he was going to sack me. Instead he offered me my own sales force and a Bedford van. I had a free rein in the warehouse to choose whatever I fancied selling that week and I was allowed to pick my own sales team. Of course, my entire staff were women. I'd set off with twelve of them in the van and target all the housewives and young mothers at home. I immediately put up the prices to enable us to give something away, like a set of teacups or a kettle. It worked brilliantly.

After a couple of months, I noticed that no one ever checked the stock. I'd walk into the warehouse with my team of girls, and as they collected the goods – anything from teddy bears to carpets – I'd chat to the cashier. I'd tell her what we'd taken out and she'd write it down. In my previous jobs, I'd fiddled my expenses. It was part of life – that's what you did; that's what everybody did. So at Dobson's I didn't think twice about taking an extra carpet, or ten.

I persuaded one of the canvassers to keep the extra stock at her house and convinced myself it was all above board. I had no idea about monthly stocktaking and no idea that half of Dobson's sales staff were doing the same thing as I was. I had a who-cares? mentality born out of years of fiddling expenses and promotions. Around the same time I rented a furnished flat for me and my wife, Norma, and thought nothing of selling off the furniture that came with it for £35 and filling the flat with things I'd signed for on hire purchase. I admit I was stupid. I didn't know the difference between right and wrong. But who cared? I was having fun.

I had some postcard-sized fliers printed advertising the carpets at £5, and one of the canvassers helped me to stick prepaid envelopes on the back of them. I posted 300 of them through letterboxes in the more affluent parts of Sheffield and waited for the response. Not only did I deliver the fliers myself, but I used Norma's mother's address, which was ridiculous.

A few weeks later the supervisor called me into his office. Once again, I thought he was going to sack me. Instead he suggested that we did the whole thing on a bigger scale. He offered to sign the docket for a load of carpets and then destroy the evidence. We started off with contacts of his in various pubs around Sheffield. He'd find the buyers, I'd drive up in my van with the goods and we'd split the profits. This went well for a few weeks, until I bumped into Ivor Bradley, a guy I'd worked for shortly before joining Dobson's, and decided to do a deal with him. One afternoon I called him from a public callbox and told him I had £40 worth of carpets. He was keen for me to bring them straight away, so I jumped in the van and set off for his office. I was met there by a short, squat guy I'd never seen before. He asked if I had brought the carpets and wanted to see them. I opened the back of the van and he said, 'Quick, let's get them inside.' He helped me carry them into Ivor's office and the moment we got inside he said, 'Are these your carpets, Peter?'

'Where's Ivor?' I asked.

'Have you brought these carpets, Peter?'

I thought the guy was daft, as he'd just helped me carry them from the van. 'Of course they're my carpets,' I said.

'OK. You're under arrest.'

Up until that moment, I hadn't considered it stealing. To me, I was doing well for the company and doing them a favour by getting rid of their surplus stock. I'd conveniently blocked out the fact that I was keeping the money for myself.

I was in total shock at being arrested. For the first time in my life I was introduced to real detectives as opposed to bobbies on bicycles. It was all Peter this, and Peter that, which lulled me into a false sense of security. I actually liked the little guy who arrested me. Throughout my life I've attached myself to men – not in a homosexual way, it's just that men seem to like me. On this occasion I misinterpreted the detective's friendliness and told him everything he wanted to know. I was totally honest. Once I'd been caught there was no holding back. I've been like that all my life. I can think of only one time when I tried to lie my way out of a situation. It was when my second wife, Coral, found a polaroid picture of my penis, captured at the point of entry with some unknown girl. Despite the fact that the evidence spoke for itself and that Coral had been married to me for fifteen years, I maintained my innocence. Coral's interrogation tactics were certainly more terrifying than those of the Sheffield police.

They were all very friendly, with lots of cups of coffee, whereas Coral was holding a hammer at the time and I was genuinely in fear of my life. The detective's approach was a gentle 'Talk to us Peter, we're trying to help you.' And of course I believed him. The whole experience was deeply shocking, but at the same time it was exciting.

I discovered that Dobson's had brought in the fraud squad because they were losing so much stock. They'd spent weeks monitoring me, and knew I was arriving that day with my load. I realised later that Ivor Bradley must have told the police. I don't hold it against him, because he wanted to save his business and didn't have a choice.

The word 'conspiracy' was bandied about because the supervisor and one other salesman had been involved. The whole thing was a nightmare, yet I genuinely believed I'd get off with a fine. When Dad came to bail me out, he walked me back home in silence. It was his way of showing his disapproval. Mum discussed the whole thing with me and ended up taking my side. Poor Norma, who was pregnant, had known nothing about it – as far as she was concerned, I was earning the money. She never questioned where it came from.

Ivor Bradley let me work for him in the weeks before I went to court. It was probably his way of relieving his sense of guilt. He was very apologetic, and kept telling me that my arrest had nothing to do with him. I've always had a forgiving nature, so it didn't occur to me to turn down his offer of temporary employment. Anyway, I thought I would be able to get out of trouble. One of the detectives had described me as glib, which was the first time I'd heard the word. If I'd known it meant 'insincere, yet plausible', I might have been less confident.

In the intervening weeks I just got on with life. I convinced everybody, including Norma's mum and dad, that it was no big deal. Out of insouciance, or naïveté, probably a combination of the two, I didn't organise a solicitor, so on the day of the trial, the solicitor acting for one of the other guys offered to represent me. He must have done it out of the kindness of his heart, because I never paid him. He stood up for me and blamed the company. He said they should never have given a 21-year-old the degree of responsibility they gave me, especially one who lacked experience and intelligence. On the surface I was a together guy, but underneath I was just a kid. I remember the whole court case like a film I once saw. Most of it is in black and white, and a lot of the details are lost in a haze. The only colourful part was my jacket. I'd gone out and bought it especially for court. I was so naïve that I chose a bright red one. It was totally unsuitable and probably antagonised the judge more than my phoney performance in the dock. I sat and listened to the supervisor and the other salesman giving their pleas of mitigation. The supervisor started crying as he talked about his wife and three kids. He dabbed his eyes with a handkerchief and looked terribly sorry. The judge took pity on him and the other salesman and fined them £100 each. As I waited for my turn I began to calculate how much I'd be fined. I reasoned that, as I was younger and earned less, I would have to stump up between £20 and £50. I also thought I might copy the supervisor's performance and have a little weep. I stood up and told the judge that my wife was pregnant and that I was very sorry. I then got out my handkerchief and wiped my eyes. It must have been the most pathetic act of contrition he'd ever seen. He peered over his spectacles and said, 'You, Mr Stringfellow, are a different kettle of fish. I think you need a sharp lesson before you go any further.' He then sentenced me to three three-month sentences to run concurrently.

At that moment my life stopped. I had no idea what concurrent meant, and thought that I'd been given nine months in prison as opposed to three. Two policemen took hold of my arms and walked me down to the cells. As soon as I saw the gates and the bars, I burst into tears. A nice old policeman brought me a cup of tea and said, 'Drink this, sonny, it'll make you feel better.'

I remember replying, 'Nothing will make me feel better. I'm going to prison.'

'It's not that bad,' he said. 'Eight weeks will go so fast you won't even notice.'

Through the haze I thought, 'Eight weeks? What is this guy talking about?' He explained that although I'd been sentenced to three months, I should get a third knocked off for good behaviour. I was relieved, but still so depressed that I refused to see Norma and Mum when they came down to the cells. In my short experience, nothing could be worse than prison. It was the depths of degradation.

With hindsight I think the judge was wise to send me down. If he'd just fined me I wouldn't be sitting here now writing my life story. I'm sure I would have progressed from petty crime to something more serious. The carpet theft was not the first time I was involved with the police, it was the third. The first incident involved stealing bread trays. My friend Jimmy Briggs had a three-wheeled Jowett (well, it was really his father's car, but his dad was too ill to drive it). We were both seventeen years old, and as neither of us had a full driving licence, we'd just sit in the back of it on the local bombsite. So we had something more comfortable to sit on, I brought six bread trays from Gillett's Bakery, where I worked on Saturdays. One day a policeman came over and asked where we'd got the trays from. I told him the bakery had given them to me. The policeman didn't believe me and asked me to get a note from my supervisor to confirm that I'd been given them. I didn't think there would be a problem because the supervisor liked me, but he refused to write a note on the grounds that the trays belonged to Gillett's and he had no right to give away company property. To cut a long story short, I ended up in court. I took the local youth-club leader as a character witness and escaped with a £15 fine.

A couple of years later I got into trouble again. On this occasion I was working in Ipswich, selling housewives photographs of their kids. I used to park my car outside my lodgings in the evenings, and one morning I found a police notice on my windscreen. It said I would have to leave my lights on if I wanted to park in that particular spot. I knew that if I left my lights on the battery would go flat, so I took two lamps from the nearest roadworks and placed them on either side of the car. The next day a policeman knocked on the door of my lodgings and arrested me for stealing the lamps. I went to court and was fined £20 for the theft.

The judge in the carpet-theft trial must have been aware of

these two previous incidents. Although he was right to give me a short, sharp shock, at the time it seemed like an eternity, especially the journey to Armley Prison. Within hours of being sentenced, I was herded into a van along with five other prisoners and taken to Leeds. I remember sitting in the back feeling totally out of place. The others talked in prison jargon and were dressed for the part; I had no idea what they were saying and looked like a Butlin's redcoat.

Arriving at Armley was like reaching the end of my world. I suffered a lifetime's humiliation in those first few hours. I was told to empty my pockets and take off my clothes. I was given a pair of prison overalls and had to walk naked to the showers. Once I'd put on the overalls, Peter Stringfellow had gone and I had become a number. A haircut with a pair of clippers completed my transformation into a 1950s prisoner.

I didn't eat for two days, but after that, the slop became quite enjoyable. It was the presentation that I didn't like. We ate off tin plates and filed past the food queue collecting lumps of bread and dollops of whatever. Even though my upbringing was poor and we didn't have a lot of food, there was a certain presentation to what we ate.

My recollection of prison life is patchy. I remember that in the evenings we'd be allowed to congregate for an hour for the news, and then we'd be encouraged to write letters, which I just couldn't do for the first few weeks. I certainly didn't want to see anybody, especially not Norma. I treated those first two weeks as a cleansing period, and once the shock had worn off, it almost became enjoyable in a funny kind of way. The hardest part was going to the toilet. The doors were two feet off the floor and the warders would walk around the bathroom checking who was on the loo. I might have grown up with three brothers and an outside toilet, but we always maintained our privacy.

Slopping out was even worse. At night you did whatever you had to do in a bucket. In Armley I was sharing a cell with three others. Two of them had been in prison before and had no problem going to the loo in a bucket, but the other guy and I simply couldn't do it. The third guy had a similar background to mine, although he was much older than me. He'd been caught stealing money from his bread round and was serving a similar sentence. Of the two experienced prisoners, one was in for benefit fraud. He had a wife and three kids and his story wasn't at all glamorous. The other was a burglar who romanticised. He told me he'd burgled a working-men's club and been caught because he went back the same night to collect something he'd left behind. He was doing eighteen months and said he would go back to burgling when he got out, even though the next time he would get five years. He planned to hide the money he stole and use it after his prison sentence. The guy in for benefit fraud said he was going to switch to robbing post offices instead. He had it all worked out: he said he'd only get three years for robbing a post office because he had kids.

I was intrigued by their stories, but the bread salesman was horrified. He told me not to listen to their rubbish and urged me to go straight when I got out. Had it not been for him I might have ended up a professional burglar. I remember going on to the second landing, where the lifers' cells were, and listening to the most fantastic stories. One of the older lifers took me into his cell and showed me his pride and joy – a window which looked out on to part of the town. Even though I was young and naïve, I could see how sad and pathetic his life was.

After two weeks in Armley I was transferred to an open prison called Thorpe Arch, which was rather like an all-male Butlin's. We slept ten to a dormitory and had our own little cupboards. It reminded me of a concentration camp with its huge barbed-wire fences, but the prisoners were very different there. Unlike the professional criminals in Armley, these guys wanted to get out and get on with their lives. Within days of being there I began to feel less depressed and I wanted to see Norma.

She arrived looking pregnant and very sexy. We couldn't touch because a long table separated the prisoners from their visitors. I remember feeling very jealous when she left because all the other men were whistling at her. She visited once more after that, and then I asked her not to come again because I didn't like the other men making sexual comments about her. For the first time since I lost my virginity at the age of eighteen, I was not thinking about sex – in fact, it was the last thing on my mind. I was thinking about my future and how I was going to stay faithful to Norma. We had been married for only eighteen months and already I'd had an affair with her cousin Cathy.

It had started in Bridlington shortly after I'd married. The three of us went on holiday together and one evening while Norma was asleep I started playing around with her cousin. Cathy was sixteen and very sexy, but we didn't have intercourse because she was still a virgin. After Bridlington I continued to see Cathy and things progressed. I would leave the house on the pretext of going selling and pick her up at the bottom of the road. We would then drive to a quiet area and have sex in the van. Norma never knew, so I had no reason to feel guilty. I remember the feeling of relief when I arrived home and she hadn't noticed any lipstick on me or anything in the first ten minutes. After that I knew I was safe and she didn't suspect anything.

My job as a salesman was not conducive to domestic discipline. Most married men come home from work at a regular time, but I could be out working until midnight. To this day I don't know why I had sex with Norma's cousin. I was in love with Norma, but I must have been sexually obsessed with Cathy. Once I'd started having sex with her, I couldn't stop. It was the start of an addiction: the more I had, the more I wanted. Just as some people get addicted to drink, I became addicted to sex, and the affair continued until I went to prison.

During my sentence my thoughts were with Norma. She was carrying my child, and I desperately wanted to get out and start providing for her and the baby.

At Thorpe Arch I earned five shillings a week, which we could spend at the prison shop. The other prisoners bought cigarettes; I bought jam, which annoyed the hell out of everyone because cigarettes were rationed and we all had more than enough jam. I was told to get cigarettes next time so that I could swap them for jam.

Along with a couple of the other prisoners, I was put on gardening duty for two weeks. We spent the entire time working out what we could get from the lady who owned the garden, but it only ever amounted to a cup of tea and a biscuit with the rest of the day spent pulling up weeds. After I'd proved myself trustworthy at gardening, I was given a forestry job, which was wonderful. I was picked up from the prison at 7 a.m. and driven to a nearby forest where I spent the day cutting up trees. It reminded me of childhood weekends at the Rivling Valley, where I'd spent hours collecting eggs and playing in the countryside. It was a real escape from prison life and made the last four weeks almost enjoyable. I'd return gratefully tired to prison in the evening, eat supper and go to bed.

The last two weeks were the longest because I could see the end. It was like the six-week school summer holidays, which seem like sixty years at the beginning; then as the return to school draws near, you begin to tick off the days and the last remaining ones are like torture. In this case, though, the torture was waiting to get out rather than trying to stretch out the remaining hours. Working outside in the sunshine helped me to recover. I had a tan for the first time in my life, my hair was cut short and I was as fit as I'd ever been. I began to feel like Peter Stringfellow again, instead of a number in a prison overall. My confidence grew as my release date approached. I was a good salesman; I knew I was good. I also knew I could make money if only someone would give me another chance.

On the day I left Thorpe Arch, I was given back my clothes and enough money to get a bus home, but as it happened I didn't have to: Dad and Norma came to collect me in my car, which meant a lot to me. She was heavily pregnant, but we still managed to make love on the back seat. It lasted a matter of seconds. Dad, being Dad, never looked round, and I never looked back. I was determined to start my life again, but this time it was going to be much harder. I would now have to overcome the stigma and prejudice which comes with doing time.

2

STREET LIFE

If you were born in jail, you wouldn't think about life outside because the jail would be your life. My childhood poverty was the same. On reflection we were desperately poor, but, thank God, we didn't know it. In fact everyone we knew was poor. The only people better off than us were the Ronksley family, who owned the shop at the top of Marshall Street. We thought they were rich because their house was always warm. We had no television and all the black-and-white films shown at the cinema were set in America, which was not the real world to us. Reality to me was Pitsmoor, in Sheffield, a small area of terraced houses surrounded by steelworks and bombsites.

On the day I was born, 17 October 1940, Princess Elizabeth made her radio debut in a broadcast to child evacuees. If only my mother, Elsie, could have known that forty-nine years later and 6,000 miles away, the Queen herself would seek me out in a line-up of dignitaries, and say, 'Oh Peter, that's where you are.' But that was in Miami in 1989, many stories and many millions of pounds away from the one-up, one-down house in Marshall Street.

Until I left home to join the merchant navy at sixteen, we all more or less lived in one room. It had a stone sink in one corner and a Yorkshire range oven with a single gas ring in the other. The floor was covered in red linoleum, which Mum kept spotlessly clean. There was one bedroom upstairs, where Mum and Dad slept, and an attic, where I and eventually my younger brothers, Geoffrey, Paul and Terry, shared a bed.

My early life revolved around an area of two square miles

where my grandmas, aunts and uncles lived. My dad had one brother, Denis, and two sisters, Sybil and Dorothy; on the Bower side, my mum had four sisters, Mary, Irene, Dorothy and Jean, and a brother, Jack. Although I loved the Stringfellows, I preferred visiting the Bowers because it was always more fun. Once a week we'd get fish and chips from Sparky's and go to Aunt Mary's. Staying over usually meant sleeping with one of my aunts or cousins. Sometimes I'd curl up on the floor covered in coats. If I slept with Aunt Jean, she used to wake me in the middle of the night to watch her dance. I'd pretend to be a man at the stage door asking to see her privately. It is strange that I'm still doing the same thing fifty years later – not sleeping with Aunt Jean, of course, but watching girls dance for me.

I spent a lot of time visiting the grandmas and mediating between my mum and her mum, who were forever shouting at each other. I'm a typical Libran so I hate disagreements. I was always knocking on some relative's door, saying, 'Mum says she's sorry.' Then I'd run home and tell Mum that Aunt so-and-so had apologised. She was always resolute. 'Well, if she's that sorry, she can come and tell me herself.'

My dad, James, was a distant figure for the first six years of my life. He was a cavalry soldier with the Royal Scots Greys, which was a source of great pride to the family. When he and Uncle Denis came home on leave, the house would be filled with an unusual smell of cleanliness from their uniforms. One day Uncle Denis took a flick-knife from his pocket and managed to spear a mouse which was running around the room. I lived off that story for weeks. It was one of the few tales I didn't embellish.

After the war Dad went back to his old job at the steelworks. He arrived with a silver Smith & Wesson gun he'd taken from a German officer, but being the cautious man he was, he filled the barrel with lead. He was the strong, silent type who never once raised his voice. Mum did all the shouting and smacking; in fact she constantly smacked me, as did most adults when I was a kid. If I came home and told her Connie whatsit had smacked me across the face, she'd smack me as well for being cheeky to Connie. Dad would threaten me silently with his belt, but the only time he ever hit me was after I ran home screaming because a man had chased me to the house. Dad saw how distraught I was and went out and thumped the man. When he found out I'd stolen some jam from this man's caravan he was so livid he threatened me with his belt.

Mum was in charge of pretty much everything in the house as well as the smacking. Some working-class husbands got drunk and beat their wives, but not Dad. He would hand over his wage packet every week and never went out drinking. When all the other parents were in the pub on Saturday nights, mine stayed at home. Looking back, I should have been grateful that they were such decent people, yet it always irritated the hell out of me. We couldn't play in our house, so we'd end up congregating at a neighbour's, where we'd run wild. One Saturday I lay on top of a girl from down the street and thought we'd had sex.

I had no sisters, and Mum never talked about sex. She wouldn't even admit to being pregnant when I saw her washing one day and noticed how large her stomach was. Obviously she was, because our Paul arrived a month later. Dad was just as reticent. If we caught him naked he'd cover his private parts with his hands. Talk of sex or bodies and swearing were taboo. I had a friend called Peter Wright who everyone called Shitesy, but I never used his nickname at home – it was too close to the word 'shit', and I knew I'd get murdered. We weren't even allowed to say 'thee' and 'thou', which were part of the Yorkshire dialect. Kids were always saying, 'Shut thee gob,' but if our mum heard us, she'd clip us round the ear.

Mum did all the arguing for both her and Dad. He was 6 ft tall to her 5 ft 2. When he'd heard enough he'd say, 'Elsie!' Nothing else, just 'Elsie!' and immediately she'd stop. I only heard him argue back once. It was such a shock that Mum left home for the day and went back to her mother's. People were always slamming doors in Marshall Street. You'd hear, 'I'm leaving!' and then someone would march out into the street. After Mum stormed out, Dad walked Geoffrey and me over the hill to little Grandma Bower's house. She opened the door and said, 'Now calm down, Jim, she's coming home.' Dad, in his usual monosyllabic fashion, said, 'Right,' and we all headed home.

Although Mum kept strict accounts, we were always in debt. Neither of them drank or gambled, but their spare money went on cigarettes. At the age of eight I tried smoking Dad's pipe, which was so revolting I never smoked again. But smoking was a glamorous thing to do in the 1950s. During the war, a whisper would go round that the rations had arrived at the corner shop. I remember running up the street to buy Woodbines for my parents and sweets.

Counting money was a big part of our lives. I can't remember my parents ever paying for anything in cash. We paid for things weekly and kept a running account at the corner shop. When Dad got paid on Fridays, I'd be sent down to settle our bill, which could be anything from £4 10s to £6. Everyone used the local pawn shop. At least once a month we'd take in someone's shoes, usually Dad's best pair. When he got paid I'd go and redeem them for the weekend.

Anyone reading this who didn't grow up in that era might think I was deprived as a child, and by today's standards, I suppose I was. But you have to remember that in Sheffield in the forties and fifties no one had anything. The biggest item you could own as a kid was a bicycle. A bike was everything. My parents actually bought me a brand-new one from Halfords when I was ten years old, the sit-up-and-beg type. It was a possession beyond my wildest dreams. For the first year, I was allowed to bring it into the house. God knows how we all fitted in with the bicycle as well. It was like a prized artefact, propped up against the sideboard. It wasn't until a year after I got it that I could bear to leave it outside, though it was unthinkable that anyone would steal your bike.

Running out of coal was our main fear in those days. An empty cellar spelled misery for everyone. No coal meant no fire and no oven. If a neighbour had coal, he'd lend you a bucketful, but sometimes we went without for a week or two. Invariably there was no money for the meters. When the lights went out, Mum would fumble for her purse by candlelight. If she had a shilling we were in the big time; if she was down to pennies, things were bad. When the meters were full or we had no money, we'd fill the tin bath using saucepans and take it in turns to wash. It was the lack of a proper bathroom, above all else, that left a lasting impression on me. Wherever I've lived, I've made my bathrooms superbly comfortable, with everything you could possibly want, including a jacuzzi, a television and champagne on ice.

I used to say Mum was a bad cook, but really she was brilliant given the facilities she had. I've eaten in all the best restaurants throughout the world, yet never once tasted a rabbit stew as good as hers. She would often talk about what we'd do if we won the pools. Her big dream was to move to Canada. One Saturday she won, so I told everyone at school that we were emigrating. Half of Sheffield won that week, which meant we scooped the grand total of £5.

There were two working cars in Marshall Street: Mr Ronksley, who owned the corner shop, had a Standard 8 which was covered in rust. If I managed to make any part of it shine he'd give me three shillings. The other car was owned by the Whitehouse family, who ran the fish-and-chip shop. Peter Cundy's dad had a big old Wolseley, but this didn't count then because no one ever saw it move, though in later years it was coaxed into life. It was a great mystery how the Cundys managed to acquire a car, because Mr Cundy never seemed to work. In those days, if a man wasn't working, he was genuinely ill – there was a lot of tuberculosis around. No one went without work through choice; in fact, it was shameful not to have a job.

Today people talk about pollution, but we were permanently filthy from playing on the slag heaps and no one seemed to bother. Mum would ask, 'Where are you going?'

I'd say, 'Oh, t'bombsite', or 'T'quarry.' If she told you not to be late, it meant come back before it was dark. I'd disappear for hours on my precious bicycle, train-spotting or egg-collecting. I'd cycle the three miles to Rivling Valley, and myself and Bob Fowler, who was much taller than me, would scour the trees for eggs. Bob's mother owned a pathetic little shop on Marshall Street with hardly any stock. If he had no money to play out, he'd take it from the till. The other small shop on Marshall Street was owned by my Uncle Denis. I remember seeing his furniture being moved one day and replaced with fruit and vegetables. He never had much stock, just a few apples and an awful lot of potatoes. Nevertheless, it gave me status for a while.

Unlike marbles and comics, no one swapped their eggs: if you hadn't collected them yourself, they didn't count. Egg-collecting is absolutely taboo today, but then it was an acceptable pastime. I had about twenty in my collection, including those of owls, magpies, lapwings and skylarks. The most swappable possessions were the American comics. Most kids got them from outside the pub on a Saturday night, but as my parents never went to the pub, I had to barter for them with my marbles.

Amid all the greyness of Pitsmoor was Woodside Common, where I'd go chasing butterflies. I shot my brother Paul on Woodside Common. I'd swapped my bicycle for an air rifle and got tired of firing at targets. Although Paul was wearing a thick coat and the progress of the pellet was slow enough to watch, it managed to rip his coat and leave a bruise on his back. I begged him not to tell Mum, and dragged him home screaming and yelling. When Dad found out he confiscated the air rifle. Mum clipped me round the ear.

The worst thing we did as children was to fill tin cans with coal ash and throw them at each other. Ash and tin cans were the only items we threw away during the war years. Jamjars could be used again and any packaging and paper went straight on to the fire. Apart from that jam-stealing incident, and another occasion when I pinched a wet fish but later took it back to the shop, I wasn't particularly naughty as a child, though I did have a vivid imagination. One day we had to call the fire brigade because of a fire in our chimney. It was incredibly exciting – like a funeral, when everybody came out to watch what was happening. I was on stage, in my mind, for the first time in my life. It was *my* house, *my* fire, and I opened the door to the firemen. Everyone was kept away except me and Mum. When the firemen wrapped up and left I was consumed with disappointment. I desperately wanted to regain everyone's attention, so I told them that one of the firemen had sat my mother on his knee. It was an out-and-out lie.

One of the high points of every year was Whitsuntide, when

everyone got new clothes. However poor you were, your mother bought you an entire new outfit. On Whit Sunday I would put on my new shoes, socks, underpants, jacket, shirt and trousers and visit all my relatives collecting money. They'd open the door to this pristine-looking child with slicked-down hair and say, 'Oh, you do look lovely,' and give me anything from threepence to a shilling. Even as a young child, clothes mattered to me a great deal, even though usually my socks and shoes were filled with holes and my trousers were covered in patches. Before I was even eight years old I remember standing in my greatcoat watching a group of kids playing marbles. For some reason I can't recall I went home and returned wearing another coat. I was amazed and distressed that nobody noticed the difference.

But it wasn't until I went to technical school at the age of twelve and saw my mother struggle to get my uniform that I realised the importance of clothes in the world in general. Long before those nightmare three years and the embarrassment of discovering that my satchel wasn't real leather, I had an uneasy relationship with school. School was like having to stay married to someone you could only just tolerate. I hated it from the start.

Monday was the most horrendous day of all at infants' school. It was the day the school dentist visited. The teachers would hand out dreaded yellow cards, marked in one corner if you needed an extraction. The extraction would take place on the Wednesday – mouth open, gas over mouth and hours of pain after having your teeth wrenched out. The waiting from Monday to Wednesday was like two days of torture, marked by sleeplessness, tears and prayers to God asking Him to somehow get you out of going.

My mum made a point of watching me walk up the road to school, especially on Mondays. One particular morning I was filled with such unspeakable dread that I clung to the wall at the corner of our street and began crying hysterically. I told Mum that my legs were paralysed. She was so worried that she carried me back to the house and called our family doctor, Dr Leddy.

Dr Leddy was a very understanding man (less so when I gave him his first case of venereal disease, but that came much later; to a terrified seven-year-old he was a kindly confidant). He sat and listened as I poured out my fears of the dentist, then asked how my legs were feeling. I said they were much better. He had a word with my mother. Instead of smacking me, she let me take the day off school. From that day onwards, Dr Leddy was a very special man to me.

Even when the dentist wasn't visiting, I'd find any excuse to miss school. Discovering the word diarrhoea was a watershed as far as truancy was concerned. It was great because it could arise suddenly and there was nothing to be done about it. Influenza was too serious for one day's absence, but inexplicable diarrhoea could come and go. To my knowledge I never suffered from the runs as a child, yet I had more 'diarrhoea' at Pie Bank Infants' than I've had in my lifetime. I did get genuine excruciating earache, but by that stage my mother had grown tired of my excuses and made me go to school anyway.

My major difficulty at school was spelling. Dyslexia was unknown in the 1950s, so children like me were singled out and ridiculed. Throughout infants' school I was bottom of the class. If there were thirty-one pupils, to be twenty-eighth was an achievement, but I was happy with twenty-ninth, which usually meant that the other two were off with diphtheria, a terrible and often fatal disease prevalent at the time.

The only thing I enjoyed was making Christmas decorations, though I didn't like art class. If I wasn't naturally good at something, I wasn't interested in learning about it. I was good at arithmetic and grammar, but lousy at everything else, including sport. Football was anathema to me. One day a leather football flew over a wall on to the bombsite where I was playing. Most boys would have kicked it back, but I took it home and hid it in my bedroom. Then I went back to the bombsite to watch the entire team looking for the ball. However, while gymnastics were out of the question because I was physically small and weak, it didn't stop me suggesting that everyone did handstands in the playground. My motive was not a sporting one: it was a great excuse to see the girls' knickers. To this day I have a penchant for girls in white panties.

The only game I was good at was marbles. Glass marbles weren't available during the war, so until 1945 we played with pitch balls. On a hot summer's day we would pick the pitch from between the cobblestones and roll it into balls. It was sensational when real marbles finally came back to Sheffield. I ended up with a whole jamjar full of them. The small multicoloured ones were the most desirable as these were impossible to buy. The only marbles on sale were the large clear-glass ones. We would have to swap six of these to get one small multicoloured one. Marbles were the first wealth I ever had, earned for myself.

Since my brilliance at marbles was not mirrored in my academic life, I failed my eleven-plus exam and went on to Burngreave Secondary Modern in the autumn of 1952. Here, for the first time in my life, I was top of the top class. At Burngreave they took a softer approach to spelling and so I began to excel. I spent only a year there, but I loved it. It was a time of pornographic magazines and dirty jokes, which usually revolved around Errol Flynn's penis being 3ft long. I learned to masturbate at Burngreave. While we were watching a slideshow in a history class one day I started playing with myself in the dark. I was totally shocked when I ejaculated. I immediately went to the toilet and did it another three times.

About the same time as I discovered masturbation, I discovered the local library. Before then, all my knowledge outside what I learned at school had come from an encyclopedia which stopped at 1932. In the library I read about the Stringfellows. For years I had hated my name. I'd get called string vest and string bean at school, which was very distressing. I wanted to be called Smith until I found out that my name had a meaning – Stringfellow meant 'from the fellowship of string-makers'. I was thrilled to learn that the Stringfellows had been involved in the first air flights – I was crazy about the air force, and spent hours poring over pictures of bombers, Hawker Hunters and Spitfires. I took tremendous pride in being British because we had the best planes in the world, and, of course, we'd won the war. I couldn't believe my luck when I found that a Robert Stringfellow had been instrumental in putting the first steam engine into an aeroplane. The fact that the whole idea had been a disaster was irrelevant: this man was famous. From then on I was proud to be a Stringfellow.

In the early fifties technical schools were introduced in Britain. A board of examiners came to Burngreave to assess its top stream, and after a brief test I was one of the few who were chosen to go to technical school that year. This was my chance to redeem myself academically. Mum and Dad had hidden their disappointment when I failed the eleven-plus, but they couldn't hide their joy at the prospect of their eldest son in a blazer. But from the moment I passed that exam, my life changed for the worse.

I'd sailed through my childhood oblivious of our poverty, but from day one of technical school, I was made painfully aware of it. I knew that Mum and Dad had struggled to buy my uniform and that it wasn't paid for in full when I put it on my back, but nothing could prepare me for the ridicule of having a phoney satchel. Being singled out as a terrible speller was one thing, but being the only child without a real leather satchel was absolute ignominy. I could have coped with the shame if it hadn't been complicated by other emotions, like the sympathy and love I felt for my parents.

It was still only the first week of term when my second rude awakening came. We were asked to take out our instruments in a technical drawing class. Those who didn't have their own could find some in a box at the front of the class. Only three of us walked to the front. My borrowed instruments were nowhere near as good as those of the boy next to me. That galled me, because I could draw better than him. The sinking feeling was compounded when the teacher asked us to take out our pens and I was the only person without a proper fountain pen.

Within this small community, which was to be my world for the next three years, I had no status, save for that provided by my uniform. And as the weeks passed, even my uniform became the cause of further mortification. It soon transpired that everyone else had two blazers, two shirts and two pairs of trousers, yet Peter Stringfellow had only one of everything. When my clothes became too filthy I would take the day off school rather than turn up without my uniform. At last I could justify playing truant on Mondays. I no longer needed my infants' school excuses because there was no answer to the excuse that your clothes were on the washing line.

I detested technical school so much that I treasured every moment away from the place. I started a paper round at the age of twelve and then became a van boy at Gillett's Bakery on Saturdays. From thirteen I was a projectionist three nights a week at the Wicker Cinema in Sheffield. When I wasn't working I'd cycle to Doncaster and go train-spotting. There were no glamorous trains in Sheffield, but the *Flying Scotsman* would pass through Doncaster on its way from London to Edinburgh. I was only interested in trains with names. Seeing *The Mallard* was out of this world. Train-spotting is now universally ridiculed, but I loved every minute of it.

Besides, there was nothing at school to stimulate or amuse me. There was no teacher or system to cater for or foster my individuality. The closest thing I had to a useful education came from my Uncle Sid, who was a real entrepreneur. He'd been promoted from a lorry driver to the manager of the depot and had his own car. In his spare time he was chairman of the entertainment committee at the working men's club in Pitsmoor. He was in charge of booking the artists, or turns as they called them. Uncle Sid was the first man to show me £1,000. He was saving up to buy a lorry with his friend and had the money piled up in the old white five-pound notes. I can still see it now, sitting on his green tablecloth. I touched it, held it in my hands and marvelled at it: there was nothing in my life to suggest I would ever have that amount of money.

The height of my aspirations was to leave school and get paid for doing a job. Leaving school was a priority; I'd thought of nothing else since the age of five. The aim at technical school was to leave with a diploma in engineering. Those who were awarded a first-class diploma went on to university. The majority got second-class ones, and there was a smattering of third-class certificates for people who had been ill. For the handful of abject failures there was a fourth-class diploma. I was surprised I even got a fourth. I actually passed in French, which was bizarre, since the French class was on Mondays, and I never went to school on Mondays.

On the last day of term I left the assembly before everyone

else. There was nothing left for me there: I felt like an outsider looking in on somewhere where I didn't belong. While everyone listened to the principal's final speech, I boldly stood up and walked out of the hall. I was ecstatic: I was free. I skipped the two miles home in the sunshine. I remember that day as one of the happiest of my life.

3

IN THE NAVY

That wonderful feeling of freedom lasted a fortnight. I wanted to enjoy my liberty for a bit and had no intention of getting a job immediately, but unfortunately I got the first job I went for, as an assistant tie-salesman at Austin Reed. I wasn't allowed to actually sell ties, only to tidy them up. Nevertheless there was scope for promotion. My ambition was to move to the shirt counter and sell one to a customer. Austin Reed was the kind of menswear shop where you called the manager over if someone wanted to buy a jacket. It was Sheffield's answer to Grace Brothers in *Are You Being Served?*

I enjoyed the first two weeks, but then a little bit of school mentality started creeping in. That dreaded word 'discipline' was mentioned. They didn't like me turning up late, and I didn't like the boredom of the job. I left after three weeks.

My recollection of 1956 is that you could get a job any time and anywhere. I remember walking through Sheffield thinking, 'I'd like to work in that building,' and going in and asking if they had any jobs. Despite my execrable qualifications I had more to offer than the majority of kids from the secondary moderns. I'd been to Sheffield Technical School, and the name carried a certain kudos irrespective of what you had achieved there; it also helped that the grammar-school boys were not applying for the same kind of jobs. So I was in competition with lesser mortals, and relished the power of asking for and being given whatever job I fancied.

After Austin Reed I became a car mechanic for half a day. My dad came down to the local Vauxhall dealer to sign the apprentice papers, and within minutes I was given overalls and a spanner. I was told to remove the exhaust from an old Vauxhall Viva. By lunchtime I was deeply regretting the whole thing. I had rust in my eyes, and oil under my fingernails, and I decided that was it and left.

I tried the local barber's shop next. The barber was a hunchback and clearly didn't want to train anyone, but nevertheless I hung around for a day and swept up after him. After that I thought I knew all about being a barber and never went back. It was only a matter of days before I found another job, as the second projectionist at the Regal Cinema in the Attercliffe area. I loved the old black-and-white movies they put on there. I remember showing Frank Sinatra in *The Man With the Golden Arm*, the terrifying story of a drug addict which left me with a lifelong fear of drugs. At sixteen I wasn't to know how important that film would be in my life, but back then the New York Mafia did not even feature in the realms of my imagination.

It was at the Regal that I fell in love for the first time, with an usherette who lived opposite the cinema. She had red hair and freckles and was very overweight. I was consumed with passion for her boobs. She would put my hand down her top and I'd get very excited, but it never went further than that. We spent our time together having supper at her mother's and walking past the local jewellery shop looking at rings. June was the first girl I took home to meet Mum. To say she disapproved was an understatement; she didn't have to say anything, it was just the look in her eyes. The relationship ended when June told me about periods. I'd seen advertisements for sanitary towels, but I didn't know what they were. When she told me about them in all the gory details I wanted to be sick there and then. It was ages before I could look at a girl again romantically.

My job at the cinema was more successful than my early occupations: it lasted for seven months, during which time I learned an invaluable lesson about music licences. Before I arrived, the Regal would play dreadful tunes like 'Little Donkey' in between the films. I went round the corner and told the manager of Littlewood's that we would mention his store if he lent the cinema ten records from the charts each week (of course, I never did). I'd play the records, miming along to Frankie Vaughan's 'Green Door' in the projectionist's box, until the manager caught me one day and explained that the cinema didn't have a licence and I was breaking the law. This was a big disappointment. I decided to find another job. I applied for a more senior projectionist's job at the Capitol Cinema at the top of Sheffield Lane, the posher end of town.

The first projectionist was so relieved that someone had come for the job that he overlooked my lack of senior experience. On my first day he offered to load the second reel for me, but I waved him off to lunch with a 'Yeah, yeah, yeah, I know what I'm doing,' and confidently started the matinee showing of *Rock Around the Clock*. The film had seven reels. The idea was to load the next reel as the previous one came to an end and flick them over so that the audience wouldn't notice. I loaded the second reel and did the flick-over perfectly. I turned my attention to the third reel, and after a few minutes I heard stomping from inside the cinema. I looked out to see the credits rolling up the screen. I'd mistaken seven for two and caused absolute mayhem. The first projectionist came roaring back and sacked me on the spot.

The end of my career as a projectionist coincided with Dad's first and only father-to-son chat about my future profession. He took me to one side and told me a story which went something like this: 'Look, son, when we all sit around eating our snap, the other fathers are all very proud of their sons doing apprenticeships in this and that. Then it comes to me, and I'm too embarrassed to tell them that you're messing around in pictures. I want you to get a proper job, and come to the steelworks before it's too late.' The thought of the steelworks filled me with dread. I'd passed the steelworks a thousand times and seen guys pouring molten steel into moulds. They wore waistcoats and silk scarves knotted around their necks and sweated like crazy. The work was incredibly hard. Many years later when Arthur Scargill tried to save the mines, I never understood why. The mines reminded me of the steelworks, they were places of purgatory. Sure, there was unemployment in the short term, but in the long term it meant a cleaner environment and longer lives for the workers who were laid off. When Sheffield's steel industry was thriving it was rare to see steelworkers in retirement because the majority had died so young. If I saw an old ex-steelworker in my youth, he was invariably hunchbacked and coughing because the constant heat had damaged his lungs. The steelworks was the last place I wanted to be, but for Dad's sake I gave it a try.

I was six months behind the other apprentice turners, so the steelworks sent me to night school, where the classes turned out to be much easier than anything I'd studied at technical school. Making isotopes was also easy, so easy that I began churning them out faster than anyone else, which didn't please the supervisor. I was introduced to restricted work practices, which dictated that I could make so many and no more. I wanted to earn £5 a week, but the manager told me he would sack me if I ever made as many isotopes as that. This left me with nothing to do on Fridays, because by then I'd completed over and above my quota. At the end of my second week someone tapped me on the shoulder and told me to turn off my machine because we were on strike. We filed out into the yard to listen to the union man talking about more pay. I turned to the manager and said, 'What's this all about? You won't let me earn more than £5 a week.'

'This is different, son,' he replied. 'This is basic pay.'

I simply couldn't understand this mentality, or the restrictions. To my mind there was nothing wrong with working harder for more money, but this was alien ideology in the steelworks. I handed in my notice after that, but I couldn't leave for another four weeks – they hoped this would give your parents enough time to dissuade you from leaving. During those four weeks the other apprentices made my life hell. There was a pecking order among the boys, and as I'd joined six months late I was made to feel like an outsider. Johnny Greaves was one of the hierarchy, despite being the greasiest and spottiest of them all. At snap time, which was what we called our break, he never spoke about his dreams of becoming a singer; it was all back-to-school rubbish about who was the toughest. When I ran into

KING OF CLUBS / 27

Johnny Greaves again, he had metamorphosed into an entirely different person. This time he was wearing eyeliner and a leather jacket. But we'll come to him later.

I wanted to do something exciting when I left the steelworks. I thought seriously about joining the air force, but Uncle Sid talked me out of it. He'd been in the army with my dad and didn't think signing up for ten years was a good idea. I took his advice and turned my attention elsewhere.

My hero at the time was Superman. Batman was fallible, but Superman was omnipotent. He lived in a city like New York, and if there was one place on earth I wanted to see, it was New York City. My other hero was Tommy Steele. From the moment I read an article about his rise to fame, I wanted to emulate his life. He'd joined the merchant navy and sailed to America, where he bought a guitar and learned to play it on the voyage back to England. When he arrived back in London he walked into a Soho bar, began singing, and the rest is history. It all sounded so glamorous. I decided to do the same.

The reality was, however, very different. For a start, I had to lie my way into the merchant navy because I had a lazy eye. I managed to embroil Dr Leddy in this deception, even though he was the epitome of morality and a good Catholic family man. I talked him into covering up my defective eyesight, although he was convinced that the merchant navy doctor would find out anyway and send me home. But the merchant navy doctor turned out to be totally uninterested. I could have walked in with a white stick and he wouldn't have noticed. During my medical, I simply covered the same eye with a different hand for the eye test and he gave me a clean bill of health.

I was ready to set sail – except that I'd overlooked the training. Tommy Steele had never mentioned anything about the Gravesend Training School. Learning how to lay table napkins was a world away from Pitsmoor. At home we put newspaper on our dining-room table – and only on Sundays would Mum bring out her best tablecloth. I might have grown up in a town where they made knives and forks, but I was ignorant when it came to eating with more than one set. Tommy Steele had made it all sound so wonderful. He'd been on a cruise liner sailing from London; I found myself on an oil tanker sailing from South Shields. I was the galley boy-cum-slave, so I spent most of my time in the hot, stinking kitchens. I'd never seen so much food: for the first two weeks I ate non-stop. I'd go down in the middle of the night and gorge myself, but instead of feasting on salmon steaks, I pigged out on the only luxury food I was used to, jam and bread.

The chef was the ugliest man in the world, half-Spanish, half-English, with greasy hair and rotting teeth. It was my job to serve him tea each morning. Before we left South Shields, I could never understand why he had a different girl in his cabin every morning. One day I brought him his tea and was awestruck to find him with the most gorgeous-looking girl. The chef told me I could have her later, so I waited outside his cabin. I remember being amazed that she was only sixteen, like me. Once I'd told her my age she gave me a little kiss on the cheek and left the ship. For a while I thought that this horrible fat chef was what women really liked. By the end of the voyage, I realised that he paid for sex.

I suffered so dreadfully with seasickness that I was already hanging over the side vomiting when the captain came to inspect the crew. In between being sick, I stuck up pictures of America in my cabin. I wept when I discovered that we were sailing to Rotterdam and then on to Dakar in Africa. I remember wailing, 'But I want to go to New York!' and the chef falling around laughing.

We were halfway across the Atlantic when the chef called me to his cabin and asked me, 'Who's your father, Stringfellow? Have you got any influence?' When I told him Dad worked at the British Steel Corporation he looked puzzled. 'Well, we've had a change of orders,' he said. 'We're sailing to America, and this ship's never been to America before.'

Of course, I thought we would sail straight into New York. We finally docked in New Jersey, where I caught a Greyhound bus and travelled through the night to the city of my dreams. It was the most magical trip of my life, like being wrapped in the pages of a Superman comic. I arrived in Times Square on the morning of my seventeenth birthday. I went into a high-tech café and put a nickel in what looked like a sandwich machine. I went back for another and got the shock of my life when a hand came through the flap.

My big plan was to buy a guitar in New York, like Tommy Steele had done. Of course, I didn't have anywhere near enough money. I ended up buying my father the longest cigar I could find and my mother a picture frame before heading back to the ship.

From that moment onwards I wanted to go home, yet we still had Philadelphia to visit, and the Tropics. The voyage back to England was interminable. I wrote every day to Mum and Dad and to a girl I pretended was my girlfriend. I'd seen her only once, when she babysat for Auntie Mary and Uncle Sid, and decided she could be my girlfriend. I put all my romantic fantasies in these letters, until her mother asked Uncle Sid to stop me writing them. Apparently, they were too sexually explicit for a twelve-year-old girl.

Before we arrived in Philadelphia I had hatched a plan with Denis, the cabin boy. We'd heard that merchant seamen could jump ship in America, work for a while and then give themselves up to the authorities and be put on the next ship heading back to England. This was the answer to my prayers. We had to revise the plan when we found out that we weren't actually due to dock in Philadelphia. We decided we would wrap ourselves in oilskins and swim ashore. Unfortunately, we arrived in Philadelphia at the same time as the Queen and the Royal Yacht *Britannia*. The entire harbour was floodlit so there was no way we could jump without being seen. Denis and I decided to stay put until the next country, which was Venezuela. As we sailed down the coast of America, one of the crew pointed out the Miami coastline. I wasn't remotely interested in Miami; it didn't mean a damn thing to me. It was 1957, I didn't have a dollar to my name, yet one day I would own a nightclub in that very place.

I remember sailing through the Caribbean and being amazed at the sunshine. No one had mentioned anything about suntan lotion. One of the deckhands told me to put butter on my face. He might as well have told me to put my head under a magnifying glass. Within an hour, I was redder than the reddest lobster you've ever seen. I spent the next three days sitting in the shower trying to cool down.

When we finally reached Curaçao, a tropical island off Venezuela, I had my first hot dog and saw my first bikini. It was heart-stoppingly exciting. I spent the whole day finding excuses to walk past this vision of beauty. The bikini girl was my second fantasy affair of the voyage; the first was with the second mate's wife, the only woman aboard the ship.

In Curaçao Denis got a poisoned thumb from a fishbone he caught it on while washing up. His hand grew to six times its normal size. The captain was worried about gangrene, so they airlifted him from the ship and flew him back to America for treatment. I was distraught and consumed with jealousy. I spent the next three days sticking fishbones in my knee (I knew if I stuck them in my thumb, they might get suspicious). After a couple of days I managed to build up a nice yellow sore. I was planning to go to the captain the following morning to tell him I had gangrene in my leg, but when I woke up the sore had burst, leaving nothing more than a little red patch.

Everyone knew I was homesick. I was always crying. I hated being on the ship, and I hated my jobs. The captain would send me out on the decks each morning to pick up the flying fish which had jumped aboard. Then I'd have to go down to the galley and scrub the chef's chopping board. It was made up of long planks of wood which I'd scrub from left to right. One day the chef grabbed hold of my hair and dragged me over to the chopping board. He ran his knife between the cracks and scraped up half a dozen maggots. 'If I ever see another maggot,' he screamed, 'I'll make you eat them.' I ran out of the galley and was physically sick. One afternoon he sent me to get a big bowl of flour which was kept in the storeroom in the bowels of the ship. I managed to carry it all the way to the galley door but then the ship rolled and I dropped it. The chef chased me around the ship with a knife. I was so frightened I hid in the funnel. I squeezed beside the water tank and sat there for hours. I knew if I waited until dark he would be drunk and would have forgotten about me.

To my amazement, Denis flew back to the ship before we left the Tropics. I couldn't believe his stupidity – he'd actually come back at his own request. But instead of going back to his cabin-boy duties, Denis swapped jobs with me. For the next two weeks, my main task was cleaning the second mate's cabin. I'd quickly make the beds and then get out his wife's underwear and play with it.

There was mass panic aboard the ship when we arrived back at Tilbury. Customs officers came aboard to check for contraband. I didn't know what the word meant. When one of the crew shouted, 'Tobacco!' I immediately thought of Dad's cigar, and tried to flush it down the toilet. I remember breaking into a sweat because the damn thing wouldn't flush. Of course, the customs officers didn't even look in my cabin.

I had earned £3 10s a week and was expecting to get about another £5 on docking at Tilbury. In fact, I was paid £65, because, unbeknown to me, we were given extra money for working overtime and on Sundays. I was rich beyond my wildest dreams. I felt like Columbus walking down Marshall Street on my way home. It didn't seem to matter that I'd been away only eight weeks. I was a hero because I'd been further than Sheffield. Everyone came out to meet me. They shook my hand and treated me like a film star. Everyone was spellbound by my stories, and after I'd told them all twenty times I began making them up, particularly the ones about the girls I'd met in New York. I was still a virgin and had no idea what sex involved. A Sheffield girl had told me about the sexual act, that a man puts his penis inside a woman, but I knew my mum wouldn't do that, and neither would the Queen. My own theory was that babies were conceived by means of an injection.

Within a matter of weeks my celebrity status had died down and I had to find a job. One day I knocked on the stage door of the Sheffield Lyceum Theatre. Although they hadn't advertised for anyone, the manager told me I could be their curtain boy if I started straight away. The matinee was beginning in a few minutes' time with a singer called Ronnie Carroll. I was quickly shown to my post and how to work the curtain wheel. I was told to drop the curtain for the interval when I heard a particular cue word. For twenty minutes I watched this man, my hand sweating on the wheel. I don't remember a single thing about his performance, only my abject terror. I kept thinking I'd missed the cue because the whole thing was taking so long. Eventually I lost confidence and shut the curtains. All hell broke loose because, obviously, I'd closed them at the wrong time. The stage manager was screaming obscenities the like of which I'd never heard before. All I remember is a chorus of '*Open the fucking curtain!*' I managed to do this but by this time I'd completely forgotten the cue word, and Ronnie Carroll was walking off stage by the time I closed them again. Amid all the bawling and yelling, the manager told me to take a lunch break and come back within the hour. The whole thing had been such a nightmare that I didn't go back.

Eventually I found a job as a van boy for Gillett's Bakery where I'd worked on Saturdays while at technical school. I earned five shillings a day and as many pastries as I could eat. It was here that I met my first wife, Norma; my first mentor, Nelson Foster; and my first rogue, Big Red. Nelson taught me how to drive and how to drop my Yorkshire dialect; Big Red taught me how to cheat and charm. His favourite word was 'whacker', which I immediately picked up. His catchphrase was, 'All right, love?' He'd also say to the bakery ladies, 'Are you getting enough? Is the old man looking after you?' He'd lie about how many loaves we'd taken. If I took six, he'd say I'd got three, and no one seemed to mind. While Nelson always wore a white overall, Big Red wore a brown one. Nelson was thin, with wispy, thinning hair, whereas Big Red was, as his name suggests, large. He had a charming smile, even though he'd lost one of his front teeth.

When Big Red left to work at another bakery, I joined Nelson's round. He immediately banned me from saying 'whacker' on the grounds that it was intensely irritating. He also put a stop to the stealing. I learned a lot from Nelson, and he straightened me out. From him I picked up his giggle.

Norma worked on the conveyor belt, putting pastries in boxes. She was one of three very pretty girls working there who all wore little white hats. The first time I tried to date Norma, I accidentally asked the wrong girl. I had to take this girl out a second time to cover my mistake before I finally got to Norma.

I fell in love. Norma was sixteen years old and incredibly

pretty with small boobs. Cute was the word. I was two years older than she was, but equally as immature. We'd do our courting in her front room when her parents were in bed. I'd take her to the cinema, then we'd go back to her house and mess around on the settee. Right up until the moment we made love, I had no idea what I was doing. I was playing around between her legs and it went in. Norma screamed, then I screamed. Talk about premature ejaculation – this preceded it. Her mum came flying downstairs and wanted to know what was going on. I told her we'd fallen asleep and Norma had had a nightmare. Her mother was far too clever to believe this. She said, 'All right, Peter, I think you had better go now.' I walked back to Marshall Street on a cloud.

Once we'd consummated our relationship, which happened within a matter of three weeks, I became obsessively jealous of Norma. I couldn't bear the thought that once she'd held another boy's hand. I'd taunt her about it and reduce her to tears.

There was no contraceptive pill in 1958, and as I didn't know how to use a condom, we relied on withdrawal. Norma and I were always waiting for her period to start. She'd say, 'I've come on,' and I'd say, 'Thank God for that.' Occasionally she'd be two days late and we'd have to start planning the wedding.

At eighteen I passed my driving test and wanted my own bread round. Gillett's refused, so I left and went to work for a small family bakery on the other side of Pitsmoor. They had two vans and baked all their own bread. I offered to build up their round by cold-calling on surrounding housing estates. Unfortunately, the bakery wasn't prepared for the speed at which I could sell. I would be flying back asking them to bake more loaves, and they couldn't keep up and didn't have the facilities to expand. I totally upset their lives. Eventually, the father called me in and asked me very politely to leave.

I wasn't particularly upset. In selling I'd found an outlet for my flashy, fast-talking, confident persona. I applied for a job supervising canvassers and persuaded my friend Peter Cundy to join me. The advertisement had asked for people with their own cars, and by this time my dad had a 1930s Hillman. Peter's dad's Wolseley, Marshall Street's third – non-operational – car in my childhood, was now in working order (or, at any rate, was less clapped out than the Hillman). We overlooked the condition of our jalopies in the hope of earning £20 a week.

The Wolseley fared better than the Hillman, which pumped out great plumes of smoke the moment I started the engine. I was stopped no fewer than five times by the police in the space of three miles. The car finally died four blocks from our destination and I had to get in Peter's Wolseley.

The guy behind the advertisement was Gus Andrews, a smart-looking Liverpudlian who was a little bit spivvy. The job was legal, but it did involve a bit of scamming. The idea was to take out a group of women canvassers in your car and send them to houses with nappies on the washing line. The women would offer housewives the services of a photographer to take pictures of their children. If they agreed, the photographer, following behind, would arrive to set up the picture. My job was to take down the colour details, such as the colour of the children's hair and clothes and so on, so that the photographs could be coloured by hand. Three weeks later, we'd return with three postcard-sized photographs and show them a large framed colour photograph which cost 59/6. Invariably the housewives didn't have the money, so we'd take a deposit of 2/6 and start a running account where they paid 2/6 a week for twenty-four weeks. I would get five shillings for every large framed photograph I sold. My target was to sell twenty a day, which made £5. If I had a good day and sold thirty, I wouldn't work the next day. If I didn't work the day after that, I'd be rushing around on a Saturday trying to make up my money. Why the houses with nappies on the washing lines? Simple. Kids under five were cuter and more lovable than older kids, and their mothers would die, or cry, rather than not buy a picture of their offspring.

As it turned out, because I was doing so well Gus Andrews gave me a company car, a brand-new Vauxhall Cresta, red with a cream stripe and incredibly flash for 1957. It was like giving a salesman a Porsche Turbo by today's standards. Peter Cundy only stayed a couple of days. I was always trying to get my friends involved in things, but this wasn't his scene.

After I'd exhausted Sheffield, Barnsley, Huddersfield and

Ipswich, Gus asked me to set up an office in Newcastle and loaned me £65 to get started. Although I had zero business skills, I managed to advertise for canvassers and started selling photographs in and around Newcastle. As the money came in I spent it, which was a bit unfortunate, as it wasn't my money. When Gus discovered this, he sacked me and took away the keys to my latest car, a Ford Zephyr 6. I fled back to Sheffield and let Mum answer the debtors' letters.

Norma and I married shortly after that, on Boxing Day in 1960. Her mother was quick to assess that the whole thing was a mistake, and my own parents weren't exactly overjoyed, because I didn't have a job. The only person who supported us was little Grandma Bower, who thought it was all very sweet. We put our names down for a council house and spent most of the next two years living between my grandma's, my mum's and with Norma's parents, Doris and Frank.

We didn't have a honeymoon. Instead, I hitch-hiked back to Newcastle and found a job as a bread salesman. I rented a one-bedroomed flat and sent for Norma. We were idyllically happy. I'd bring home steak and kidney pies which had been damaged at the bakery and we'd sit and eat those every night. I thought we had a little palace. OK, so we slept on a fold-away bed because the bedroom roof leaked, but it was still our own home. Not for long. We'd been there only about six weeks when my mother-in-law came to check on us. She was happy with the tiny kitchen and lounge. When she saw the sky through the hole in the bedroom ceiling, she marched Norma back to Sheffield. I sold the hire-purchase furniture and headed back home.

It was then that Ivor Bradley, who played a part in my arrest for fraud, gave me a job, selling canvassers' address books. We'd sell addresses and debts to retail companies like Dobson's. Ivor also gave me a green Austin 35. But I didn't like the irregular hours the job involved, so I moved to Sutherland's potted-meat company. That lasted about a month. I was so brilliant at selling their meatpaste that I thought the boss was going to make me the area manager. When he called me into his office I decided that while I was there I'd ask for a ten-shilling advance on my wages. But he'd called me in to tell me that no one wanted to work with me and to ask me to leave. He lent me ten shillings anyway, to show there were no hard feelings. I burst into tears. I was a brilliant salesman, yet I couldn't keep a job.

My next job was to follow up leads for an agent for Nova Sewing Machines. He would run a competition with ridiculously easy 'trick' questions, like, 'What colour is red cotton?' According to the literature, the prizes were fifty Nova sewing machines, a hundred £10 vouchers and 500 vouchers for £5. Of course, everyone won a £10 voucher.

I'd go to the addresses of the entrants, carrying a brand-new sewing machine, and say, 'Hi, I'm from Nova Sewing Machines.' I'd wait a second for them to notice that I was holding a spanking new machine before asking, 'Can I come in?'

The first rule of door-to-door selling is to get into the house. Once inside, I'd sit down and invariably the housewife would ask me if I wanted a cup of tea. The second rule is to always accept tea, as this buys time. She would be quite excited by now, and say, 'Have I won?' Of course she thought she'd won – I was carrying a brand-new sewing machine, for God's sake. I'd tell her she hadn't won the sewing machine, but I'd get it out of the box anyway. Before she could register her disappointment, I'd tell her she'd won a £10 voucher towards buying a new one. The machines were ridiculously priced at £40, so I'd offer them money off for their old sewing machine as well. Some old Singers were worth a lot of money, so this would bring the price down by another £5 or £10.

The only problem at Nova was the boss's daughter, who worked on the reception desk. She was only sixteen and a virgin, and even though I was married, I dated her and made love to her. One day I dropped her off home in one of her father's vans and he saw me. He went berserk and sacked me the following day.

I tried selling car covers next. This proved to be a disaster, because the few people who had cars could barely afford to keep them on the road, let alone buy a £45 plastic cover for them. I was looking around for something more stable when I saw the Dobson's advertisement. I thought a respectable company like that would be the answer to all my problems. Nothing could have been further from the truth, as I discovered to my cost and my shame.

4

WALKIN' BACK TO HAPPINESS

Having been to prison seemed to give me a weird fame, more than mere notoriety; a kind of respect, which I enjoyed in a perverse way. The reality of my situation didn't sink in until I tried to get work. I remember going for an interview for a factory job and showing the manager my merchant navy passport, which had an 'excellence' stamp in it. They all had this stamp in them, but he didn't know that, so he was quite impressed. He looked at the date and then asked me where I'd been for the past eight weeks. When I told him I'd been to prison, I might as well have said I'd raped his wife. The shock on his face was total. He left the room and came back a few minutes later, shaking his head. His reaction was echoed at the next three firms where I went looking for work. The moment I mentioned prison, they didn't want to know. After the third refusal, it began to dawn on me that, far from being a source of respect, my prison record was a burden which I would have to carry for the rest of my life.

It was a real anti-climax to the confidence I'd built up towards the end of my sentence. I'd left prison feeling enthusiastic about getting a proper job with regular wages. We were living at Norma's mother's, so I desperately wanted to get a place of our own and to start living as a real family. My only ambition was to find nine-to-five employment, avoiding the instability of selling, but nothing was coming together. Yet if someone had given me a job, I would not be the man I am today. I would have settled down to regular employment and got on with my life. Instead fate dealt me a very different hand.

Out of absolute necessity, I was forced to go back to selling. I contacted Ivor Bradley and went back to work for his company, in the offices in which I'd been arrested. Although Ivor had assisted the police on my case, he was actually a very nice guy, and he had given Norma money when I was in prison. Despite everything that had happened, I liked him. He told me that his company was the first in the area to gross a quarter of a million pounds a year, and that his accountant was very impressed. I knew that was a lot of money, but I had no idea what an accountant was. Ivor lived in a superior council house on the outskirts of Sheffield. He once took me there to show off his collection of miniature liqueurs. I remember thinking, 'Wow,' when I saw them. He gave me one of his Austin 7 vans to use and a job as a tallyman.

I should have been ecstatic, but my heart wasn't in it. One day I drove up to an area called Crooks, which was a hilly part of Sheffield, and got out of the van. I was trying to find a house for Norma and me to live in, but I kept thinking that there must be more to life than this. Prison had unsettled me. I'd spent the summer in the forest, I'd been fed, I'd had nothing to worry about apart from getting out. Now I was back in the real world. Part of my unhappiness stemmed from the situation with Norma's cousin, Cathy. During my prison sentence, she'd met her future husband and didn't want to see me any more. Norma was about to have our baby, so I should have been feeling excited, but something was missing. I was hankering after the discipline of a real job. I felt trapped between the unappealing prospect of discipline and my inability to handle the freedom which came with selling. I had no financial security with Ivor – one week I might make £12, the next £20, but there were no guarantees. I was deeply unhappy. For the first time in my life I'd experienced rejection, both in love and in work. Before going to prison, every job I asked for I got; every girl I chatted up said yes. Now it was all no, no, no. My confidence had taken a knock and I couldn't see a way out of the situation. I didn't know that this low point was in fact to be a turning point in my life.

I was always looking for ways to make extra money on top of my irregular wages. One day I was looking through the small ads when something caught my eye. It was an ad for a driver with his own van to take a band to gigs for £3 10s a night. My friend Billy Oldham and I both had vans by now, so we went along to the address. The house was on a council estate on the outskirts of Sheffield, and the group's name was Johnny Tempest and the Cadillacs. I got the shock of my life when a young guy opened the door and said his name was Johnny Tempest. Beneath the eyeliner, mascara and rouge were the unmistakable features of Johnny Greaves, the spotty, greasy apprentice turner who had made my life hell in my final weeks at the steelworks. I stifled my laughter and told him I'd come about the job. He recognised me immediately. 'Well, thou won't get it,' he said, and shut the door. Then Billy knocked on the door and Johnny gave him the driving job.

A couple of weeks later I asked Billy how it was all going. He told me that he took Johnny and the Cadillacs to different venues about three times a week and that he made £3 a trip after petrol. He said that once he'd plugged in their equipment he just sat and waited until they had finished, then loaded their stuff back into his van. I had no idea what a group did or was. I'd gone straight from the bakery into the merchant navy and missed out on the teenage coffee-bar scene, where everyone sat around listening to the jukebox. The only records I knew were Cliff Richard's 'Move It' and Tommy Steele's 'Rock With The Caveman', which I'd heard while doing my bread round, and I was totally naïve when it came to new bands like Johnny Tempest and the Cadillacs.

I found out that the band played at the Chesterfield Town Hall and got £13 for going on stage three times in an evening. If they were good, they were given an extra £2. Billy told me the place was full of kids and that pretty girls followed Johnny all over the place. According to Billy's reckoning, the Chesterfield held about 800 people, each of whom paid 2s 6d to watch the band. Now, I may not have known anything about music, but there was nothing wrong with my adding up. I worked out that 800 people at 2s 6d made £100; subtract £15 for the band, if they played well, and you were left with £85. I asked Billy who got the money. He said the man on the door put it in a box.

I thought the whole thing sounded incredible. I wanted to go to the Chesterfield that same night. Johnny Tempest was not playing there for another three weeks, but I went along anyway, and saw a band called Dave Berry and the Cruisers. The excitement was too much for me – it was like being back in New York again. Dave Berry was a very sexy guy on stage. He wore leather trousers and a fringed leather jacket, and he was so tall that he seemed to crawl around the place like a spider in slow motion. I was overwhelmed. I'd spent the last few weeks feeling unhappy, and suddenly all the misery had lifted. After everyone had filed out, I asked the man on the door who owned the place. He was a bit suspicious, but he gave me a name and number.

Two days later I called and asked if there was an evening free for me to book the hall. Unfortunately, every night was taken. I didn't know where else to look. I didn't even know where teenagers went out in Sheffield, so I asked my seventeen-year-old brother, Geoffrey. The following Saturday night, Geoffrey took me to two of the most popular venues, Mecca and Club 60. I wasn't impressed. Club 60 was packed out, yet it was nothing more than a damp cellar with old wine bottles hanging from the ceiling. OK, so they had red lights, but it was hardly glamorous.

I spent the next two weeks driving around Sheffield, selling goods for Ivor and looking for a suitable venue at the same time. St Aidan's church was local to our estate and often had dances on Friday nights. I went to see Vicar Jerome to ask about renting it, but he wasn't very keen. He said that someone had once tried to put on jazz evenings and that the whole thing had been a flop. Eventually, however, he agreed to rent the hall for £2 10s an evening. My next step was to find a band. I tried to book Johnny Tempest, but he couldn't play for four weeks. I then tried Dave Berry, but he wasn't available for three weeks. I started to panic. I had only three days in which to scour all the pubs looking for someone to play. I went to the Cannon Inn in Sheffield and saw a group called the Pursuers. They had two drummers, which I thought was very impressive. In the middle of their act, a tall guy with glasses started singing Buddy Holly numbers. I was blown away. I booked them that evening for two Fridays. The next day I hand-painted a sign using some old bicycle paint. I wrote, 'DIG

THIS, DADDY'O' in big black letters and drew Andy Capp dancing in one corner. I printed some fliers and handed them to people leaving the local cinema.

The following night, 17 August 1962, I went to St Aidan's at 6.30p.m. and waited. The Pursuers arrived with their drumkits and set up their equipment on the small stage at the back of the hall. At 7.30p.m. I opened the doors, not knowing whether I would see a crowd of people or an empty street. To my amazement, people were queuing outside. As the hall began to fill up, I realised that I'd overlooked one crucial element to any venue: the atmosphere. As it was mid-August, the light was still streaming through the windows. The Pursuers could have been the most fantastic band in the world, but they still needed the right environment. After twenty minutes they stopped playing and told me to put on the music while they took a break. Music? What music? The only thing I could think of was Mum's radiogram. I jumped into my van and drove to her house to fetch it. I only had two Tommy Steele records, so my cousin, Betty Brightmore, went home for her collection of about six. In Mum's living room, the radiogram was loud; in St Aidan's church hall it was barely audible.

I learned three important lessons that evening: first, I needed atmosphere; secondly, I needed lights; thirdly, I needed sound.

After I'd paid the Pursuers their £12 fee and paid for the fliers and the advert I was £25 down. My wages from Ivor was £20 that week, so I had to borrow £5 from Norma's mum. The evening had been a disaster. If I hadn't booked the Pursuers for the following week, and Dave Berry and Johnny Tempest respectively for the third and fourth weeks, I might have given up there and then. As it was, I was committed. I quickly bought some red lightbulbs and sheets of chipboard to block the windows in the hall. I found some speakers in the roof which had been used for the choir, and connected them to the back of Mum's radiogram. The next time the Pursuers played, there was more of an atmosphere, because at least the place was in darkness, but the music was still inaudible.

After I'd deducted the cost of the lights and the boards, I was once again in deficit by £25. I was charging three shillings to see the band, but clearly they weren't a crowd-puller. I borrowed another £5 off Norma's mum, who was by now losing patience with me. She came out with the old cliché, 'Get yourself a proper job.' She said I ought to be more sensible because Norma was pregnant. 'Your wife can't pay her debts and I'm keeping you both,' was another thing she said, along with 'Why don't you go back to the bakery as a driver?'

The only encouragement came from my Uncle Jack and Auntie Jean. I'd call in for cups of tea and chat to Uncle Jack. Their house was always full of kids and animals – they had more dogs and cats than any family I'd seen. They told me to stick with it. Against all the odds and with everybody screaming at me, I persevered for one more week. I had Dave Berry next, and I knew that he was bound to pull a large crowd. I was convinced it would work, but just to be sure, I took out a big £6 advert in the *Sheffield Star*.

Friday 31 August 1962 was the day my life changed. For the first time ever, I experienced the euphoria of walking on stage in front of an audience. The place was packed out for Dave Berry and I couldn't resist taking the microphone and introducing the band. I made £65 that night, and I managed to pull a girl. I gave her a lift home and made love to her in the van. I'd discovered the pulling power of the spotlight, and from that day onwards I never looked back. On the Monday morning I returned Ivor's van and never worked for anyone else again.

Until now, I have always maintained that Johnny Tempest and the Cadillacs were the first band to make me money. This is not actually true: it was Dave Berry and the Cruisers. I've repeated this over the years because Johnny Tempest became a great friend of mine and I wanted him to have that accolade. Johnny did play the following week, and I made another £65, so he was a close second. Johnny's music was very different from Dave Berry's. Berry played Chuck Berry, while Tempest was more mainstream pop, like Cliff Richard. Tempest would sing, 'Do not forsake me, oh my darling', whereas Berry would rather have died than sing something like that. Berry was more, 'Long-distance information, give me Memphis Tennessee'. He also wanted to know that he was getting paid more than anyone else;

even if it was only £1 more, £15 to Tempest's £14, it made him happy.

By the time Johnny Tempest played on the fourth Friday, I had renamed St Aidan's church hall the Black Cat Club and painted a new sign over the door. Why the Black Cat? I've no idea, it just sounded good. I'd spent the week looking through music papers like the *New Musical Express* to see if there were any other interesting bands in the Sheffield area. We had two local groups which could bring in the crowds: the Vantennas, because they sang whatever was in the Top 10 in the charts that week, and Dean Marshall and the Deputies. If they were good, I decided, I'd leave a three-week gap and then book them to play again. The first group that came with three microphones was Frank Kelly and the Hunters, but they weren't a big crowd-puller. They stayed the night at my mum's.

From the very beginning, my whole family were involved in the club. Mum was the cashier, Dad was the doorman and Geoffrey helped to book the bands. Paul and Terry were too young in the very early days, but eventually they helped too. Some local boys lent a hand for ten shillings a night. I wanted to involve Billy Oldham but it wasn't his scene. We fell out a year later after I played around with his girlfriend. For some reason I went to her house looking for Billy. I don't know how it happened, but she ended up in my car and one thing led to another. When I next saw Billy he was furious. I said, 'Hi, mate,' as if nothing had happened; he retorted, 'Don't "Hi, mate" me, we're finished.' He was so angry I thought he was going to hit me. I felt bad about it because I never saw him again, from that day to this.

Although Dave Berry, who had given me my first profits, was known throughout the Sheffield area, I had yet to experience a real crowd-puller. Screaming Lord Sutch and the Savages changed that. They were hugely popular, and probably one of the best rock bands around in the early sixties. I paid Dave Sutch £50, which was a fortune compared to what most other bands got. Today, people know Screaming Lord Sutch as the joker who fronts the Monster Raving Loony Party, but back then he was a serious rock singer. Peter Green, who became a legendary guitarist, regularly played with Dave Sutch's band, and was part of the line-up the night I booked them for the Black Cat.

I was amazed to see their van outside when I went to open the club. It was a huge relief, because even the local bands were usually late. I was always on tenterhooks waiting for them to arrive. Dave's punctuality surprised me, and so did the state of his van. It was the scruffiest, filthiest thing I'd ever seen, with old posters stuck to the side. All our local bands had pristine transit vans. When they opened the back I nearly passed out from the smell. Talk about scratch your bum and pick your nose, it was rancid. The Savages had been eating, sleeping and doing God knows what in the back, and for a long time, by the look of it. I was equally shocked when I met Dave. I was used to glamorous pretty boys like Dave Berry, and here was a horrible little scruffy guy. I'd put up a huge sign in black and dayglo orange advertising their gig, but having seen them, I wasn't so sure that anyone would turn up.

In fact hundreds of people came, and the show was fantastic. It was a real horror show, with hatchets and pig's blood. They had the first strobe lights I'd ever seen and mind-blowing special effects for the time. Unlike every other band, which did two or three twenty-minute slots, depending on how good they were, Dave did one long set. He played for an hour and no more. The Savages' finale was chopping up a chair and setting fire to it on stage. The audience went wild, and I knew that I would have to book him again.

The success of the Black Cat marked the beginning of the end of my marriage to Norma. While I was caught up in the excitement of finding and booking new bands, Norma stayed at home. She couldn't understand what I did, and wished I would get a proper job. By the time our daughter Karen was born, in October 1962, the Black Cat was thriving and I was changing.

The minute the spotlight hit me, I became good looking. It was obvious from the reaction I got that women liked the power the stage gives a guy. Women like power, whether it's sexual power, financial power or showbiz power. Power brings confidence, and confidence is a big factor when it comes to sex appeal. When I was up there with the microphone, my personality shone out above everyone else's. Those sparks of charisma I'd shown during my early selling days were finally being put to good use. The flamboyant, glib side of my personality which, up until now, had only succeeded in getting me into trouble had now found an outlet.

Every night at the church hall there were girls waiting for me. I defy any man, put in the same situation, to resist that kind of attention. The sex I was having with these girls was fast – I don't think staying power was one of my fortes. On reflection, I must have been crap, because I didn't know the first thing about foreplay. I was offered instant sexual gratification, so I took it, any way and anywhere I could. I'd make love on the stage when the band had gone home, in the emergency exit, in the loo, in the back of vans, front of cars, wherever. I'm often confronted by women who say that their husbands have been faithful for fifteen years or whatever. I think that's great, but the husband is usually a bus driver or something, so what chance has he had for extra-marital sex? Yes, I was married, but I didn't see this as cheating on my wife. I wasn't cheating on her emotionally, and I tried to be a good husband, but we were both emotionally immature. Norma's mother was the mature one in our marriage.

As I have said, we were living at Norma's parents' house, in Kingly Street. I quite liked it there, as the house was bigger than my mum's. We'd tried living with Grandma Bower, but, looking back, it must have been quite hard work for Gran. She had to cook for us because Norma couldn't cook. After that, we lived with my mum, but she only knew about sons and wasn't very nice to Norma. She certainly didn't give her any emotional support. Norma had a miscarriage at Mum's house, before Karen was conceived and I went to prison, but it wasn't until later that I even knew what a miscarriage was. I'm horrified to think that that little girl went through all that on her own, without any sympathy from me or my mum.

We were at Doris and Frank's when Karen was born on 13 October. I didn't know what to expect, and completely panicked when Norma went into labour. I kept going to the phone box at the bottom of the street and asking when the midwife would be coming. I remember rushing out and dragging this poor woman into the house. There was no way on earth I was going in that room to watch my daughter being born – in those days such a thing was unheard of. Karen was big and orange when she was born, perhaps because of all the orange juice Norma had drunk to satisfy her cravings in the last few months of her pregnancy.

I can't say that I changed significantly after Karen came along. I was too wrapped up in the club. Putting on new bands was a matter of trial and error. One of the local bands, the Citadels, were good, but they couldn't draw a crowd. Count Lindsay was the same. Lindsay was a lugubrious-looking kid who did impersonations of Elvis Presley. He looked to me a bit like a cadaver, with hollow eyes, so it was me who christened him 'Count'. He could sing one of Screaming Lord Sutch's numbers, so I'd make him wear white make-up and a top hat and occasionally put him on as a warm-up act. One day I had a brilliant idea for a band. I asked the Citadels if they would change their name to the Skeletons and back Count Lindsay. I billed them as Count Lindsay III and the Skeletons. They had got a cheap strobe light from the Army & Navy store and basically copied Dave Sutch's act. The crowd loved it. I loved them, too, because I had to pay them only a fraction of what I paid Dave.

Around the same time I was being hassled by a guy called Ray Stewart. Like Lindsay, Ray also centred his act around Elvis, except that he looked even more like a cadaver than Lindsay. His music was good, but because he was tall and ugly, he didn't go down at all well. After he saw Count Lindsay he said he could do a better impression of Dave Sutch because he'd sing it for real instead of miming it which is what Lindsay did. He had a big, square face so I called him Frankenstein. I renamed his band the Monsters, and they went down a storm. The only problem was that Ray didn't want to be Frankenstein, he wanted to be Ray Stewart the Elvis impersonator. He played along because it was the only way I would let him on the stage.

It was only a matter of weeks before the crowd got bored with Frankenstein. By now Dave Sutch had taken his act all over Sheffield, so the horror bit was getting passé. To liven things up one night, I suggested that Ray should run into the audience waving a chain and frighten everybody. I'd rig up a bull rope with a loop on the end so that he could put his foot in it and climb up the rope into the roof. In theory it sounded brilliant. Everything went according to plan until Ray tried to climb the rope. He was wearing a rubber mask at the time and sweating like crazy, so he couldn't see what he was doing. Halfway up he tried to remove his mask and lost his grip. Thank God his foot caught in the loop. As he was dangling upside down, the Black Cat audience went crazy and started swinging him. Ray was going berserk; I could see from the look on his face that he'd lost his temper, so we put on the lights and Geoffrey, my father and I stopped him swinging and let him down. But it was too late. Ray had totally lost it and went at the crowd like a madman the moment he got to his feet. Here was a 6ft 3in guy who wanted to do Elvis Presley impersonations. He didn't want to be Frankenstein, and he certainly didn't want to be hung upside down from the rafters of a church hall. He was livid. If he'd caught anyone he would certainly have killed him. The whole club cleared in less than ten seconds. It took Geoffrey and me considerably longer to calm him down. I thought that would be the end of the Black Cat Club. I was wrong. Word spread about Frankenstein and I was bombarded with requests for more.

Two weeks later Frankenstein was back. This time I arranged for him to run into the crowd and grab a girl from the audience. I told him I'd put three guys at the front to catch the girl when he threw her back – he just had to wait for the cue. He ran out and got the girl, which went down really well as she was very pretty and wearing a particularly short skirt. While he was struggling with her on stage, I started calling the catchers to the front. I could see we were running out of time, so I was shouting, 'Dave, Alan, John – now, now.' Unfortunately, when Ray heard the word 'now', he hurled this girl from the stage. The audience scattered and she fell flat on her back. I thought she was dead. It was one of the most terrifying moments of my life. By the time the ambulance arrived she'd got her wind back, but she was still very dazed. I asked her to stay around so that I could check that she was OK. I ended up making love to her in the club that night.

After those two calamities I couldn't involve Ray in any more acrobatics, so I thought I'd copy another of Dave Sutch's stage acts instead. Part of his finale involved an explosion on stage, but I hadn't been able to track down the necessary equipment to imitate it. Eventually someone found some primitive pyrotechnic devices and I decided we'd have two explosions to mark the end of the Frankenstein act. My job was to connect the battery so that the devices would go off. When the time came for the explosions I put the connections together, and nothing happened. As I was sitting at the front, I couldn't see inside the tin boxes, so I shouted to the drummer to have a look to see if the wires were OK. The moment he peered into the tin, the whole thing exploded. It blew his spectacles off his face and threw him off his seat. While he was fumbling around, the second tin went off and knocked Ray off his feet and into the drumkit, which collapsed. It was a complete disaster. My ears never recovered from those explosions; the drummer never found his specs and Ray refused to play Frankenstein ever again. But for two months Frankenstein and the Monsters were one of Sheffield's biggest draws.

I was making a living running the Black Cat, but I wasn't accumulating wealth. I never had more than £100, which was always kept for booking the bands. It wasn't money that changed my personality, it was the power of the stage. All the qualities which had made me a brilliant salesman, like my exuberance and my fast talk, were perfect for fronting a nightclub. One of the things I'm often asked is, 'How did you find the courage to start?' I didn't. It just happened. I had nothing to give up: I wasn't at the end of an apprenticeship, I hadn't just finished college, or qualified for a profession – I was a salesman. My mind was scattered all over the place. What if I did this? What if I did that? I wasn't focused. As a salesman you never focus, because you have to be able to sell anything to anyone. I didn't have a 'proper' job to give up, which is what I always tell everyone. Solicitors say to me, 'Oh Peter, your life is so exciting, I wish I'd gone into your business.' Unfortunately once you're in a profession, it's almost impossible to give it up. You don't see many doctors chucking it all in to become a pop singer, guitar player or club owner: they've invested so many years in training. My training involved wooing and selling to people in and around Sheffield, and running the Black Cat Club was no different: I was simply selling something else: entertainment. I'd progressed from selling things to people on their doorsteps to selling music to a mass of people on *my* doorstep. It was much more fun, and certainly more lucrative. I could make more money in one night than I could in three weeks as a salesman. All I had to do was put everything into that one night and introduce the bands.

The Black Cat was on the border of two housing estates, the Intake and the Arbithorne. One housed the steelworkers and the other the coalminers. When the bands stopped playing, the crowd would start fighting. The only way to stop this was to entertain them. I'd get up on stage with the microphone and organise silly games. I'd have piccalilli sandwich-eating competitions and give the winner ten shillings. The sandwiches were totally lethal, but it kept everyone amused until the band came back on. When the piccalilli ran out I'd organise dancing competitions. I learned very quickly that generosity brings rewards, and I've adhered to that maxim all my life, although these days I find it works better with champagne. Being on stage and getting attention was a huge ego boost. I remember that whole period as being incredibly exciting and free – but at the same time it was unsettling.

I'd been brought up with the working-class work ethic and now I didn't have much to do on Mondays, Tuesdays, Wednesdays and Thursdays. My life revolved around Fridays. Running the club was more precarious than selling, but I didn't worry about that. From the moment Dave Berry made me money I had no fears for the future. The Merseybeat was about to explode and I was perfectly poised for the blast. It was November 1962 when I booked a little-known band from Liverpool. By the time they played for me in February 1963, they were a worldwide sensation.

5

BLUE MOON

The first record request I ever got was for 'Love Me Do' by the Beatles. Every Friday night I'd play it about three times during the band breaks. The Beatles were still unknown outside their native Liverpool, but their popularity was growing. In January 1962 they had been rejected by Decca Records because the company didn't believe they would ever make it into the music charts. Ten months later they had produced their own single and were being regularly written about in the *New Musical Express*. In November 1962 I was coming down from the success of Frankenstein and the Monsters and looking for something new to give the Black Cat crowd. If I hadn't seen an advert for the Beatles in *NME* I might never have got round to booking them.

As we didn't have a telephone at home, I did all my bookings from a public callbox on the council estate where Mum lived. I rang the number in the advert and got the Beatles' manager, Brian Epstein. I told him I wanted to book the Beatles and he said it would cost me £50. I was totally shocked. I remember saying to him, 'Excuse me, I only pay Screaming Lord Sutch £50, and nobody has heard of the Beatles.'

Epstein's justification for the fee was that they had a record in the charts. I knew that in fact it was moving out of the charts, but he wouldn't reduce the price. I told him that I'd think about it and call him back the following day. When I rang back to say I'd take them at £50, he said they'd gone up to £65. It wasn't a heavy negotiation – I think Epstein was as nervous as I was. From the start it was Brian and Peter, no Mr Epsteins or Mr Stringfellows. He wasn't like other managers I'd dealt with, he was more laid back. He'd rustle papers and rattle around his desk looking through letters. I could hear music in the background from his record shop. He was first and foremost a shop owner, not the hard-headed music manager everyone had assumed. Despite what he said, the price wasn't cut and dried. The Beatles were genuinely in demand and I don't think he could cope. He'd taken on something he thought was a candle and it turned into a fire-cracker in his hand. Everybody was ringing him demanding dates and the man was in a turmoil. At £65, the Beatles were too expensive for me. Once again, I told him I'd think about it.

Two days later, I called back again. Brian sounded even more anxious and told me the price had gone up to £100. This was an unbelievable sum of money. He told me they had another single coming out which would go to the top of the charts. I was excited, but I didn't know why. It wasn't as if Brian Epstein was giving me a hard sell – he sounded almost panic-stricken. We haggled back and forth. I wanted to pay no more than £65 but Epstein was adamant he wouldn't take less than £90. Eventually we agreed on £85, and I came out of the telephone box in a sweat. I'd never paid that amount of money for a band before.

The Black Cat could legally hold 210 people. I regularly let in 600, which went beyond sardines. I thought I could squeeze in 100 more at three shillings a head, which would make an extra £15. To earn £65 profit on a Dave Berry night, I would have to let in 609 people. The club cost £3 10s to hire; it was £2 to print the tickets and £2 for an advert in the *Sheffield Star*. We'd make a bit more money selling pop at sixpence a bottle.

I worked out I'd need to charge my usual three shillings to barely cover myself, even if I let seven hundred in. I was convinced that nobody, other than Dave Sutch, Johnny Tempest and Dave Berry, could fill the club to capacity. If I charged four shillings it would make me another £35, but the risk was even greater. The Beatles had a flat period between the exit of 'Love Me Do' from the charts and the release of 'Please Please Me' in February. I was starting to panic until I mentioned their name to a couple of girls at the club. They went crazy.

Encouraged by this reaction, I put my first advert in *NME*

which announced that the Beatles would be playing at the Black Cat Club on 12 February 1963. I then produced my first batch of tickets which had four shillings printed on them. When I started getting postal orders from Scotland I put the price up to five shillings. Between Christmas and January, I lost count of how many times I went back to the printers. My last 500 tickets were for sale at six shillings each. By January, I knew I'd sold in excess of 1,500 tickets. I also knew that the Black Cat could hold only 700, and then if everybody didn't breathe at the same time. I would have to find another venue.

Mecca laughed at me when I tried to book their dance hall, so I was forced to look on the outskirts of Sheffield. The nearest place with any space was the Azena Ballroom. The Azena was Sheffield's poshest dance hall. It had a beautiful pristine floor and plastic flowers on the surrounding tables. The owner, Arnold Fiddler, was a funeral director who had built the club for his ballroom dancer wife, Zena. She was always beautifully manicured and wearing some sequinned number, whatever the time of day or night. Mr Fiddler, also immaculately dressed in a little black suit, was a very sharp businessman. He told me they'd once had 450 dancers on their floor. I remember looking over his balcony doing mental calculations. Where he could accommodate 450, I could fit in 2,000. The moment I left him, I went back to the printers and ordered another 500 tickets.

Of course, Mr Fiddler had never heard of the Beatles. 'Well, what kind of music is it?'

'Oh, very nice, Mr Fiddler.'

'Well, what kind of dress?'

'Really nice.'

'What about the dancing, Peter?'

'They're really good dancers.'

'OK, let's say £29.'

It was such a relief to have found somewhere to put on the show. I took another advertisement in *NME* to announce the change of venue and by the time 12 February arrived, I'd sold 2,000 tickets. On the night the Beatles played, the Azena was mobbed. Apart from the 2,000 people with tickets, another 1,000 turned up from all over the country. Epstein could easily have pulled my date, but the man was true to his word and the Beatles turned up.

I drove into Sheffield to collect the band from their hotel and they all squeezed into the back of my Ford Anglia. That day their new single, 'Please Please Me', had gone straight to number one in the *NME* chart. In 1963 there were several charts, but the *NME*'s was probably the most respected. They were all incredibly excited at having their first number one. In the back of my car they passed around the telegram of congratulations from *NME*. I still get goose pimples when I hear the song. When I listen to it I remember a magical musical explosion. It was an epic event in my life. It was perfect timing for the Beatles, and perfect timing for me.

I remember them as lovely guys, laughing and screaming that they were top of the charts. John Lennon was just an ordinary bloke then, certainly not the man he became, in any shape or form.

When we arrived at the Azena, there were people crawling all over the roof trying to get in. The Beatles went in by the fire exit and set up on the stage while I tried to placate the crowd.

Mr Fiddler and his wife had dressed up specially to see this famous band. Zena was draped in jewels and sequins, and he was wearing a dinner jacket with dickie bow and cummerbund. They had no idea that there were already 2,000 people in their ballroom. All the Fiddlers saw were the 1,000 people shouting and yelling outside. When Zena caught a dozen fans trying to climb in through the toilet window, she called me over. 'When are you going to let them in, Peter?'

'Er, they're already in.'

With that she fainted. Mr Fiddler, desperately trying to bring his wife round, was at the same time desperately trying to increase the £29 booking fee. We renegotiated while she was still out cold. He used one hand to waft air to her face and the other to gesticulate for more money. We finally settled on £40, on the condition that I didn't let any more than 1,000 people in.

Meanwhile, the crowd outside were hanging off the roof, chanting my name, 'Stringfellow. Stringfellow. We're not coming to the Black Cat any more.' I realised that I was going to lose a lot of custom if I didn't do something quickly. I told Geoffrey to open the fire-exit doors. I shouted above the chanting, 'Don't blame me if you find a door open at the back!' Within seconds the throng had cleared. It was a total fire hazard, but nobody cared. The atmosphere was electric. I swear to this day that no one can have heard a thing because of all the screaming. The Beatles had only two hits, 'Love Me Do' and 'Please Please Me', so their set was only forty minutes long.

I was totally blown away by the glamour and the excitement. That evening changed my life. I knew that one Black Cat Club wasn't enough. I wanted more; I wanted what I'd had that night, every night.

After they played for me, the Beatles went on a UK tour. For some reason they were missing out Sheffield. I got my first bit of local publicity by asking Brian Epstein personally if he'd put the Beatles on at the Sheffield City Hall. Brian added another date and I got all the credit for it. I also got to go backstage. The Beatles were superstars by then, yet they came across as the same regular guys who had sat in the back of my car. That same year Epstein asked me to join his stable and become the Beatles' compere. He was such a friendly guy. I had no idea he was gay – I just thought he liked my style!

There were always hordes of people waiting outside his office. The day I went to see him, Ringo Starr was sitting outside. I was amazed that Brian called me in before Ringo. There was none of this 'wait outside and I'll see you in three days' business. Brian told me I'd have to give up my clubs if I wanted to join him. By then – this was some time after the Azena gig – I had the Black Cat, the Blue Moon and the Mojo club, which was a lot to give up. He actually advised me not to let the clubs go. He equated my life with his own, except that he'd had only the one record shop to sacrifice when he started managing the band. We were calling them clubs, but they were in fact two church halls and a bombed building. They were my livelihood nonetheless, and I decided not to join Brian. Regrets? None whatsoever. I loved the freedom of being my own boss. And anyway the Beatles had already given me the impetus to expand my own operation. They came through my life like a shooting star and changed it forever.

It wasn't long after the Beatles played the Azena that I found another church hall about two miles from the Black Cat. Unusually for my clubs, this one was on the first floor. I booked it for Sunday evenings because I'd already tried Saturdays at the Black Cat and it hadn't worked. I was always asking Vicar Jerome for Saturday nights, but invariably his hall was booked up with charity events. One Saturday it was free so I booked it. I remember thinking, 'Wow, if I can pack this place on Fridays *and* Saturdays, it's going to make a lot of money.' The evening was a disaster, but nevertheless it taught me a lesson: Saturday was the big night out for my local crowd. They went straight into the centre of Sheffield, usually to the Mecca, and didn't want to hang around near home. So instead of Saturdays I asked the vicar for Tuesday nights. It was a good night to try out up-and-coming bands. I would pay them no more than £7, and I'd be lucky to make £20. I knew I could not fill my clubs on two consecutive weekend nights, so I was happy to have the Blue Moon for Sundays.

The Blue Moon was just another church hall, like St Aidan's, but this time I did more than just board up the windows. I constructed a dressing-room area at one side of the stage using old railway sleepers and planks of wood. On the other side I built myself a small boxed-in area with a curtain round it, which was where I'd play my records in between the groups' sets. For the opening night I booked the Marauders on the strength of their record 'I Don't Want Your Money'. It sounded Mersey-beatish and they managed to pull a crowd.

For the second week I had the Kinks playing. Once again, I'd booked them on hearing their single, 'You Really Got Me', which had reached number one by the time they came to the Blue Moon. The Kinks drove up from London and behaved like archetypal pop stars. Their lead singer, Ray Davies, oozed sex appeal. He was still in his van making love to his girlfriend when the band started playing. They were halfway through their first number before he climbed out of the van and got on stage. He had a 'who gives a fuck' attitude which I'd never seen before. The Kinks packed the Blue Moon for the first time. It was so full no one could move.

When I went on stage to announce the band I noticed something very odd: all the small people seemed to be standing in the middle. It wasn't until I made my way to the back of the room that I realised the floor had collapsed. I couldn't stop the band; I just prayed to God that the floor would hold out. If I'd mentioned it there would have been mass panic, so I just had to bite my lip and sit through the longest forty minutes of my life. I knew that everyone would start stamping their feet for an encore when the set was finished, so the moment the Kinks left the stage I put on a Cliff Richard record to drive the audience away. Miraculously, the floor bounced back after a couple of days. I never filled the Blue Moon to capacity again.

The following week I booked a Mersey group called Freddy Starr and the Midnighters. Although Freddy was handsome and looked the part, he kept stopping to tell jokes. I was annoyed, even though the audience was falling about laughing. I wanted a sexy Merseybeat, not a comedian.

At about this time I booked Gene Vincent for the Black Cat and the evening was a spectacular failure. I was carried away with the idea of getting a big name to play. I paid Vincent £100 because to my mind he was a fantastic superstar and very exciting. I learned another big lesson from that: what was exciting to me was not necessarily exciting to everyone else. I'd proved I was capable of hitting the bell and I went on to do it many times, but I could miss it, too. By the time Gene Vincent played for me he was well past his prime. Everyone was into the Merseybeat from Liverpool, the Hollies from Manchester and the Rolling Stones from London; Vincent belonged to the 'Be-bop-a-Lula' era of the late fifties. I remember him from that period, dressed in leather and standing with one leg cocked, singing to the sky – for some reason he never looked at the audience. I was totally in awe of him because he was American and had been in one of my favourite films, *The Girl Can't Help It*, with Jayne Mansfield.

When Gene arrived at the Black Cat, I could see he was shocked. On his contract, the name Black Cat looked great; it certainly didn't conjure up the image of a church hall on the City Road in Sheffield. I remember talking to him outside the club while his backing band were setting up. He was very quiet and reserved. Looking back, I can see that he was probably weighing up whether to go on stage or not. To me, he was very, very cool. With hindsight, I should think he was probably wondering what the fuck he was doing there. Hardly anyone turned up to see him. Believing he was still a big star, I charged six shillings, which contributed to the half-empty hall. I took no more than £40 that night, and lost a lot of money.

I had to be careful not to lose money two weeks running. While I could make £100 or £200 in one night, a mistake like Gene Vincent could wipe out £100. It was always a gamble with completely new bands. A few months after the Beatles played I went to the Cavern Club in Liverpool and met Bob Wooller, a famous Liverpool DJ in those days. He looked so ordinary I remember thinking that I could do his job better than him. I turned up at the Cavern Club wearing a leather jacket that wasn't quite right. Bomber jackets were all the rage, but I couldn't find one in Sheffield, so I bought the next best thing. It was the wrong style, but what the hell, it was leather.

That night, Brian Epstein suggested that I book Gerry and the Pacemakers. He showed me a photograph of Gerry and I said no without even giving their music a hearing. He didn't look right. He had a little fat face and was not at all glamorous or sexy. Of course, their first record went to number one, as did their next two records.

The Iron Gate Club in Liverpool was another good venue for finding bands. The owner took me into his office and played me a tape of a group called the Searchers. The song was 'Sweets For My Sweet', and the moment I heard it I booked them, for £80. Once again, the record was at number one when they played the Blue Moon. I wasn't smart enough to make three bookings at the same time, but I soon learned. Once a group had been at number one they were impossible to book. The flipside to this was overbooking a band that couldn't bring in the crowds. I once booked Wayne Fontana for six nights after hearing 'It Was Easier To Hurt Her', but it didn't make the charts until four months later. Even Shane Fenton and the Fentones didn't pack the place, and they were big in the early sixties. Shane Fenton subsequently became Alvin Stardust and came back into my life later.

The first time I ever met Rod Stewart was at the Blue Moon. I'd booked Long John Baldry and the Hoochy Coochy Men, and Rod came along as their second singer. When Long John took a break he let Rod do a couple of numbers. Rod was the first person I'd seen with backcombed hair. He always had a scarf round his neck and looked a bit effeminate. A lot of people thought he was gay – although, I hasten to add, I wasn't one of them. In fact it was Long John who was homosexual, but nobody suspected him because he was 6ft tall and very masculine with a deep voice. I could never understand why Rod was called a poof, because he always had a beautiful girl with him; I never once saw Rod without a beautiful blonde. They were what we called 'London-groomed'. He would get on stage and pretend he had a sore throat so he only had to sing two numbers. After the Coochy Men had played a few times, the crowd were really waiting for Rod to come on.

I was the first person to put Rod's name on the bill. I put an advert in the local paper announcing, 'Long John Baldry and the Hoochy Coochy Men, starring Rod Stewart'. Long John went berserk. He told me any advertising should mention only him and his band. Not long after that, Rod left the band and formed the Soul Agents, which I'd bill as Rod Stewart and the Soul Agents. I liked him because he was different from a lot of the other singers. He was no mad raver in those days. Whereas the other guys, including myself, used the power of the stage to attract girls, Rod always came with a girl already in tow. He would sit in the dressing-room area at the Blue Moon holding hands with his girlfriend. When it was time to go on stage, his blonde would sit and watch him, then he'd go back and sit with her again. He would go on, get a reaction, then get off. My mother Elsie adored him. He was very image-conscious, always touching his hair and holding his scarf, which became a trademark.

As the Black Cat and the Blue Moon became more popular, their success reflected directly on me and I became hugely popular with the girls. I no longer had to chase around after them. Up until I started the clubs, I hadn't had many one-night stands. I used to take a girl out a couple of times, and maybe on the third date I'd make love to her in the back of my car. The first time I ever had a one-off experience was in Manchester, when I was about seventeen. Billy Oldham and I had gone cruising for girls in the city centre in the car. We pulled up beside two girls and started chatting. They lived above a pub in Manchester, so we gave them a lift home. Their parents were out, and we ended up in their bedrooms. It was the first time I went down on a girl. I was seeing Norma at the time, but she was my girlfriend, and I didn't think you did things like that to your girlfriend. The whole experience was rather dismal, and not much better for Billy.

We didn't know *anything* about sex. I'd read *Lady Chatterley's Lover*, which had given me some education, but I'd been turned off by the roughness of it. The book was banned because the language was too explicit for the time. I'd never heard words like 'fuck' used in a sexual context before. There was no sex in the papers – well, certainly none in the *Sheffield Star*. The *News of the World* was the only paper that carried any 'naughty' stories. It took me ages to work out what the word 'intercourse' meant because the dictionaries of the time didn't make any reference to sexual intercourse. The *News of the World* would refer to people being found in 'compromising positions', which was just as baffling. I knew a lot of vicars did it, and got into trouble for doing it, but I still couldn't figure out exactly what it was they were doing.

There is a myth that door-to-door salesmen get off with all the young wives stuck at home, but in all my years of knocking on doors, I never once had a sexual encounter. To me, it was unbelievable that a married woman would want to have casual sex with a salesman. For a short time I sold lingerie door to door, but even with such a risqué product my sexual expectations were nil. I was working for Ivor Bradley at the time, and although I was supposed to be selling carpets, I'd keep a suitcase full of lingerie with me just in case. If I found a lady attractive, I'd tell her I had something special in my van and show her the suitcase full of underwear. I found it exciting showing these women lingerie, but I never once tried to seduce any of them. As I say, I didn't think married women did things like that. I knew that Norma would never do it. Sure, married guys did it, but it was different for women. Once Norma and I were married, she joined the holy trinity of those who didn't do it: my mother, the Queen and my wife.

The girls who came to the club were different. They were young, single and very impressionable. The dancing at the club was what I call 'proper' dancing, which was more sexy than dancing is today. We were twisting and doing rock 'n' roll, which usually involved the girls being thrown over some guy's shoulder. Their swirly skirts would fly up and you'd see their panties underneath. All the girls wore stockings and suspenders because there were no tights in those days. Panty-girdles were the in thing; every girl wore one, regardless of her shape. Norma was thin, I mean thin, and even she wore one. The atmosphere in the club was sexy, too. Sex was everywhere, and the girls were available.

I met my second wife, Coral, at the Blue Moon. I was in the middle of talking on the microphone when I felt a finger run down my back. Once I'd got the record playing, I turned round and saw a blonde figure disappearing into the crowd. A big guy called David Knowells was standing behind me. He said, 'Oh, that's Coral. She came with me, but she's a bit flirty. Don't take her seriously.' I looked around for Coral and saw her sitting on the edge of the stage in a little dress, but I didn't talk to her that night because she was with David, who had a crush on her.

The following Sunday she was at the Blue Moon again and at the end of the night I started talking to her and offered to walk her home. It was a long, long way, probably the other side of Sheffield, and I regretted the suggestion. In the end I didn't take her all the way home. I went halfway (and that was about three miles) because I knew that otherwise I'd never get back. Coral, who worked at the local printing works, was very slim, very sexy and, even though she was young, she was glamorous. She was also cleverer than a lot of the girls I'd met.

The next week we started playing around together when the club closed. I wasn't at all serious about her. To me she was just another girl. The last thing I wanted was an affair, because I was married, but Coral kept coming back week after week. After a month or so, I tried to palm her off on a friend of mine who ran the local record shop. I was putting on a show at Sheffield City Hall, and Norma was coming with me. Obviously, I didn't want her to know about Coral.

I'd seen a talent competition in a local pub and decided to stage a similar event at the City Hall. I called the evening 'Thank Your Lucky Stars' after the television show. The BBC found out about it and wanted to put an injunction on me. They sent a solicitor to Sheffield to get me to change the name, but when he realised how naïve I was, he let me keep it. I even talked him into being one of the judges. I rang Pye and EMI records and asked them to send up representatives to judge the competition. Johnny Tempest, Dave Berry, the Vampires, Joe Cocker – who was then Vance Arnold of Vance Arnold and the Avengers – and Dean Marshall and the Deputies played that night. As Vance Arnold, Joe Cocker wasn't even in the running. He was a poor man's version of Dave Berry – except for the two Ray Charles numbers he did, which he sang better than anybody.

Geoffrey and I also performed that night. We went on before Dave Berry, which infuriated him. I sang 'I Saw Her Standing There', one of the Beatles' early songs, and brought the place down. I sang it like John Lennon, with a growl, and all the kids started screaming on cue. I remember to this day the tremendous feeling you get from a standing ovation. It was mind-blowing. If I'd been able to sing that song properly, I would have been a singer instead of a nightclub owner, but I had one humongous problem: I had no sense of timing.

The Cadillacs, Johnny Tempest's band, backed me and I couldn't get the timing even though we'd rehearsed the song. The drummer, Johnny Hall, suggested that I start off facing the band so that he could count me in and give me a nod. Geoffrey was fine, because he could pretend to play the guitar, but there was no way I could mime the song in front of an audience. When it came to our turn I held the microphone and stood with my back to the audience. It looked fantastic. The moment Johnny gave me the nod, I turned round and launched into 'I was standing there . . .' They screamed so much, I ended up singing it three times. Each time I turned round and faced the drummer. Dave Berry was furious because he had to follow me on to the stage. He was *the* star in Sheffield – he had 'Memphis Tennessee' in the charts – and he didn't appreciate the fact that his photograph wasn't on the programme cover. Geoffrey and I had bought ourselves leather jackets and I thought we looked so good I put our picture on the programme. It was years before Dave Berry mentioned his irritation. He said it was the first time he'd been asked to do a show where the promoters' photographs were used instead of those of the stars!

I tried singing in public only once more after that. I booked the City Hall and put on the Hollies, Wayne Fontana and the Rolling Stones. I'd planned to sing 'I Wanna Be Your Man', a Beatles song recorded by the Stones, their first Top 20 hit, but I couldn't get the key. Coral and I drove into the country so I could practise. We ended up having a row and in the event I sang 'Walking The Dog', an R&B number by Rufus Thomas, instead. I remembered all the words, but it didn't go down well. The crowd clapped, but there were no cries for an encore. God played a big joke on me. He gave me everything that goes with being a rock singer – the image, the lifestyle – except the voice to go with it.

To my dismay, the judges at the City Hall chose the Vampires instead of Johnny Tempest. Tony Hatch, who was representing Pye Records, saw something in the band I hadn't seen and wanted to make a record with them. On the night of the talent competition they had introduced a new member, a guy who played the harmonica. He was brilliant, and he was the reason Tony Hatch picked the Vampires ahead of Johnny Tempest. Tony changed their name to the Sheffields and asked me to manage them. They went on to make two records before fading into obscurity.

Even though I was supposed to be the Sheffields' manager, I was far more interested in Johnny Tempest. After the talent night I managed to get the Cadillacs a meeting at EMI. The company sent me a telegram telling me where and when to arrive. I got confused (as I still do) between a.m. and p.m., and

we arrived twelve hours early. We drove through the night for
what I thought was a 6a.m. appointment. The M1 motorway
didn't go as far as Sheffield then, so it took us seven hours on the
A1. Driving to London was a big expedition in those days. It
gave you a working-class version of jet lag, you were so tired by
the time you arrived. We ran out of petrol three times on the
journey – in those days we only bought petrol a gallon at a time
because nobody had any money. We'd never driven to London
before, so we had no idea how much petrol we'd need, and we
kept grinding to a halt and having to walk to the nearest garage.
So as well as being exhausted we were freezing cold.

We finally knocked on the door of EMI at 6a.m. and woke up
the night security guard. I told him we had a meeting to make
a record. When the guy asked to see the telegram, and told us the
meeting wasn't until six that evening, I thought the band were
going to kill me.

The girls in London looked different from Sheffield girls.
They wore what looked like yellow face make-up and we
thought they were much more sophisticated. With the rest of the
day to kill, the first place we wanted to see was Soho, of course.
We set off in search of a strip club. We wandered around Soho
until some guy invited us into one of the so-called strip joints.
We were just a bunch of Sheffield lads, so we must have looked
totally naïve. The owner told us the stripper would be coming
on shortly so we ordered a drink. We weren't to know that they
didn't have a licence for striptease. We sat and waited. After
about twenty minutes it was obvious there was not going to be
a stripper so we asked for our bill. It was £8 for four beers, a
staggering sum in those days. We were horrified. Quite apart
from the fact that we had been ripped off, we had no more than
£20 between us and we still had to get back to Sheffield.

Johnny Tempest and the Cadillacs did eventually make a
record, but the Cadillacs had to change their name to the
Stallions because there was already a band called the Cadillacs.
Their single never made the charts, and although they recorded
two more numbers, they were never released. The band toured
for a few more years before fading away. Chris Stainton, the
guitarist, went on to play with luminaries like Eric Clapton and

Joe Cocker, and made a lot of money. Their drummer, Johnny Hall, became my driver in the seventies and ended up finding God and moving to Greece. Malcolm Townsend joined the fire brigade, and Johnny Tempest became a carpet salesman. He eventually committed suicide in 1987.

Johnny Tempest and the Cadillacs were just one of a number of Sheffield bands who never made the big time. They rose, like myself, out of northern poverty, but somewhere along the line they lost sight of their dreams. In 1964 mine were only just beginning. I had the Black Cat and the Blue Moon, but what I wanted was nothing short of an empire.

6

GOT MY MOJO WORKING

Between 1964 and 1968 the youth culture of Great Britain exploded. One band came after the other: the Who, the Small Faces, the Yardbirds. Up until then, I'd played bopsy-wopsy music, but I wanted to be part of the rhythm 'n' blues sound. From the moment the Beatles had packed the Azena Ballroom, I wanted something bigger and better. One night a little fat guy came into the Blue Moon Club with a blonde woman who must have been three feet taller than him. They were the most incongruous couple I'd ever seen. He was balding with a little moustache and she was covered with make-up and wearing a fur stole. I remember thinking that this woman was a vision of beauty, but looking back, she must have been as common as hell. The little guy was called Ruben Wallis. He was the first Jewish person I'd met in Sheffield. There was no such thing as anti-semitism where I came from because we knew as much about Jews as we did about Mongolians.

Ruben spoke with a strange accent, punctuating each sentence with a shrug of the shoulders and an 'All right, my son.' He wanted to sell me the Day's Dance Hall, which was at the top of Pitsmoor. 'It's not for me, son,' he sniffed. 'If you're as good as they say you are, it's for you.' He was asking £5,000 for the premises, which was a ludicrous amount. He wouldn't believe I didn't have that kind of money. In his eyes I was an affluent nightclub owner who had managed to get the Beatles. In reality, I owned nothing and my clubs rarely generated more than £100 between them.

Ruben owned a hotel in a good part of Sheffield. He also

owned, among other properties, the Café Ocelot, which he leased to a friend of mine called Ivor White. The Café Ocelot had bedrooms upstairs, so it became a regular haunt after the Mojo Club opened. The Mojo started out as a derelict house which had once been Day's Dance Hall. The bombsite next door eventually became the Mojo car park. Ruben was keen to get rid of the dance hall, so he suggested I give him £1,000 immediately and pay the rest in monthly instalments. Eventually I convinced him that I didn't have £1,000, either, which was true. In the end he agreed to rent it to me for £30 a week.

By now I was paying £6 a week for the Black Cat, so £30 was an awful lot of money. But my optimism and propensity for signing anything took over. Ruben presented Geoffrey and me with a twenty-page lease agreement which we never read. We found out later that we'd signed a lease for thirty years.

Part of the agreement was that we kept pictures of the Queen and the Duke of Edinburgh on the wall. He also asked us not to touch the Steinway grand piano in the house. Once a month Ruben would come and count the mugs and the teaspoons, and each time he came, he had a new blonde on his arm.

I called the club the Mojo, after the song 'Got My Mojo Working', one of the numbers Long John Baldry sang at the Blue Moon Club. In the next four years the Mojo went through many changes. We started off painting African warriors on the walls and putting bits of mirror in their eyes. I asked everyone to bring in little dolls and we covered the stage with them.

The club later became the King Mojo, and we repainted it with pop art. I wanted it all striped black and white, but I forgot to tell the painters to leave the piano. Ruben's precious Steinway suddenly disappeared under the stripes in a mass of monochrome. The next time he came to count the mugs, he said: 'Where's the piano?'

'It's there, Ruben.'

'Where?'

'Look, there.'

He was furious. 'Oh, my God,' he kept saying as he tried to rub the paint off its legs.

The Mojo got off to a shaky start because I opened with the

wrong band. I booked Buddy Briton and the Regents. They sounded good, but for some reason they just didn't go down at all well.

The Mojo was not only my first move into trendiness but also my first attempt at running a proper business. I started banking money for the first time, at the Yorkshire penny bank. I would take in the takings, which Mum had counted, and hand over bags of coins to the cashier. I drove the bank crazy because I never knew exactly how much was in the bags. The cashier would say, 'Count it,' and I'd say, 'No, you count it.'

The Mojo opened on Thursdays, Fridays and Saturdays, and the Blue Moon on Sunday evenings, though it didn't make money unless I put on a major band. I closed down the Black Cat because I didn't want two clubs competing on a Friday evening. I thought that my old crowd would follow me to the Mojo, but they didn't. Instead I got a new crowd who were into the whole spectrum of music at that time – blues, rhythm 'n' blues and soul music. The Mojo made me ambitious, not for money, although I did begin to make more, but for fame. I didn't drink or go to restaurants; I was into fame, or at least, potential fame. I liked the response I was getting on the telephone from agents and I liked the reflected glory from all the big names, like Jimi Hendrix, for example. I'd never heard Hendrix play, but I was told that he was a brilliant, wild guitarist and someone I had to book. So I did, for £50.

He arrived in the Mojo's linoleum-covered dressing room and took up a position in front of the mirror. He didn't say very much, he just combed his hair. If I knew nothing about Hendrix's music, I knew even less about his reputation for taking drugs, but somebody in Sheffield must have known, because someone, somewhere, tipped off the local police that Hendrix would have drugs on him. It was well before the police brought in specialised drug squads, so the Sheffield constabulary sent the fire brigade instead.

Two burly firemen turned up and demanded to see the black guy with the drugs. As there were only two black guys in Sheffield – one was called Puffy Jimmy; the other, Ron Ron – Jimi Hendrix wasn't that difficult to miss. The firemen walked into the dressing room and said, 'Come on, blackie, where's these drugs?' In typical laconic manner, Hendrix said, 'There's no drugs in here, man.' The firemen were unconvinced. They had no idea what drugs looked like, but nevertheless they had a look around before they left. As they were going, I suggested that they should apologise to Mr Hendrix, as he'd flown in from America especially to come to Sheffield. They put their heads round the dressing-room door and said, 'Sorry about that, laddie.' Hendrix looked up from what appeared to be a six-inch joint and said, 'Hey, cool, man.'

When a very stoned Hendrix finally took the stage, no one had heard anything like him before. It was loud, screaming and yelling, and left everyone completely stunned.

After Hendrix, I had a succession of big-name bands. I booked Wilson Pickett, who came along with an organist called Reg Dwight. Dwight played keyboards for a band called Bluesology. No one ever took any notice of him – he was just a quiet, nondescript little guy who wore spectacles. He certainly wasn't the flamboyant performer we all know today as Elton John. I booked out-and-out legends, like Ben E. King and Sonny Boy Williamson, who was the Elvis of rhythm 'n' blues. Sonny Boy took one look at the Mojo and us young white kids and started laughing. He'd seen it all, done it all. 'Well, boys, where's de booze?' he said. He couldn't believe that we didn't have a bar. I sent out for a bottle of whisky and he drank the lot before going on stage. He played fantastically.

By now I'd got my crowd used to encores. Some of these groups made a whole act out of coming back on stage, and the audience expected it every time. When Ike and Tina Turner played, there was no way they were going to let her off the stage without an encore – or three. Ike and Tina packed the place with a show that had to be seen to be believed. They came with the Ikettes and a thirteen-piece band. They all crammed on to the 25ft by 6ft stage, so, as you can imagine, the atmosphere was intense to say the least. There was no air-conditioning, so it was just like being in a sauna – wall-to-wall sweat.

After the second encore, Tina gasped, 'Peter, get me the fuck off this stage.' I pleaded with her to do just one more, because

I knew the audience wouldn't let her get away without an encore. In any case, in order to leave the stage the performers had to walk through the audience, and they were unlikely to let her pass. But Tina was giving me such a look that there was no way I could insist. I knew I could control my Mojo crowd, so I told her to faint and said I would catch her. I announced to the audience, 'Ladies and gentlemen, let's hear it for the fantastic Ike and Tina Turner and the Ikettes,' and then gave her the nod. Now, Tiny Turner is a big, energetic lady, and I was just skin and bones, so I suppose the upshot of all this was inevitable. The moment she threw herself forward, I collapsed under her weight and we both fell off the stage and into the audience. Neither of us were hurt, and the audience carried us both on their hands to the back of the club.

I could never get Tina Turner to play again, not because of the encore incident, but because like many bands of the sixties, she became too big. Roy Tempest, who was the booker for Tina Turner and other big bands, rang a couple of weeks later and asked if I wanted the original Drifters. I agreed a date, the Drifters arrived, and they were fantastic. The significance of his use of the word 'original' didn't become clear until I'd booked the Terrific Temptations, the Fabulous Four Tops and the Irresistible Isley Brothers.

Roy Tempest had been getting big stars over from America for years, but he wasn't making any money because they wanted to stay in the best hotels and have the best backing bands. When he offered the stars crappy little backing bands and cheap hotels, they refused to come. His solution to this problem was to find other black American artists who were prepared to play for less in return for the chance to visit England. To get bookings he used these familiar-sounding but crucially different names. By the time I'd discovered this, it was too late. I'd already booked the 'Terrific' Temptations and the Mojo regulars were really excited.

For the first time as a club owner I was faced with a moral dilemma. It didn't matter that I hadn't known myself that this band was not the real McCoy, I didn't want to con the Mojo crowd. On the night they played I went into the dressing room and asked the fake Temptations who they really were. 'Man, we're the Velours from New Jersey,' said one of them. They performed a little routine for me, singing in harmony and clapping, and they sounded great. I decided there and then to be honest with my crowd. After all, they had paid £1 to see the Temptations and £1 was a lot of money. I knew the Velours would get a cool reception, but having heard them perform in the dressing room, I was confident that they would eventually win over the audience.

I went on stage and announced that there had been a mix-up. Before the audience could start booing and hissing, I told them that the Velours were brilliant and that they'd come all the way from New Jersey, USA. The band went on and were fantastic. In fact, I was so impressed that I asked the singers if they fancied changing their name to the Fantastics, which would sound more Motown and help get them a record deal. The Velours seemed a nothing name: velvet, smooth and meaningless. The following week I spoke to a producer at Pye Records, who suggested that we went for an audition. The producer was impressed, but he'd just signed up a similar all-black band called the Foundations. Although the Fantastics were better, they were too similar.

Before we left the studio, the producer mentioned to me that he was looking for some white Supremes. I immediately said I knew of just the group. I had in mind three dancers from Chesterfield, sexy showgirls who were seeing my brother Geoffrey, Johnny Hall, the Cadillacs' drummer, and me. They called themselves Tiger, Spider and Copper.

The next time the girls came to the club, I took them into the back room and asked if they could sing. They only knew a few bars from the Wilson Pickett number 'Land Of A Thousand Dances', but they sounded good enough for me to call the producer at Pye and get them an audition. All the way down to London they practised in the back of my van. For five hours, I heard 'ner ner n' ner ner ner n' ner ner ner ner ner ...' and then the whole thing would collapse because they didn't know how to end the song in harmony. The girls were beginning to panic, but I had an idea.

When we got into the studio, the producer asked the girls what they'd like to sing. Tiger, who was a small blonde with big boobs, said, 'Well, one of our favourites in our act is "Land Of A Thousand Dances".' The producer found a backing tape and the girls started their routine. I remember thinking how terrible they looked as I planned my response if the producer asked them to sing another song. I decided I'd say, 'Well, shall we hear that one again?' Suddenly the producer yelled, 'Stop!' I was convinced that he'd sussed out that the girls weren't really singers, but instead he said, 'Great, girls. I don't need to hear any more.' He was so excited that he arranged for them to make a record in four days' time and immediately named the group the Paper Dolls. He even promised that he would record the Fantastics as soon as the Paper Dolls were on their way to success, in spite of the fact that he already had the Foundations.

This was my first introduction to band management, and it was going so well that I even considered selling the Mojo to become a full-time manager – until the reality of the situation hit home. The next time we went down to London, I was introduced to the Paper Dolls' agent, who'd been appointed by the Pye producer. Slowly but surely, I was being eased out of the picture. The agent got them on *Opportunity Knocks*, which was beautifully semi-fixed up, to my mind, because they won four weeks running. By that stage they were wearing wigs, short skirts and boots and enjoying every minute of their new-found fame. They'd also become as hard as nails. Their single, 'Something Here In My Heart', went to number four in the charts, but the 5 per cent I'd been promised never materialised. In retrospect, as a naïve Sheffield kid, I had great ideas but no contacts. In those days I was in awe of London. I could speak to Brian Epstein on the telephone and get hold of record producers, but I didn't know how to take anything further than that. These people could see my limitations.

At the time it hurt. I was a victim of southern prejudice because I spoke with a northern accent and came from Sheffield. I didn't yet understand the north–south divide, but it wasn't the first time I'd experienced prejudice of this type. During the early days of the Mojo, I got involved with the television programme *Ready Steady Go* and encountered similar problems. It was shortly after the Cadillacs, or rather, the Stallions, as they became known, released a record, and I was desperate to promote them. *Ready Steady Go* had been launched in 1963 at the height of Beatlemania and was Britain's most popular and influential music show, and I wanted to get the Stallions on it.

I drove down to London, found the ITV headquarters and talked my way into the office of a woman called Vicki Wickham. I'd been told that she edited the programme, so I set about charming her into featuring the Stallions. I showed her photographs of the group and chatted to her about the Mojo Club. By the end of the afternoon, I'd met Francis Hitchin, the programme's producer, and had been asked to audition as a presenter for the show.

A couple of weeks later I arrived with twenty-five supporters from Sheffield, ready to take *Ready Steady Go* by storm. I was utterly dismayed to find that I had competition from two disc jockeys, both of whom were from London. We had to take it in turns to warm up the audience before the cameras started rolling. I went first, and talked about how Sheffield looked to London for style and musical trends and so on. I at least managed to get everyone to listen. The guy after me was a jack-the-lad Cockney who must have brought a hundred people with him. He wasn't as good as me, but he got a rave reception by the sheer number of his supporters. The third DJ was a young Jewish chap of whom no one took any notice.

After the show I went looking for Vicki Wickham to see if I'd got the job. We sat in the green room and she told me I was by far the best, but I'd have to get used to the audience. I realise now she was alluding to my broad Yorkshire accent, which was alien to their audience. If I'd spoken with a Cockney twang, I know I would have been given the presenting job. Instead, I was given the warm-up role, which basically involved relaxing the audience and making them laugh before filming started.

I did this for a whole year. I'd travel down to London on a Thursday morning with Johnny Hall, do the show in the afternoon, then collect my £35 fee and spend it in Charlie Chester's casino. Johnny and I would drive back to Sheffield in the early hours of the following morning and I'd be ready for the Mojo that evening. As the warm-up guy, my job was always off camera, but at every available opportunity I'd try to get my face in front of the lens. I have a video of me hogging the camera pretending to hold the crowd back when the Rolling Stones played one week. They were singing 'Paint It Black', and when they went off stage I jumped on, the camera following me, to make it look as if the crowd were running after the Stones. Unfortunately, I managed to put my foot through Brian Jones' sitar. I didn't just bend it, I destroyed the whole bowl of the instrument. One of the roadies said, 'Fuck, Brian's going to go crazy.' I thought the best thing to do was to apologise immediately, so I went up to their dressing room.

I had met the Rolling Stones about a year earlier when I put on a show at Sheffield's City Hall. The Four Cities Road Show had bands from Liverpool, Manchester, Sheffield and the Stones from London. Mick Jagger may sometimes give the impression that he is all 'all right, mate' friendliness, but he isn't a bit like that. In fact, I'd never met anyone like him before. I paid the Stones £125 and I was the one putting them on stage, yet he couldn't be bothered even to speak to me. I remember going up to the dressing room in Sheffield and seeing Brian Jones and Mick Jagger having an intense conversation. They didn't want to talk to me or anyone else, so I left them to it.

So here I was in their dressing room again, a year later, except this time I was full of apologies. I said, 'I'm really sorry, I was trying to hold back the crowd and I just . . .' There was a stony silence as the four of them looked at me with utter disgust. Brian Jones didn't say, 'Get stuffed,' 'Fuck off,' or even 'It's OK.' They all just stared at me and said absolutely nothing. I crept out of the dressing room, utterly embarrassed.

Looking back, I was probably too northern and a little bit raw for everyone, but of course, I couldn't see this at the time. I thought I was the best, and I couldn't understand why I was off camera when, as far as I was concerned, I should have been fronting my own television show. Vicki Wickham and the show's presenter, Cathy McGowan, eventually took up my invitation to come and see me at the Mojo. They were really impressed with how I handled the crowd, and after much cajoling from me, they agreed to give me one shot at presenting with Cathy. I was given a script, which immediately put me on my guard. I was so stiff during the rehearsals that I told Vicki I'd prefer to ad lib and use the script as a prompt. She wasn't happy, but as we were ten seconds from going on air at the time she was not in a position to argue.

The stars of that week's show were Herman's Hermits. I remember introducing Peter Noone, the lead singer, as the 'toothy wonder'. It just came out of my mouth, and it really upset Peter. He came up to me in the green room after the show and said, 'What do you mean, "toothy wonder"?' I thought he was going to hit me. I told him I hadn't meant it nastily, but he still took offence. Shortly afterwards he went to America and had his front teeth capped.

At the end of the show I put up an umbrella and held it over my head and Cathy's. The producer thought it looked great, but Cathy completely freaked out. She said it was unlucky, and oddly enough it was, because I didn't get the show. The guy who was eventually given a presenting job was the young Jewish boy I'd met at the first audition. Compared to me he had no personality, but he did have a very straight accent.

In spite of these frustrations, my year at *Ready Steady Go* did wonders for both my ego and my reputation. I started to be recognised in Sheffield city centre, which, I confess, I liked very much. Every girl I made eyes at in the club I would make love to that same evening. Then I'd either go straight home to Norma or I'd see Coral, who was clever enough to hang in there. Although I hadn't taken the relationship seriously at the start, after about a year I eventually fell in love with her. It was inevitable that someone would see us together and tell Norma, and so it proved. When Norma confronted me, I burst into tears. We were still living with her parents, so things were a little awkward. Norma and I went into the back room to talk. She wanted me to promise that I would never see Coral again. I told her I didn't think I could do that. In my ridiculous way, I even ventured to suggest that all three of us could work something out. Norma, of course, was having none of it.

About six months later, Coral became pregnant. We didn't know what to do, and even discussed having the baby adopted.

But eventually it became obvious that I would have to get a divorce, even though such a thing was virtually unheard of in Sheffield in 1965.

Once I'd decided to leave Norma, Coral and I moved in above the Mojo Club and furnished the place on HP. I'm still amazed that I could have walked out on Norma and Karen, who was only two years old at the time. Leaving my daughter was incredibly painful. I still wonder how I did it. But I can also remember the love I felt for Coral at the time. It was all-consuming, a powerful, passionate love. Thank God, Norma didn't stop me from seeing Karen. I stayed close to her throughout her life and eventually she came to live with Coral and me.

On the night Scott was born, 7 January 1966, a week early, I was gambling in a casino in Manchester. I won £64, which was an absolute fortune then, and came back home to find the flat empty. I phoned Coral's mother to ask if she'd stayed the night there. 'No,' said her mother. 'She's in hospital, having *your* baby.' I went straight to the hospital and saw Scott, who was very pretty and very small. Then I went out and spent my winnings on toys, nappies and everything we needed. While Coral stayed at home and looked after Scott, I continued to build up the Mojo.

A new phenomenon was about to arrive in the form of the all-nighters. It all started because I couldn't afford to book the big names for a whole Saturday evening. Singers like Wilson Pickett, who had the hit 'In The Midnight Hour', were now only affordable at 2a.m., after they'd already played a major venue. I'd charge £1 entrance, and if I had 600 people for the night, I was well in front. I would make more money from these all-nighters than I would for the rest of the week.

During this period I booked the legendary Bo Diddley. Once again, my enthusiasm took over and I agreed to pay him £200. It was an astronomical sum, but I thought I could pack the place. By now I was used to seeing 200 or 300 people waiting outside for the all-nighters. The length of the queue was my barometer for the success of the evening. I could charge ten shillings for a session which started at 12p.m. and finished at 11a.m. It was a lot of money, but there again, the crowd got a lot for it, so they didn't mind paying.

But on the night Bo Diddley was due to play there was no one queuing outside. Most of the bands were late in those days, so I was praying he wouldn't be the exception. Half an hour before we opened a handful of people wandered in. I was panic-stricken. Maybe I hadn't advertised it well enough; maybe there'd been a disaster in Sheffield I hadn't heard about. The truth was, nobody wanted to see Bo Diddley. I remember sitting in my office looking over his contract. It had come from Barry Marshall, one of the big agents, and it was watertight. The only clause I could find which would enable me to cancel was the one covering the closure of the premises in the event of an 'act of God'. That meant a hurricane or an explosion at the very least, and I knew I couldn't conjure up either of those in half an hour. My only hope was that he would arrive too late and I could cancel and tell him I'd sent everyone home. As I pondered this, his van pulled up.

I immediately told Geoffrey to go downstairs and throw the electricity switch. I went outside to shake Bo's hand and just as I was saying, 'Welcome to the Mojo,' all the lights went off. I feigned absolute shock. I guided Bo and his crew into the office, where I phoned the electricity board by candlelight.

The guy on the phone said: 'Have you checked your switch?'

'Yes, yes, we've checked everything.'

'We'll send someone straight away, Mr Stringfellow.'

'No, no, that won't be necessary.'

'No, we can send someone now.'

'Well, I appreciate that you can't get here until tomorrow.'

'I said tonight. We can send someone tonight.'

'Well, thank you for trying. We'll just have to do our best until tomorrow.'

The guy on the other end of the phone must have thought I was either deaf or mad. I waited a few more minutes before remarking, 'Well, I think it must be an act of God.' Bo sensed something wasn't right. He just said, 'Right, the only thing we can do is get in our van and fuck off.' His final words were: 'You'll be hearing from me.' We never did. I waited until his van was out of sight then I put the lights back on. An hour later the electricity board turned up.

After the all-nighters came the discotheque, yet another new phenomenon. In London, I'd been to a club called Le Discotheque and was shocked to find there was no band playing. All I heard was blue-beat music all night. I started disco night the following Tuesday at the Mojo. I put an advert in the local paper announcing: 'Tuesday: discotheque, starring the Beatles, Ike and Tina Turner and Charlie Fox'.

The next week the place was packed, so I put the price up from a shilling to 1s 6d. Up until then, records had been used merely to fill in between the groups – though during the all-nighters, the groups would only play for forty-five minutes, so we listened to hours of records then anyway.

My next innovation was the all-dayer. Once again, this new concept was introduced for financial reasons. I wanted to book Stevie Wonder, but the cheapest I could get him for was £200, and even then the only time he could play was on a Sunday afternoon as he was passing through the city on his way to his next venue. But Stevie Wonder was so hot that it wouldn't have mattered what time he played. I charged £2 entrance and made a fortune. Little Stevie Wonder turned up with a twenty-piece orchestra and several aides. We'd never seen so many black people in Sheffield. It was extraordinary to watch them all pile out of their tour bus.

We all knew that Stevie was blind, of course, but we didn't know that he had other peculiarities. He must only have been about fourteen years old and I remember thinking he was quite mental because he was so unco-ordinated. His limbs were all over the place. On reflection, having met him many times since, I realise he was simply over-excited about going on stage. When he spoke he'd sway his head and his arms would flail around. The orchestra leader took me to one side and said, 'Stevie needs to use the john.' As if to confirm this, Stevie kept saying, 'Man, I gotta go to the john.' The toilets were at the back of the Mojo Club, so I took him up to the apartment. Coral was in the bathroom. I tapped on the door and asked Stevie to wait a moment. 'No, man, I can't wait,' he said.

Coral shouted, 'I'm in the bath!'

I explained that Stevie Wonder needed to use the toilet. 'Coral, let him in,' I said.

'I'm in the bath!' she shouted.

'Baby, he's blind, he won't see you.'

While all this was going on, Stevie was humming and shuffling around the flat, repeating that he had to 'go to the john'. After a while I told Coral that I would break down the door if she didn't open it. 'OK,' she shouted, 'but don't let him open his eyes.' We left Coral and Stevie in the bathroom. Stevie then proceeded to play the mouth organ and sing to himself while he was on the toilet. 'Peter, get this man out of here!' yelled Coral. I told her she had a choice: either she could come out wearing a towel, or stay inside. She decided to stay in the bath. Stevie might not have been able to see Coral, but she could see him. For half an hour he sat on the toilet with his trousers round his ankles, playing the mouth organ, while she sat in the bath. When he finally went on stage, he was superb.

It was during the Mojo period that I met my friend Roger Howe. A group of us went to a student dance on the outskirts of Sheffield one night. It was after I'd met the Rolling Stones, and I was dressed in flared jeans with bells on. We all had long hair and looked like a bunch of hippies. The student at the door refused to let us in, but then Roger came out and recognised me. I remember thinking he must be a young, affluent farmer because he was dressed in a waistcoat and tweed jacket. We immediately nicknamed him 'Town and Country'. Roger had organised the dance, which was all folk music, so we looked and felt very out of place.

We started talking and it turned out that he was from Attercliffe, which is not far from Pitsmoor, and that his father was a steelworker. Despite the disparity in our appearances, we actually came from very similar backgrounds. From that first meeting, we became lifelong friends and Roger eventually came to work for me. He is now the operations director of String-fellow's. He still dresses 'town and country', but at least his wardrobe suits his age these days. Back then, he could have passed for a ballet dancer, or even a rich man's son. However, he actually worked as a welder, which was a very tough job. It was only at night that he put on his tweeds and became affected.

It was Roger's idea to start a country-and-western night at the Mojo Club. We tried it for three weeks, but we couldn't generate enough interest so we gave up. Until he met me, Roger only ever had one girlfriend at a time, so I take the credit for showing him how to womanise. He'd chat up the girls I'd slept with the night before and tell them that I was too busy to see them. I used to admire him for coming to the all-nighters on Saturdays and then going straight off to his welding shift the next day, while all we did was to go off swimming in the country. We'd drop him at work and he'd do a full day's graft, even though he'd been up dancing all night. I should add here that, like me, Roger never took drugs to stay awake.

So much happened during those Mojo Club days. Geoffrey and I thought we could do anything. My own notoriety as a DJ spread throughout Sheffield and the north. I soon began doing star spots at other clubs, like the Dungeon in Nottingham, for £50 a night. I enjoyed the fame it brought me. I became obsessed with keeping up my image as a single guy. If Coral and I went into town to buy records, I'd ask her to walk behind me, not at my side, because I didn't want my reputation tarnished by the presence of a regular girlfriend. We certainly never held hands in public. One day I was driving my Vauxhall Wyvern with Coral, Scott and a bag of washing in the back when the police stopped me. It was hardly surprising. I'd paid £32 for the car, even though it was so wrecked that the body was tied to the chassis with a piece of rope. The top half was at a 25-degree angle to the bottom, and any passengers automatically felt sick. I remember telling the policeman I couldn't abandon the car because I had my girlfriend and 'this baby' in the back. I loved Scott dearly, but my overinflated ego didn't want anyone in Sheffield to know I had a girlfriend and a baby. It wasn't too long before everyone knew, and I began to revel in my new image as Sheffield's hippest dad. At that particular time it didn't fit in with my image, so Coral had to put Scott on top of the washing and catch a bus home. I rattled off in the Vauxhall and scrapped it the next day.

We'd drive anything in those days. Bald tyres were the norm;

you were lucky if your car *had* tyres. If we got a puncture, we'd mend it with a patch. I blew up the engine on the first motorbike I bought because I didn't know that you had to put oil in it. Geoffrey and I were always getting cars from leasing companies and not paying for them. We both got brand-new Minis and only paid the first instalment. It would take the leasing company a couple of months to get the car back, by which time we'd have moved on to another company.

I remember buying a Bentley for £300 and getting my friend Johnny Hacket's brother to paint it cream and brown, which were Rolls-Royce colours. He used soft paint which flaked off the moment anyone touched it. By the time I got rid of the Bentley, it looked like it had been to Vietnam and back.

From the moment Scott was born, Coral wanted to get married. I wanted to keep the whole thing a secret, but was eventually persuaded. Even so, it took us a while to get round to it. We decided to go down to London to get married at one point, but the registrar needed forty-eight hours' notice so the whole trip was pointless. I think we had three attempts in three different cities, but as we weren't residents in any of them, they wouldn't allow it. Scott was eighteen months old when we finally set a date for August 1967.

The day before our wedding a film crew came to Sheffield to shoot a movie starring Stanley Baxter. The Italian producer came to the Mojo looking for extras. He wanted flower-power types, in kaftans and beads, so Roger (abandoning his tweeds for once), Johnny Hall and I all volunteered. I was convinced this was going to be my break into movies. Peter Stringfellow, nightclub owner, super DJ and now film star. It was Johnny who reminded me that I was getting married the next day, so it wasn't exactly convenient. Undeterred, I checked what time the filming started, which was 10a.m. I knew I would have plenty of time to get to the register office by 2.30p.m., so the following day, my wedding day, all three of us went down to the shoot in my Triumph Herald.

The director told us to park our car and wait for Stanley Baxter to run past. He would ask us if we'd seen anybody, and that was our cue to say, 'He went that way.' We were so excited.

All of us were wearing kaftans and had flowers in our hair. In fact I was already dressed in my wedding clothes, which as luck would have it were exactly what the director wanted. As this was my first movie (and my last, I hasten to add), I had no idea that a 10a.m. start on a film shoot doesn't mean that they actually start filming at 10a.m. We didn't realise that nothing ever happens for hours. We sat and waited patiently until Roger looked at his watch and said, 'Peter, it's 1p.m. You've got to go now.' I was adamant I wanted to stay. The director kept saying, 'Any minute now,' but the minutes kept ticking by and it was soon 2p.m. Roger and Johnny went crazy, but I still insisted on staying another five minutes. With only twenty-five minutes to get to the register office, we left the set and I never got to appear in the film. I did manage to get married, however.

Afterwards we all went back to the Mojo for a party, where the Alan Bown Set played for us. Scott wasn't impressed; he cried all afternoon.

On the night of my wedding I was booked as the star DJ at the Dungeon in Nottingham, so Roger and I left the party early and headed off there. The same night I made love to a girl from the Dungeon Club. Then I drove back to Sheffield and consummated my marriage with Coral.

I never had any discipline in my sex life. I never once thought of it as immoral because Coral was my wife. She was different, completely separate from the beautiful, attractive, sexy girl I picked up in Nottingham. Coral and I had a wonderful sex life, but even during those early, heady days of our relationship, that didn't stop me making love to five virgins in one week at the club.

The Mojo days were truly wild. The Merseybeats, the Who, the Herd, the Spencer Davis Group, the Pretty Things, Manfred Mann, Ben E. King, the Small Faces, Georgie Fame, Edwin Starr ... the list goes on and on. Just about every major band of the sixties played at the club. It was one long party, but the party couldn't last forever. While I was dancing the night away, two important events were unfolding: a journalist at the *Sheffield Star* was writing a front-page story about drugs and a club boss; and officials in Whitehall were letting the ink dry on a new licensing bill. One would colour my reputation; the other was to end my livelihood.

7

KING OF THE ROAD

In the 1990s, they were called raves; in my day they were all-nighters. Apart from the music, the only difference between them was twenty-odd years. The image of all-nighters, like that of raves, was drug-induced dancing from dusk to dawn. But I swear to this day that I never took drugs. While the majority of kids were taking their mother's slimming pills, I kept going on natural adrenaline. Black bombers and purple hearts were the Ecstasy of the sixties – they kept everyone wide awake and wide-eyed. I was totally naïve about drugs, so naïve, in fact, that it took me months to work out why we weren't selling any chips at the all-nighters. Eventually it dawned on me that two-thirds of the crowd were taking appetite suppressants. The only drug I was eager to try was LSD – the Beatles' album *Sergeant Pepper's Lonely Hearts Club Band*, released in 1967, was full of references to LSD. It gave you dreamy thoughts and made you into a pop star, so I wanted some of that.

One evening, Chris Stainton, the bass guitarist with the Cadillacs, who went on to play with Joe Cocker and become a millionaire, and a few others, including the drummer, Johnny Hall, decided they wanted to try some LSD. We sent one of the band's groupies to look for some in Sheffield but she didn't have any luck. I was in the kitchen when she came back empty-handed. As everyone sat upstairs waiting for their trip, I had a brilliant idea.

Coral and I had a huge monster of a mountain dog at the time, called Fune McCool. Someone had asked me to look after him for a week, but the guy never came back so we adopted him. At the time he had an ear infection. The vet had given me a phial of drops to treat it. I found the drops and took them upstairs with a bag of sugar lumps. I let everyone in on the joke except Chris Stainton. He, of course, thought I was putting LSD on the sugar and didn't notice that he was the only one to actually swallow the cube. I turned off the lights and we all sat and waited. After about ten minutes someone said, 'Yeah, the trip's really coming on now,' and one by one we all joined in. Eventually Chris said, 'Yeah, I can feel it happening too.' When we asked him what he was getting, he went off on a wild fantasy about all the shapes he could see and how brilliant he felt. He was about five minutes into his soliloquy when everyone started screaming with laughter. We switched the lights back on and told Chris he'd just eaten Fune's drops. That was the closest I ever came to an LSD trip. A few weeks later we read some reports about the side-effects of the drug and it put everyone off.

In Sheffield, we weren't part of the psychedelic drug revolution that was happening in London. If they took anything at all, Sheffield kids were mainly into amphetamines, but I don't remember any drug casualties among the Mojo crowd. Even so, by 1968 the local police were concerned enough about the situation to start a drug squad. The Favorita, one of the trendy coffee bars where people congregated before coming to the all-nighters, was also a favourite haunt of the newly formed drug squad. One evening, around midnight, when the club was beginning to fill up, someone warned me that the café had been raided. I took the microphone and said, 'If you're carrying drugs in my club, get rid of them or get out.' An hour later someone was picked up by the police in the middle of town. He told them about my warning and they then told the *Sheffield Star*. The next day its front-page headline ran: 'CLUB BOSS GIVES DRUG TIP-OFF'.

I was devastated. I thought my club would be closed; I thought the whole of Sheffield had seen it and I'd be ruined. It turned out that three out of four people didn't know about the story, which taught me a big lesson about awareness of the press.

To this day I don't take drugs, yet I've lost count of the times people have asked my friends, 'Where does Peter get his cocaine from?' They assume that I'm high all the time because I bounce into Stringfellow's and chat to people all night, every night of the week. I know people think I take drugs; I also know that no matter how many times I deny it, there are always going to be a few who don't believe me. But what would be the point in writing my life story and lying? Paul McCartney, Mick Jagger, Eric Clapton and many other stars have admitted taking drugs in the sixties. I was either too scared to try them or too highly strung to need them – probably both. The only drug I use is alcohol. I like vodka, and it's legal. As for marijuana, I've never even smoked cigarettes, so it didn't interest me. My early experience with my dad's pipe pretty much put me off smoking anything.

I don't deny that I have tried marijuana, but not with any great enthusiasm. I was thirty-seven years old before I even took a puff of a joint. I was at a party in London, where everyone was lying around slumped on the floor. I'd had quite a lot of vodka and someone handed me a joint. I said, 'Cheers,' and took a couple of puffs. To this day I don't know whether it affected me, because I was high anyway from drinking. The next time I was offered marijuana was in 1993. My New York girlfriend, Christine, thought my fear of drugs was ridiculous. Like lots of girls in New York, she occasionally liked to smoke a joint, but I would never allow it in my apartment in London – not because I disapprove, but because it is still illegal. She told me it would relax me, and that if we were to have a relationship, I should at least try to appreciate some of the things that she liked. She insisted that I didn't drink any wine or vodka – that it was just me, her and the joint in a New York hotel room. My natural state is one of excitement and stress, and my idea of unwinding is to stay at home with a bottle of wine and a beautiful woman. Nevertheless, I entered into the spirit of things and smoked some of her joint to please her. All I remember is feeling incredibly sloppy. I told her I loved her, asked her to marry me and then, zzzzzz – I fell asleep. In the morning I woke up and said, 'Is that it?' She said, 'Yeah, it's cool.'

Along with the drug culture which pervaded much of the

sixties came the sexual revolution, sparked by another drug: the contraceptive pill. While the Beatles were singing predominantly about drugs, the Rolling Stones were singing about sex. The contraceptive pill was a wonderful invention, but the sexual freedom it created did have some unpleasant side-effects. Through the astounding promiscuity it permitted, diseases were spread. If you caught a venereal disease in the sixties, you would have to put up your hand and admit that you'd been unfaithful. I couldn't insult Coral's intelligence by telling her I'd caught gonorrhoea from a loo seat. The first time I found I couldn't urinate because it was too painful, I went to see Dr Leddy, our family doctor, who, if you remember, was a childhood hero of mine because he'd saved me from the clutches of the school dentist. The last time I'd seen him was just before I joined the merchant navy ten years earlier. I had no idea about VD: all I knew was that I couldn't go to the toilet. He asked me to take out my penis and the moment I did, he jumped back. 'My God, you've got it!' he exclaimed. In all his years as a doctor I was the first case of VD he had seen. My complaint turned out to be non-specific urethritis, one of the less serious forms of VD, which was rife in those days.

Of course, I had to tell Coral that I had slept with someone else. I tried to convince her that it was a one-off and I'd never do it again, but of course, I did. It became a numbers game for myself and Roger, in which wives and regular girlfriends didn't count. Looking back, I must have been a lousy lay. I was certainly super-fast, worried that Coral might catch me. I'm sure Roger and I were instrumental in setting up Sheffield's first VD clinic. I remember a doctor going berserk with Roger when he told him he'd had twelve partners in one week. The doctor said that he was the perfect candidate for syphilis. Another doctor found a mole on my back and got very excited because he thought I'd caught it.

If I wasn't making love to girls in the back of my car, I would be at the Café Ocelot, where Ivor White let me use his room upstairs. I remember going over there one night and seeing a girl I'd made love to the previous week having sex with an entire cricket team one after the other. I was with a friend of hers and had no idea what was going on until we found her on a bed with a queue of eager men all waiting outside. She seemed happy, so we left her for half an hour. When we went back upstairs the cricket team had already left and she was making her way through a band called the Alarm. I'll never forget seeing one of the band members lying naked beside her in tears. I thought they'd had a lovers' tiff or something, but it turned out he couldn't get an erection. For some reason it had just dawned on him that he was gay, which was a great shame because the girl was a beautiful, tall blonde.

I was threatened twice at Café Ocelot, not, as you might imagine, by irate boyfriends, but by beautiful girls. The first time was when a girl threatened to kill me if I made her pregnant. I told her not to worry. Being killed was in the future: at that particular moment in time she could have threatened anything and I wouldn't have stopped. The second time was when I slept with the girlfriend of a girl called Tessa, whom I'd made love to the previous week. While we were in the throes of passion she said she would kill me if I ever told Tessa.

Roger and I weren't the only ones having sex everywhere and anywhere during this period. The car park beside the Mojo Club would be littered with condoms after the all-nighters. The Mojo days were four years of pure hedonism. They came to an end with the introduction of the Private Members' Club Act in 1968. Up until then, anyone could open up a club and play music all night, but the new law required club owners to apply for a music and dancing licence. Other permissions were needed as well. When I opened the Mojo in 1964, I cleared a space at the side of the club for a car park. I knew nothing about planning permission, but when the new Act came in, I had to apply for permission for my car park, and even for the sign above the Mojo. As it turned out, that was the easy bit. At the time the new law came in, it never once occurred to me that the Mojo would have to close – if anything, I hoped to expand the club and turn the house at the front into a bar.

To do this I had to apply for a drinks licence. I went to court with Roger and a girl called Jilly, who was working as my secretary. I thought the pair of them would give the Mojo credibility. I was wrong. Jilly stood up and told the magistrates that there was nowhere else in Sheffield where she could have a drink and hear good music. One of the magistrates asked her what she did for a living. 'I'm a secretary,' she said.

'And who do you work for?'

'Peter Stringfellow,' she replied.

'Er, thank you. No more questions,' said the magistrate. John Neilson, my solicitor, looked slightly baffled. He was the first man to use the word 'shit' in my company. He would say, 'Peter, I know you think I'm a shit,' and every time he said it I would shiver because I hated the word. Roger stood up next, and immediately I could see that the magistrates didn't like him. He was wearing his usual regalia – hat with a feather and tweeds. 'The only place I like to be seen, outside the Regency Hotel cocktail bar,' he said with affected aplomb, 'is the Mojo Club.' It was like saying 'I only go to the Savoy and McDonald's.' My solicitor was cringing at this point. He must have known we had no chance, but nevertheless he battled on. 'You may think my client and his friends are oddballs,' he said. 'And so they are. But why don't we let these oddballs play in the same place together? That is what they are asking.'

The magistrates were like aliens from another world. They must have looked at me, with my hippy clothes and long hair, and thought exactly the same about me. Needless to say we didn't get our drinks licence. I wasn't that bothered, as I didn't drink then. I was more concerned with getting the music and dancing licence. The next time we went to court I was fighting for the lifeblood of the club. This time I thought I'd make my own plea. I stood up and told the magistrates about the wonderful youth of Sheffield. My speech was a little over- dramatic, to say the least. Half the local residents were also in court, along with several police officers, all with a list of complaints about the all-nighters. They were moaning about kids coming up from London, taking drugs, making noise, having sex – the objections went on and on. One resident, Dougie Birge, said he'd counted fifteen used condoms in the car park one morning. His *pièce de résistance*, though, was his budgie story. Dougie, an avid budgie breeder, claimed that his hobby had been ruined by the Mojo Club. He kept his birds in a cage next to the wall. According to Dougie, not a single egg had hatched in four years because the volume of music had cracked them all. The court was shocked. Forget mass orgies in the car park – the budgie breeder had a very good point. The magistrates suggested I took my club to another part of Sheffield that wasn't so residential. When we left the courtroom I couldn't believe that it was all over.

The Mojo Club was all I had in my whole life; it was my job; it was everything to me. It was also everything to my family and friends. I wasn't the only one who would be losing my livelihood. It was Geoffrey's, too, and my younger brother Paul, who'd joined me straight from school, was also left without a job. I felt paranoid and persecuted. I even took out an advert in the *Sheffield Star* to say that I'd been victimised and that the club should never have closed. Despite the unanimous opposition, I appealed. I just couldn't accept that this was the end. Ever the optimist, I convinced myself that we'd win on appeal. That way I could put off facing up to the reality of the situation and do something else to fill in the time until I got my club back.

Geoffrey and I had £2,000 in the bank when the club closed, and that was eaten up in a matter of weeks. There was a sadness and a kind of headiness about the whole period. Up until then my life hadn't really had much of a direction. If anything, I wanted to become a radio DJ. As a result of the all-nighters I'd become quite famous: I was King Mojo, the guy who had brought the big stars to Sheffield. There was little for me to do but go back on the road. I took the sound system out of the Mojo and started taking bookings in Nottingham, Leeds, Stoke-on-Trent, Barnsley and York.

Around this time I was invited to compere for Humble Pie, who were on tour in Leeds. Peter Frampton had joined Steve Marriott from the Small Faces to form the band. They had only one hit, 'Natural Born Bugie', which made number four in 1969. Peter Frampton was face of the year in 1967, which really annoyed me because we looked alike (except that he was ten years younger). He used to play at the Mojo with his original band, the Herd. When he formed Humble Pie I went to their launch in Liverpool. I remember opening a bottle of champagne and deliberately aiming the cork at Frampton's head. When it shot across the room and hit him I said, 'Oh, sorry, Pete.' I would eventually see the advantage of looking like Peter Frampton, but that didn't happen until many years later, in New York. My main memory of that evening in Leeds, however, is of an unknown singer called David Bowie. He wore blue jeans and a navy blue sweater and looked nothing like a pop singer. When he came on stage he even asked everyone to be kind to him because he wasn't used to playing in front of an audience. We were used to rough, tough musicians, like the Who and the Action. As far as I was concerned, this guy with an acoustic guitar asking people to be 'kind' to him was heading for the dustbin. My eye for talent was not infallible, to say the least.

While I was earning money at night as a mobile DJ, I returned during the day to the one thing I thought I'd never have to do again – selling. Ivor White, who leased the Café Ocelot from Ruben Wallis, had just taken over Ruben's hotel as well. I went over to have a look at it. In one of the rooms I saw all these baths, sinks and toilets stacked up. Ivor said that a guy rented the room once a month after placing an advert in the *Sheffield Star*, which read something like: 'Bathroom suite for sale. Made mistake in buying. Willing to sell at a loss. Value £60. Wanted £30.' In fact the guy was buying the suites for £10 from a local wholesaler, and according to Ivor, he was selling between seven and eight of them in a weekend. It sounded a brilliant idea. I put a similar advert in the *Star* myself. I had four replies, which was a start. Unfortunately, when I went to the warehouse to fulfil the orders, I didn't have any proof that I worked in the trade. My letterhead read 'The Mojo Club': any fool could see it wasn't a plumbing company. So I had a new letterhead printed, using the name 'Nice Kitchens', and went back. I got my four bathroom suites. Over the next few weeks, I filled the lawn at the front of the Mojo club with kitchen and bathroom fittings and Roger and I went as far as Darlington to deliver them. We'd make £10 on a suite and split the money. In between selling kitchens and bathrooms and being a mobile DJ, I eventually came to terms with the fact that the Mojo was finished and began the search for new premises.

During this whole period, I had been sure that I would get my music and dancing licence on appeal. My optimism was ridiculous. I wouldn't accept that the fact that the club was in a residential area made it a non-starter. I thought the judge would be impressed by all the names who played there, but he wasn't remotely moved. He still refused to grant me a licence, and now there's a block of flats where the old Mojo used to stand.

I found my first proper premises below Stylo's shoe shop in the centre of Sheffield. It was a disused cellar with huge potential. A local designer wanted £7,000 to refurbish the place, which was a lot of money to someone with nothing. I had no money, no collateral, no backing and no guarantee that I could pay any rent, so it must have been sheer confidence that carried me through the meeting with the owners of Stylo's. I told them that I was going to spend a lot of money on their premises; that I was a superstar in Sheffield; that the nightclub would be a brilliant success, and so on. They didn't take much persuading, largely because no one else wanted the place.

While the designer set about finding a building contractor I began negotiating the sale of the Mojo. Out of the blue I got a call from Jack Walker, a Conservative councillor in Wakefield. He owned a printing company which produced the tickets for a huge bingo hall called Mecca Locarno. He'd seen how much business they were doing and wanted some of the action. The Mojo by now consisted of only an empty hall with a stage. He planned to put in rows of seats and re-open it as a bingo hall called Lucky 7. I was a bit wary of Walker to begin with: he was so damned nice he was almost too good to be true, though I think he did genuinely like me. He took me to his mansion in Wakefield, introduced me to his family and treated me like a son. His own son was a nice kid, but a bit introverted – the antithesis of me, in fact. I suspect Jack wanted him to be more confident like me, or at least to show some sort of aptitude for his father's business, so that he could take it over one day.

Walker and I agreed a price of £5,000 for the lease, on the condition that he could have a six-month option on it. He said he would pay me the £5,000 up front, and if he didn't want to keep the premises at the end of the six months, I could pay it back to him in instalments. He also agreed to allow me to carry on living in the flat above the Mojo. He wrote out a contract on a piece of A4 paper and I happily signed it – as I've said, I'd sign anything in those days. It made no difference to me. Signing a hire-purchase agreement for a car and actually paying for it were two entirely unrelated actions as far as I was concerned, as you've already seen. This laid-back attitude to legal documents would eventually come back to haunt me, but for now I was £5,000 richer, I'd sold the lease on a club I didn't own and I'd found the perfect site to open a new club.

As yet the new club didn't have a name. I thought about 'Looking For A Fox' – a fox was slang for a girl in those days; 'Sock It To Me One More Time' was another sixties cliché but it was far too long. In the end it became Down Broadway, as America was still on my mind. After I'd paid off my legal fees and taken out living expenses, Geoffrey and I were left with £2,000 which we gave to the designer and building contractor in instalments.

While the club was being built, I carried on selling bathroom suites during the day and became a travelling DJ in the evenings. I was hoping to struggle on until the club was finished, but things didn't go quite according to plan. The developer ran out of money. I didn't have any more money to give him after the £2,000 was used up, so we had to come to an agreement. He suggested that we formed a company with the designer. That way, the developer could use his own money to complete the project. I was so desperate to finish the club that it was a case of 'Where do I sign?' I was still confused as to what a company was, and neither Geoffrey nor I read the contract – we were far too desperate to bother about that. To make matters worse, Jack Walker decided he didn't want to buy the lease on the Mojo after all; he wanted to rent the place instead. All the talk of repayment in instalments went out the window: he wanted his £5,000 back immediately. What was more, he wanted to rent the club for a pittance on the condition that I paid *him* rent for the flat upstairs. He waved the piece of A4 paper I'd signed at me and said I had no alternative. The dream deal had turned into a nightmare in less than four months.

The following day I bought a load of chains and padlocks and sealed the entrance to the old Mojo Club. His equipment was inside; his staff and customers outside. I ignored his threat of legal action and immediately put a 'bingo for sale' advert in the *Sheffield Star*. Within days I had a buyer. The guy who managed the local Mecca gave me £5,000 on the condition that he could have the flat. Work had resumed on Down Broadway and we were nearly ready to open, so Coral and I found a house to rent in the centre of Sheffield.

Fortunately, Down Broadway was an instant success from the night it opened. It was licensed to hold 120, but most Saturday nights we'd let in 400 people. During the day it was a 'bistrotheque', selling pies and chips. Oddly enough, no one's ever used the word I invented since. We were one of the first places to have microwave ovens. For a while we tried selling gourmet microwave food in a bag, but it was too advanced for Sheffield. Ernest Marples MP, who owned the company which sold us the gourmet food, invited me to his home in London once. I dropped a glass of vintage port on his carpet and he refused to give me another glass on the grounds that it was too expensive. After meeting me he realised that his food would never sell in my club. I was pure Sheffield: I didn't know what the word 'gourmet' meant. My favourite food was, and still is, a fried egg sandwich and spam. I love them so much I once ate six fried egg sandwiches in one go.

Down Broadway opened four nights a week and every daytime. On the second Saturday we were short-staffed on the daytime shift, so I helped out selling coffee at 6d a cup. It was the hardest day's work I'd done in a long while. At the end of the afternoon we'd taken only £50. After we deducted the overheads and staff wages, it left a profit of £10. The following week I introduced an entrance charge of two shillings during the day and we made £75 profit. I was good at seeing ways to make money, but I was even better at spending it. When the club opened Geoffrey and I immediately paid ourselves £35 a week. I was on stage, as usual, every night, having a brilliant time. It was just like the Mojo days – except this time I had partners.

After four months they started doing the books and realised

we weren't making any money, even though the place was packed every night. They sat me down for two hours and bored me with a whole load of figures. I wasn't putting money away for this and for that – of course I wasn't; I'd only just accepted I had to pay tax, for God's sake. When I'd concluded the sale of the Mojo, the taxman wanted to know where my returns were for the last four years. I wrote them on the back of a brown envelope and gave them to an accountant. The result was that the taxman took a chunk of the second £5,000 I'd received for the Mojo. The contract I'd casually signed to complete Down Broadway gave me only 49 per cent of the company. After the umpteenth meeting over finances, I realised that it was not my club. My partners were telling me to bring in receipts when I bought records, how much I could draw, what I could spend. All the things I hate, hate, hate. The moment all this started I wanted out.

At the same time as the Down Broadway contract came back to haunt me, I had to appear in court over the Jack Walker contract. I told my solicitor, John Neilson, that Walker's contract was no bigger than a sheet of A4. His reply has stayed with me always: 'Peter, as far as I'm concerned, the smaller the contract, the more powerful it is.' While he was looking at the contract he noticed the letterhead – Bingo Ltd. John disappeared for a few minutes and made a telephone call. He came back with a smile on his face. When the court proceedings began, he agreed that his client (me) owed Bingo Ltd £5,000. 'Who owns the company Bingo Ltd?' he asked.

'I do,' replied Jack Walker.

My solicitor looked at him smugly and said, 'Well, I'm sorry to say there is no such name registered at Companies House.'

It was true. Jack Walker hadn't registered the company, so that was the end of that. As we left the court Jack Walker was threatening to sue me personally. I told him he could try, but I'd let the whole of Wakefield know about his business dealings. As a councillor, I knew he couldn't afford the damage to his reputation, and sure enough I heard no more about it.

Despite this stroke of luck, I felt demoralised about Down Broadway. I wanted out because I wasn't in control. In trying to tie down the wild card in me, the bit of me they had originally liked and which made me good at what I did, my partners were taking away my fizz. The club had been open only five months when I found some more premises, only 200 yards away, above Burton's. I asked one of my partners, the designer who had refurbished Down Broadway, to have a look at the site. It was a whole floor, seven flights up, overlooking the High Street. I could visualise a club there from the moment I walked into the place.

I went to the headquarters of Burton's in Leeds and asked to lease the top floor. Once again I had no money, but the directors must have liked something about me because they agreed to rent it to me. I had no problem naming this club: it could only be called the Penthouse. I wanted something different this time. I wanted to sell alcohol, which was a big step forward. I invited someone from the Hole's Brewery to see the premises at the same time as I put in my application for a liquor licence, and the brewery promised me £2,000 if I got the licence. I'd seen a developer build a club without any money and knew that I could find another one to do the same again. The designer from Down Broadway had drawn me up some plans and his rough estimate of what it would cost to realise them was £10,000. At that stage he assumed he would become my partner for this venture too, but I had other ideas.

I advertised for a developer to build a nightclub, offering stage payments, and as a result met up with the son of a wealthy builder from Chesterfield. I told him I had £2,000 from the brewery, but he wanted to know how much I was putting into the project myself. I didn't have any money, of course: the only thing I had to offer was my reputation. He was agog that I was asking him to build me a club on the promise that I would make it a success. But the moment I took him to Down Broadway and put on my super-DJ act, he agreed to take on the project.

Everything was going well until the designer, my so-called partner, wanted to know what his percentage would be. I was happy to let him design the club, but I didn't want the guy as a partner. When I told him this, he offered to buy me out of Down Broadway. Up to then I hadn't thought I had any money in the club. I'd seen so much paperwork and debt that I was more than happy to walk away with nothing rather than have to pore over any more of it. My partners offered Geoffrey and me £1,000 for our 49 per cent. We took it immediately. They thought they were getting a great deal. They saw us as merely a drain on their profits; they couldn't see that I was the person who brought the money into the club. Without Peter Stringfellow they didn't *have* a club. I didn't care.

The Penthouse, as I mentioned, was only 200 yards away, and it was beginning to look good. It was being decorated on a Greek theme. No one ever understood the logo – I had a figure of a discus-thrower next to the sign above the door, which I thought was brilliant. The disc was actually a record, but unfortunately that was obvious only to me. I put in a parquet dance floor and flashing lights, which had to be hand-made. Instead of positioning the DJ decks facing away from the audience, I put them in front, so that everyone would see me. I had a small restaurant area built with six tables, and, for the first time, a bar.

By the time it was finished the Penthouse had cost £12,500. All we needed now was the liquor licence. In view of my previous disasters in court, John Neilson suggested that Geoffrey should represent the club instead. In spite of my various brushes with the law, I didn't know how to behave in a courtroom in those days. I'd put my hand up and interrupt the judge, and on more than one occasion I'd been asked to shut up or leave. While Geoffrey was in court, I drove around the centre of Sheffield. I was fully expecting a refusal. I didn't think the club could get a licence without me. To my surprise, Geoffrey came out beaming. We'd done it.

I thought the liquor licence would be a step forward, but I hadn't bargained for the effects of the alcohol on the crowd. For four years I'd entertained teenagers high on adrenaline and occasionally pep pills at the Mojo, but drink was something different. I was in for a very big shock at the Penthouse.

8

MOVE ON UP

The Penthouse was my first foray into real business. It was no longer 'Oh, we've made a bit of money, let's go fishing.' I owed the developer £12,500, so the pressure was on to make money. It was 1969, I was twenty-nine years old and I was about to enter a crucial period of my life. The Mojo had been closed a year, yet I had still not left behind that groovy-kids-dancing mentality. Down Broadway had been similar to the Mojo in that the crowd were young and didn't drink. I hoped they would all follow me to the Penthouse, but instead I got an entirely different group. They were men and women, as opposed to boys and girls. Many of them had grown up in a working-men's-club environment and were used to drinking, but they hadn't experienced drinking, dancing and live music. I began attracting the kind of clientele I should never have let in the place. They were known as the West Street crowd. West Street was an area of Sheffield full of pubs. Every Saturday night there would be several fights, so decent people never went near the place. In fact 'West Street' was used as a derogatory term for anything uncouth. I was introduced to beer-drinkers and I didn't really enjoy being around them.

Half the crowd were great. They'd come and see the acts, have a drink and leave without causing problems. The other half were rowdy and rough. Placating a bunch of brawling teenagers with piccalilli sandwich-eating competitions was one thing; trying to stop fifteen drunken fighting men was something I didn't enjoy. Financially, the club did brilliantly. I gave myself a pay rise, which improved my lifestyle. Coral and I rented an ultramodern flat in a upmarket part of Sheffield called Healey. We even had a garage, which was a big luxury, to go with my 1948 Bentley R. Everything was great except for two things: the fighting and the police.

From the second week onwards I was hounded by a policeman called Sergeant Monday. He appeared at the door one Saturday night and said, 'Mr Stringfellow, do you know what your limit is in this club?' I didn't know exactly, but it was a ludicrously low figure, something like 260. We were seven flights up, for God's sake, with only one fire exit halfway up the stairs. The magistrates must have been lovely people to have granted me a licence. Sergeant Monday looked at his notepad and said, 'Well, according to my notes you've let in 620 people.' I knew we couldn't move in there, but I gave him a blank expression and asked Mum how many she'd let through. Sergeant Monday said he would give me an hour to count everyone, then he'd be back. I went on stage and told the crowd that if anyone wanted to leave, I would give them free tickets. No one left. Sergeant Monday didn't return that night, but over the next few weeks he turned up regularly. Unbeknown to me he brought a special clicker and stood outside counting everyone in. I would shout down to Mum, 'How many are in?' She'd say, 'Five hundred,' and I'd say, 'Let in some more.' On occasions the sergeant would find me and ask me how many I'd counted. I'd usually tell him something like 280, and he'd say, 'No, there are 608.' I had no idea how this guy was doing it. At one point I thought that Mum was telling him before he came up the stairs. After he caught me out for the fourth time, I knew I'd never get my licence renewed. In retrospect, I was stupid to ignore the safety aspect, but I didn't think about that at the time. The club was packed and people were having a good time, despite the fights.

I'd already come a long way from the raw excitement of the Black Cat and the Blue Moon to the sophistication of the Mojo crowd and the big names. The Penthouse was exciting in some respects, as my fame from the previous clubs was beginning to consolidate. I had lots of publicity in the *Sheffield Star*; I was putting on big names, like Yes, yet for some reason I felt uncomfortable. Some nights were fantastic; others were so edgy you were glad to get through them. By now I was employing two doormen. One of them was a monster of a guy called Barry, the other was called Brian Turner. One evening Barry, or Baz, as we called him, threw a guy out for fighting. I was furious when I saw that he had this guy pinned to the bonnet of my precious Bentley. To be fair, Baz had three men hanging off his back at the time, but I wasn't interested in that, I was fuming about the blood on my car. This incident should have been a warning of the way things were going.

Not long afterwards I employed another doorman called George. He'd only been with us a couple of weeks when the club was burgled. Someone had kicked the safe down seven flights of stairs. I didn't personally suspect him, but the police were convinced he was responsible. When they went to interview him, George attacked them. He went to prison for the assault and we never found out who had robbed the club.

The next time I lost money from the safe was in a game of poker. During my days as a mobile DJ I would often play poker at the Dungeon in Nottingham with the owner, Mick Parker. In fact it was Mick who first taught me how to play. He would give me my wages and then invariably win them all back at poker. One night two smart-looking guys with slicked-back hair walked into the Penthouse. They introduced themselves as friends of Mick Parker and said they knew I played poker. They suggested we had a game after the club closed. We played for a few hours, and I won some and lost some. Of course, they were building me up for the sting. I can still see the hands. It will sound stupid to any poker players, but they might understand how it happened. I was dealt four queens, which I thought was stunning. I sent Johnny Hacket, a friend who'd worked on the door for me at the Mojo, to empty the safe and put £1,000 on the table. I turned over the queens and one of them turned over four aces. They wiped me out, shook my hand and I never saw them again. A few weeks later, I bumped into Mick Parker and told him that a couple of his poker friends had taken me for everything. I described the guys, who turned out to be the two best card sharps in Nottingham. I should have learned my lesson that night, but I didn't. I went on to lose £47,000 in one game – but that comes later.

The Penthouse lasted only one year. On balance, it wasn't a great fun time, but I compensated for this by chasing girls. Roger Howe had a small cottage four miles from the centre of Sheffield which we both used for entertaining. It only had one bedroom, so we'd literally race each other there to avoid being left with the sofa. I'd tell Roger I was taking a break from the decks, grab a girl, rush downstairs and get into my Bentley. It would take Roger about twenty minutes to realise where I'd gone, and by the time he arrived at the cottage I'd have bagged the bedroom. If we left the club at the same time Roger would win, because he drove a Lotus Elan, which was faster than the Bentley. One night he managed to get away before me. I was so mad I phoned the police and told them Roger had left the club drunk and would be driving a yellow Lotus down the Moor Road. Roger only ever drank tea, so I knew he was safe. I passed him as he was being stopped by the police. Of course, I waved and tooted.

The only nights I didn't go to the cottage were when Coral joined me at the club, which, thankfully, was only once a week. We would put on an act of wild dancing under ultra-violet light, which was very sexy.

The business side of things at the Penthouse was much more serious than it had been at my other clubs. I'd been pretty devil-may-care at Down Broadway, but now the responsibility was all mine and Geoffrey's. He was my partner in those days, keeping the books and making sure the money went into the bank. During the evenings I'd be up front, pushing the image of the club, and more often than not Geoffrey would be at the bar. He'd always liked a drink, even as a kid. I remember on his stag night in 1963 he got so drunk he started fighting my father. I was so angry that I pushed him down some steps. It was a sign of things to come.

Even though we sold beer at the Penthouse, I disliked the image of men standing around with pint glasses in their hands. I wanted my club to have a particular look, which probably harked back to the Mojo days, when I wanted everyone dancing, not a dozen guys standing on the side of the dance floor. One evening a stag party of fifteen miners arrived from the village of Maltby. They stuck out because they all congregated on the dance floor, not dancing, just holding pints of beer. When I think back, it was probably my fault that the fighting started. I didn't like the look of them so I asked Brian Turner to move them away. Before long they were all pushing and shoving each other. Oh no, here we go again, I thought. The shoving then developed into punching, with Brian trapped in the middle. I had kept a baseball bat underneath my record decks since my days as a mobile DJ, although I would never have used it in a million years. I got out the bat and went towards the fighting, hoping it would scare off the Maltby crowd. It was all bravado. Johnny Hacket took the bat off me and threatened them with it.

By now the brawl had moved towards the top of the stairs, leaving a trail of blood in the club. Johnny bonked them all on the top of their heads with the bat and they tumbled like skittles down the seven flights of stairs, fighting and shouting as they fell. Then Geoffrey appeared at the top of the stairs with a gas-gun one of the bands had left behind. It was like a scene from a film. One of the miners ripped open his shirt and shouted, 'Shoot me.' Then I heard someone else scream, 'My leg, I've lost my leg.' At the bottom of the stairs there was a guy holding a severed leg in his hand. For one horrific moment I thought it had somehow been amputated in the fracas. It turned out to be a false leg. The police turned up and arrested everyone, except me.

The club had closed by this time, so I sat alone in the restaurant, reflecting on what had happened. My brother was at the police station, along with the doorman, and I knew this meant big trouble. We'd already been reported four times for overcrowding, there had been numerous scraps both inside and outside the club, and now this. I decided there and then to sell the Penthouse and leave Sheffield. It was unusual for me to make such a snap decision, but I'd had enough.

While I was sitting there thinking about selling up, the police came back. They wanted to know who owned the bat, which was covered in blood. Johnny had owned up to using it, but he wouldn't tell them who it belonged to. I couldn't let Johnny take the rap, so I went down to the police station to put them straight. The moment I said that the bat was mine, I was arrested for owning an offensive weapon, questioned, then let out on bail. I hardly had time to catch my breath. Geoffrey and Johnny were released at the same time, so we all went back to the club and sat around looking at each other. The final curtain had come down on Sheffield.

In the months before we went to court I let it be known that the Penthouse was for sale. A little Scotsman called George Hendry came to see me. I couldn't understand a damned word he said and I still can't. He took me to lunch at Sheffield's first hamburger place. I remember being incredibly impressed by the bundle of notes he carried with him. I was used to having about £10 or £15 in my pocket; George must have had about £500. I told him I wanted £35,000 for the Penthouse. By the end of lunch we'd agreed on £30,000. It was less than I'd hoped for, but it gave me enough money to pay off the brewery, settle a few debts and find another club in another city.

Leeds was only thirty-five miles away from Sheffield, but it might as well have been another country. A lot of people had travelled to the Mojo Club from Leeds, so I knew I had a following there. It was also a more sophisticated city than Sheffield in many ways. Where Sheffield was full of blue-collar steelworkers, Leeds was a cleaner place, known for its fashion. Not fashion as in Jean-Paul Gaultier, but they did make clothes there.

Before the agreement was signed on the sale of the Penthouse, I had to go to court to reapply for my annual licence. Without it, the club would have to close, and Hendry wouldn't want the premises without a licence. I was actually in court fighting for it when the deal was finalised. George Hendry sent a letter to the courtroom stating that he'd agreed to buy the club, and immediately I took it to the magistrates, telling them I was withdrawing my application. They put a hold on the licence to give Hendry time to reapply and have it transferred into his name. George was a nice guy. He could have taken advantage of the situation, but he behaved decently and didn't try to steal the club from me. He agreed to pay me £28,000, plus £2,000 as a consultancy fee over a period of six months. After I'd paid off the £12,500 loan to the developer and various other debts, we were left with £8,000.

In the middle of Leeds there was a big shopping mall called the Marion Centre. Nearby were the city's two nightclubs, Time Out, which was smaller than the Penthouse, and the Phonogram. Beside the shopping centre there was a long building with a TO LET sign in one of the windows, 15,000 square feet on two levels. I made an appointment to meet the developers of the Marion Centre and went before the board to ask about leasing the space. With my long hair and flared trousers, I was probably the last person they expected to walk through the door. It took me about an hour to convince them that I could turn the space into a brilliant nightclub. It was obviously a white elephant. As with the Penthouse, no one wanted the place, so they were open to suggestions.

I met a local designer, Johnny Franks, who worked for a large design firm, and showed him the site where I wanted to build the club. I told him I'd just sold a club in Sheffield for £30,000, but I didn't tell him how much money I had left from the sale. I didn't lie to the guy abut it – I was just economical with the truth. I also told him I had a brewery involved, which wasn't strictly true. I did eventually get £8,000 from a brewery in Leeds, but at the time I was negotiating the premises, I hadn't even made an appointment to see them. The designer sat me down, told me he wanted to start a new company of his own to build my club and asked me what I thought about the idea. I didn't care. I liked the guy: he hadn't asked for any money, so he was my kind of designer. I took him to the Penthouse to give him an idea of the kind of things I liked in a club. I'd had a taste of running a restaurant, albeit with only six tables. I wanted something bigger for Leeds. I also wanted to move upmarket. I wanted Johnny to design a nightclub like no one had ever seen before. It was to have a kidney-shaped dance floor with a stage at the back for live bands. Johnny suggested that we decorated it in purples and lilacs, which I thought was a great idea. They were rich, glamorous colours which would give the club an opulent feel. I wasn't so keen on his suggestion for a name, which was Shades of Purple. I wanted a name that would conjure up glamour and make you feel good; a name that sounded sophisticated when a guy said to his girlfriend, 'I'm going to take you out tonight. I'm going to take you to . . .' I decided on Cinderella's. It was a magical name that everyone knew from the fairytale. It sounded good; it made you feel good. It was perfect.

Johnny Franks introduced me to a developer and work began on Cinderella's. Neither of them knew that I didn't have all the money. The £16,000 I did have (when the brewery had given me another £8,000), I eked out very slowly. There were lots of things I could get without paying for them immediately – the carpets, for instance. I would put down a minimum deposit and agree to pay on delivery. We did deals with everybody – including the developer, after he realised that I'd run out of money. It came as a big shock to him, but he had no alternative other than to finish the club. Once I'd explained the situation I handed him over to Geoffrey, who was very adept at dealing with people who wanted money. He managed to talk the developer into accepting stage payments. That was how Geoffrey and I worked together: I'd lead them on and once they'd stepped into the quagmire, Geoffrey would throw them a rope.

Within a matter of months the cost of Cinderella's had escalated to £60,000. It was a daunting debt in 1970, but I had nothing to lose. Throughout my life I have always been a total optimist. When I start a project I see nothing but success; I never think about failure, I leave that to other people. Yet those six months were one of the most nerve-racking periods of my life. In my bleaker moments, I'd sit down and work out the worst possible scenario: if it all fell apart, I could always go back to being a DJ, which I loved anyway. I'd tasted success already, so I was able to convince myself that everything would be fine once Cinderella's opened. I just couldn't worry about money, and I'm still like that today. It's a maddening trait, I know. It goes back to my childhood, when Mum and Dad bought everything on a weekly basis. I wasn't brought up to be careful with money – the situation simply never arose, because we never had any. No company or individual could get money out of me if I didn't have it – it was as simple as that. With Cinderella's, there was no point in the developer stopping halfway through building the place and taking me to court over payment. He knew I didn't have the money.

The licence for Cinderella's was different from the one I had for the Penthouse in that I couldn't admit anyone who hadn't been a member for forty-eight hours. While the club was being built this was fine, because I began collecting membership fees. I put an advert in a local newspaper asking people to send £1 postal orders to a box number for their membership cards. Geoffrey and I would drive to Leeds each week to empty the box and cash the postal orders. Some weeks we'd get £40, which gave us money to live on. It was exciting to watch the club being built from scratch, but we lived from hand to mouth for the entire six months. By the time Cinderella's opened on my daughter Karen's birthday, 13 October, in 1970, I owed £65,000 and was down to my last pound.

Coral and Scott were still living in Sheffield so I planned to commute the thirty-five miles to Leeds each evening. Up to now, Mum had always been my cashier, but there was no way she could travel back and forth to Leeds. In truth it was an excuse to get her to step down. The time had come for me to get a proper cashier. Mum was very upset for a while. She felt as if she'd been put out to grass. For a long time afterwards she would bring it up in conversation. If I mentioned any problems with the club she would say, 'Oh, I could do that job,' or 'I could always come back as the cashier.' Mum was a very vigilant cashier. During the Mojo days we were always falling out because she wouldn't let *anyone* in free. My friends would come to the door and say, 'Peter has said it's OK – I helped him out this week.' Mum would never believe them. They'd tell me, 'Your mum's made me pay again,' which was embarrassing. I'd say to her, 'Mum, when I say they can come in for free, they can come in, OK?' She never took any notice. We had big arguments, but they were always forgotten the next day. I was never a mummy's boy, but always my mother's boy, which is different. My brothers won't mind me saying that I was her favourite. I was her first-born and naturally the one who took the lead. If

Mum didn't like the look of somebody, she wouldn't let him in. There was no way I could have that with Cinderella's. I owed a lot of money and needed to get it right from the opening night. I booked Georgie Fame and the Blue Flames for the grand opening. I'd collected 500 members, so I knew I would have a crowd. Cinderella's was set for success from the moment the doors opened; I was in for a shock.

My idea was to put on top bands people could dance to and to create a kind of upmarket Mojo. I thought people in the restaurant area would be able to eat and listen to the music. They would see Georgie Fame on stage, think, 'How nice,' and carry on with their meal. Unfortunately, when Georgie Fame came on stage all the diners went crazy because the packed dance floor was blocking their view. Meanwhile the crowd on the dance floor were moaning because they had to stand all night. Everywhere I turned, I could hear people saying, 'I'm not coming here again . . . I want my money back . . . We can't see the band.'

They'd come to see Georgie Fame, not Cinderella's. At the end of the first night I sat with my head in my hands, convinced I was going to go bankrupt. I had gambled everything on the opening night and got it all wrong. The one thing that saved me from utter despair was the cashflow. After I'd paid the band £1,500 I still had money in the till. It meant I was taking money and didn't have to pay it out automatically. If I'd deducted the cost of the electricity and the staff's wages, I would have been in deficit, but I didn't take that into account when Geoffrey and I divided up the takings from the till.

Georgie Fame was booked to play for four more days, by which time I knew there was no point in getting the big names. As his fans were leaving, I had another crowd wanting to get in to see Cinderella's. They'd heard that the club was brilliant, but because they weren't members, I couldn't let them in. I remember standing at the door pleading with them to fill in the membership forms. Not surprisingly, they weren't interested in coming back in forty-eight hours. If they couldn't get in that night, they didn't want to come at all.

Within three weeks of opening I was back in court asking for a public licence. I stood in front of the magistrates and said, 'Gentlemen, if you don't grant me this licence the club will go bankrupt. I've just opened the biggest nightclub Leeds has ever seen but I can't go on like this.' The magistrates understood the situation and gave me the licence. The very same night the club was packed out for the first time.

After Georgie Fame I never booked a big name again. I went for good bands who weren't famous. Madrigal were a band everyone loved. Their singer, Peter Tyler, eventually became a DJ at the club. Although I was brilliant on the decks, Peter Tyler's musical talent meant he could mix two records beautifully, which is something I never really mastered.

Cinderella's introduced me to two things I'd never encountered before: married couples and affluence. There was no money in Sheffield and the only married couples I knew were people's mums and dads. It was the beginning of the seventies' glam-rock period – big shirt collars and velvet suits. It was real glamour, not the chintzy glamour of the Mecca. For the first time I was in a position to sell champagne. Every night I would take the microphone and cajole the crowd like a ringmaster. I started introducing games and giving away champagne to the winners in between the groups and the records. I would take one of Scott's Noddy books on stage and ask the crowd to fill in the missing word – for example, 'Noddy said to Big Ears, I like your big ***' The real word was 'car', but in Cinderella's, of course, it would be 'willy'. I introduced 'The Mucky Shot' which was a spoof of the television programme *The Golden Shot*. I'd give the husbands a children's bow and arrow with suckers on the end and ask them to shoot at their wives and girlfriends on stage. The girl had to take off a piece of clothing from whichever bit of her her husband or boyfriend hit. The first one to undress to her bra and panties won the champagne.

On some nights the games were more popular than the bands. One evening I offered a bottle of champagne to the person who could name Gene Autrey's horse. I thought the horse was called 'Lady', but one of the guys insisted it was 'Champion'. I bet him six bottles of champagne and dinner if he could prove it. The following week the club was packed with people waiting for this guy to come in with his cowboy book. I didn't believe him until I'd seen it in black and white. Hen nights on Thursdays were the wildest. There must have been more brides-to-be in Leeds than in any other city in the country. The first bride to strip to her bra and panties would get a bottle of champagne. We would normally give away twelve bottles a night, but one night we ran out of house champagne, save for one bottle. Rather than give away the expensive Dom Perignon we took the game further and suggested that the first one to strip off entirely would win the champagne. But within seconds, there were twelve naked girls on stage. Rather than disappoint them we had to give them the bottles of Dom Perignon.

For the first three months I was under enormous pressure to pay back the money I owed. By Christmas 1970 I had almost cleared the £65,000 debt, but the developer nearly went bankrupt while waiting for his money.

By the end of the first year I had decided to leave Sheffield. Rather than move Coral and Scott to Leeds, I rented a bungalow halfway between the two towns. With Coral away from the club I could freely play around with other women. If I couldn't find anywhere in the club to have sex, I'd do it in my new E-type Jaguar, then take them home.

For the first year of Cinderella's I had a steady girlfriend called Susan. She was sixteen when I met her at the Down Broadway. She was absolutely gorgeous, with long blue-black hair; it was my first proper affair after marrying Coral. Within a year Susan was pregnant. I don't think we even discussed whether she would keep the child. We arranged for her to see a little old lady who would induce a miscarriage. This was in 1969, before abortions were legal. Everybody knew 'little old ladies' in those days. You hoped they were former nurses, but looking back we were very naïve. After the abortion Susan and I carried on seeing each other on a regular basis.

When I opened Cinderella's she would travel over from Sheffield every Tuesday and Friday. If we didn't book a hotel room, I drove her back to Sheffield, made love to her in her parents' front room, then drove back home. A mistress was the last thing I wanted, but if it hadn't been for Coral I know I would have married Susan. She was such a beautiful person, both inside and out, that I couldn't let her go. Then one day I took a girl to the swimming pool at Selby Fork Motel, a place we all used. She mentioned that she'd seen Susan there the previous day with a guy called Alan. I asked the girl what had happened and she casually said, 'Well, in the morning we all had breakfast.' I was consumed with jealousy. The thought of Susan making love to another guy was too painful to contemplate. It didn't stop me making love to the girl I was with, but the moment I'd dropped her off home I phoned Susan and called her a slut. She burst into tears. She told me that I never paid her any attention; that I was always on the microphone, or going home to Coral. She was absolutely right, of course. I had taken her completely for granted. She said that this other guy was serious about her, even though she hadn't meant to sleep with him.

As far as I was concerned, however, this was extreme disloyalty and I didn't ever want to see her again. It took me months to get over Susan. A few years later I heard that she'd died in a car accident. I was devastated. It was the second time in a year that one of my regular girlfriends had died in a car crash. I had to hide the pain because I didn't want Coral to know about our relationship. I blocked out the hurt by burying myself in my work.

Other girls didn't mean anything to me. Susan meant a great deal, and Coral meant everything. Susan came along at a time when Coral's hold over me was so strong that no one, however beautiful, could get close. There was never the slightest chance that I would leave Coral. We had a fantastic marriage, except for the fact that I couldn't stay faithful. My sexuality was a driving factor. It went hand in hand with the nightclub business, like lights and music. I was on a roll, sexually and financially. The club was an enormous success, but I wanted more. I couldn't ignore the space next door.

9

CINDERELLA ROCKAFELLA

After the first year of Cinderella's I was amazed to find we had £50,000 in the bank. Decimal coinage made a big contribution to those profits: the moment it was introduced, on 15 February 1971, we put up our prices along with everyone else. We mourned the demise of the half-crown coin, the threepence and the sixpence, but the up side was being able to round everything up to the nearest ten. We could raise the prices of our drinks by five new pence – the equivalent of a shilling – whereas before decimalisation there would have been riots over an increase of sixpence. Between 1971 and the introduction of VAT on 1 April 1973, business boomed. I went back to the landlord and agreed to lease the space next door to Cinderella's. The actor Robert Powell suggested the name Rockafella's, which was the perfect complement to Cinderella's, in an echo of the hit single 'Cinderella Rockafella' which had reached number one a few years earlier.

I wanted Rockafella's to be the first supper club in Leeds. In contrast to the lilacs and purples of Cinderella's, Rockafella's was to be decorated in honey-browns and creams. I wanted a softer, more romantic feel to the place. We put little lamps on each of the tables and built a smaller dance floor. The building of Rockafella's was a hugely exciting time. I like seeing concrete, fresh wood floors, air-conditioning and carpets being laid. It was the beginning of a brand-new club and what I thought would be a brilliant new concept, too.

While the club was being built, I continued to build up my reputation next door. Cinderella's introduced me to 'real' celebrities. I'd moved on from meeting potential rock stars and would-be soul legends to television stars, like Robert Powell, who was starring in a show called *Doomwatch* at the time. Diana Dors began coming in, too. She was starring in a sitcom called *Queenie*, which was set in a council block in Leeds. Diana Dors was a film star in my eyes. When I was a kid she had been Britain's answer to Marilyn Monroe. I was taken aback when I saw how much weight she was carrying in those days, but she was still a beautiful, voluptuous, sexy lady. The little restaurant that had almost bankrupted me in the first few months had now become a place where celebrities sat and drank champagne. The actors Anthony Valentine and Alexandra Bastedo regularly came into the club. We all suspected they were having an affair and would use Cinderella's as their meeting place. This would have been hot gossip then, but I was too naïve to realise that – I couldn't even spell Nigel Dempster in those days, let alone know how to get him on the telephone.

Once again the clientele at Cinderella's was very different from those of my previous clubs. Eighty per cent of them were fantastic; the other 20 per cent were dangerous, criminally dangerous. One night word went round the club that 'Fuzz' was in. People were saying, 'Don't go over there, Fuzz is over there.' I saw a very big guy standing at one of the bars. He was like a tough-looking Omar Sharif, without the charm. He had a thick grey thatch on his head and a big square jaw. I went over and asked him, 'Hi, you're Fuzz. How come everybody is frightened of you?'

'I don't know,' he said. 'I'm OK.'

In a funny way, he was OK. He might have looked a bit scary, but I liked him. I left him alone because nobody could have thrown him out. Later that night a big, fat, blubbery man appeared at the top of the steps without his jacket. We had a rule at Cinderella's that everyone had to wear a jacket. He had a pint of beer in each hand and was deliberately blocking the stairs. The doormen were trying to move him without success and I just knew something was about to go off. I went over to Fuzz and asked him if he'd like a job as my number-one doorman.

'How much?'

'As much as I pay the doormen.'

'When do I start?'

'Tonight. You see that fat guy up there? I want him out.'

Fuzz wasted no time. He took off his jacket, walked up the stairs and took the pints of beer off the fat guy. Then he hit him and smacked him and punched him all the way down the stairs and out of the club. To this day I don't know whether that guy died. Fuzz came back in, put his jacket back on and said, 'What time do you want me to go home, boss?'

'Not yet. Wait until I've left the club.'

From that night Fuzz became our resident FBI–CIA man. It was like having Mike Tyson as a bouncer. Even my friend Roger Howe had an encounter with Fuzz. He was on the dance floor minus his jacket when Fuzz came over to him and said very loudly in his ear, 'Put thee fucking coat on.'

Not long afterwards Roger came to work for me. He'd taken over my kitchen and bathroom business in Sheffield, but he hadn't made any money from it. He spent all his takings on a Lotus Elan, which wasn't the smartest move in the world. He'd also opened a boutique called 'Lift Up Your Skirt And Fly', which went bankrupt. Roger had style, but zero business acumen. I offered him a job and told him we would still be friends even if it didn't work out. He has been with me ever since. Roger took over the management of the kitchens and helped out with shampooing the carpets. (Only a brand-new nightclub owner would buy lilac carpets for a club. They were a complete disaster, which is why I've had black carpets ever since.) Malcolm Metcalf, who I'd brought in as my general manager at Cinderella's, loathed him and would do everything in his power to try to get me to sack him. I trusted Malcolm because he'd worked at the Mecca Locarno in Leeds and had invaluable experience, but of course I trusted Roger more because I'd known him longer and we were friends.

One night Malcolm went into Roger's office and told him that all the takings had been stolen. He wasn't accusing Roger of stealing, he was just making the point that Roger should have locked the office door. I went down to the office and could see that something wasn't quite right. I knew Roger hadn't stolen the money, but neither did I believe that Malcolm had taken it. While I was looking around the room I noticed that one of the tiles in the ceiling had been moved. I pushed it aside and found the money. Someone had hidden it there in order to take it home later. I didn't accuse anyone, because there was no proof. Not long after this Malcolm went off with one of the office secretaries and we didn't hear from him again. But within a week of his departure a telephone engineer arrived to empty the payphone in the club. He asked me who had taken over from Malcolm. He wanted to know what to do with the money he'd taken out of the payphone. For three years I'd been paying the telephone bills and Malcolm had been pocketing the money from the payphone. It was another lesson learned. Now, at the age of fifty-six, I know just about every fiddle in the nightclub business. If we employ a new barman today, Roger will tell him that there is nothing he can fiddle that we won't find out about. It's a constant war in any business where cash is involved.

But the nasty incidents at Cinderella's were minor compared to the fun everyone was having. One night Fuzz told me there were a couple of jokers outside claiming to have Engelbert Humperdinck and Tom Jones in their cars.

'Oh, really? Tom Jones *and* Engelbert Humperdinck?'

'Yeah. I told them to piss off, but they wanted me to find you.'

'Well, what do their cars look like?'

'They're two big, long Mercedes with black windows.'

'For God's sake, Fuzz, get out there and let the buggers in.'

It was obviously them. They'd both been singing at different cabaret clubs in Wakefield and had decided to meet up at Cinderella's. The first thing I did was to hit the microphones and announce that they were coming in. It's something I wouldn't dream of doing today. Eventually I found that the benefits of the presence of stars in my clubs were mutual. The stars would use my clubs for their enjoyment and indirectly to publicise their latest film, book, television programme or whatever, and I would use them to enhance our reputation – 'Hey, guess who was in my club last night . . .' There was heavy rivalry between Tom Jones and Engelbert Humperdinck, although they put on a show of being friends. They took over the back of the restaurant when everyone had gone and drank champagne into the early hours. Did I ask Tom to sing on stage? No. Did I play his number one 'She's A Lady' non-stop? Yes, I'm afraid so.

After that, the word went round and every star who came to the area would visit Cinderella's. In the north both Batley Variety Club and the Wakefield Theatre Club, massive venues where all the big names played, were less than half an hour away from my club.

Cinderella's was a personal ego trip for me, too. I was being fêted for the first time in my own right, as Peter Stringfellow, the up-and-coming celebrity. It was all, 'Hey, Peter, sit down, let's talk, have a drink.' It was heady stuff, and I can't deny that I was flattered by all the attention. I began to find my own power and to hone my act with the microphone.

I was giving a lot of fun, and at the same time I was having a lot of fun. Leeds introduced me to wife-swapping, which was not something I'd come across in Sheffield. One night I was introduced to two couples who wanted to congratulate me on the club. They went to Spain every year, they said, and Cinderella's on a Saturday night was like being back on holiday. One of the husbands was a salesman and the other was a sergeant in the police force. They invited Coral and me to have dinner with the four of them. We decided we'd go as they only lived round the corner. The moment I walked in the house I knew there was something going on because the dining room was lit with candles, which is usually intended to give out some sort of message. By the end of the meal, after we'd drunk lots of wine and were all screaming with laughter, they invited Coral and me to swap partners with them. I told them I wouldn't share Coral, so we made our excuses and left. Quite apart from anything else, I didn't fancy either of the wives.

By the time we left Leeds both these couples had divorced. Their lifestyle was a recipe for ruining your marriage. One of the wives had fallen in love with the other husband, but he didn't want to leave his own wife. They all got hurt, and one husband lost his wife, his girlfriend and his best friend. The next time I was invited to swap wives was in the affluent Jewish community in Manchester. This time I was more keen on the idea – or on making love to the wife, at least, because she was gorgeous. The only problem was working out how I could have her without letting her husband have Coral. I was ready to take Coral to dinner with them but only if she swore on everybody's lives that nothing would happen. I think this guy worked me out, and nothing ever happened in the end.

While Rockafella's was being built, Coral and I went on our first foreign holiday, to the Canary Islands. A friend of mine called Asga and his beautiful girlfriend, Lesley, joined us on the trip. By now Coral had settled into life as my wife and Scott's mother. She'd always had trouble with her eyes, and she'd taken to wearing thick glasses. To put it bluntly, she'd become dowdy. One afternoon on holiday we were sitting by the pool and Lesley, who was a top model in Leeds at the time, turned to her and said, 'You know, Coral, it's really nice coming on holiday with you, because I don't have to compete.' Coral will always remember those words. Lesley might just as well have said, 'Oh Coral, you're so ugly – what a relief that I don't have to make an effort.' The words hit Coral like a stone, and the moment we got back to Leeds, she underwent a metamorphosis. She got contact lenses, dyed her hair blonde and went out and bought a whole new wardrobe. She became glamorous once again and took to vamping. It was good to see her flirting again. It excited me and fitted in with the kind of image I wanted for her.

It took six months to build Rockafella's and cost £95,000. Although I'd put down £50,000, I was once again in debt. Having burned my fingers with big names at Cinderella's, I decided to book 'international' cabaret acts, which meant, 'You don't know who they are, but they're good.' I advertised my opening night with the promise: 'New York, London, Paris comes to Leeds. International cabaret at Rockafella's.' It was a huge mistake. It frightened everyone away and hardly anyone turned up. It was the same thing for weeks. The first time I saw a crowd was when Mike and Bernie Winters played. They had their own television show at the time, so I kept them on for three weeks. Most Saturday nights only a handful of people came. Occasionally we'd reach the 300 capacity, but it was rare. A hypnotist called Edward Heath could pull a crowd, as could the magician Paul Daniels. He was a peculiar little fellow, but he had a great act. I'd seen him on television, but he wasn't a big star in those days. He did truly amazing card tricks and then he'd round off the evening with some hypnosis. I remember him telling the audience that only the most sensitive, intelligent people could be hypnotised. He asked them all to clasp their hands above their heads and said that when he clicked his fingers some people would not be able to open their hands. There was always a bunch who couldn't open them, and he'd pick six of these to come up on stage. He ran through the usual hypnotist's act, getting people to pretend to be dogs and so on, and then he'd tell the participants that they wouldn't be able to stand up and leave the stage when he snapped his fingers. I watched for two weeks and was astounded that indeed no one could get off their chairs. After the show I asked Paul what he did to them. He said that he simply whispered in their ears: 'I'm going to ask you to do one thing for me, which is not to get off your chair.' To his own surprise, he said, nobody ever did.

After his performance Paul would show us card tricks. He could do anything with a pack of cards. At the time I regularly played poker with Asga and a couple of others. I asked Paul if he would deal for me one night. He said he couldn't do that because he was a member of the Magic Circle. When I explained that I didn't intend to defraud anyone and had only asked him to do it as a joke, he agreed – but even then he'd only play if he could warn the players beforehand. I got my poker friends round and told them how close they'd come to losing all the money they had, and for half an hour Paul dealt the most amazing hands. He gave three queens to one guy, four kings to another, and every time I got the winning hand. I had the brilliant idea that Paul and I could team up and become professional poker players. I realised that if he could manipulate a pack of cards, there must be hundreds of people out there doing the same thing. I also realised how stupid I'd been to play with those two strangers the night I lost my takings at the Penthouse. Of course, Paul Daniels had better things to do than play poker. He had his sights on international fame, which he eventually found.

I booked the singer Danny Rivers one night and was wildly excited about him coming. He was an English Johnny Mathis, slick and good looking. I'd seen him on TV as a glamorous, sophisticated entertainer, always immaculately dressed in dickie bow and dinner jacket. He'd been off the circuit for quite a while when he came to Rockafella's, but he was still well known. He turned up to rehearse in an open-necked shirt and jeans, then went to his dressing room to get ready for the show. After about half an hour I went to see him. I was horrified to find him still wearing his jeans and shirt. I couldn't believe he was going on stage looking like that. He told me he wanted to change his style. I said, 'Danny, you can't do that. If you go on stage you have to go on as Danny Rivers, because people like to see you like that.' Eventually I talked him round and we sent out for an evening suit. He walked on stage and stormed the place. Afterwards he shook my hand and thanked me. He'd got his confidence back.

I've learned over the years that if you're going to be a star, you have to act like one. It's no good making apologies for it. I don't go with the ones who want to be like everybody else. If you entertain the public, you have to be larger than life or completely outrageous – people don't want to see someone just like them. Stars literally can get away with murder. The more starry entertainers make themselves, the bigger they're likely to be. The stars from those days who can still pull a crowd today know this; people like Tom Jones. He's glamour, glamour, glamour. He keeps his tracksuit for lounging around the house, not for wearing on stage. When Mick Jagger walks out in front of an audience he doesn't look like the guy next door, he's sexier than him. If he throws on a rag, it's a designer rag. I recognised this in the sixties, and I'm still seeing it work for bands like Oasis, Blur and Eternal in the nineties.

There were times when I got it wrong, as I've said. A scruffy little group called Mud would sometimes play for me. I hated their name, but I loved their lead singer, Les Gray. I was forever telling him to do something with his hair. I'd say to him, 'Grow it, cut it, dye it, perm it – wash it, even – but do *something* with it.' He didn't take any notice and neither did he change the name of the group. At the time he was recording 'Tiger Feet', and he'd get my crowd doing a silly little dance to it. I would say, 'No, Les, don't get them doing that.' 'Tiger Feet', of course, reached number one and the dance became a hit. A month later I made a similar mistake when the manager of Paper Lace came to the club and played me a demo tape of their new song, 'Billy, Don't Be A Hero'. I told him it would never be a hit. On 23 February 1974, it went to number one and stayed there for fourteen weeks.

Despite the odd packed night at Rockafella's when I booked good acts, in general it wasn't full and lost £36,000 in the first nine months. I tried and tried to make it work, but it wasn't what Leeds wanted. At times in my life I've had to stop and admit that I've made a mistake, however expensive that might be. And to me Rockafella's was fabulous. It had a warmth about it that I'd never felt in another nightclub. The night I decided to close it down was the night Matt Monro was due to perform. The local group who backed all the stars told me that he'd missed the rehearsal earlier in the day. I should have called his agent there and then, but I didn't. I just assumed he would turn up.

Two hours before we opened I got a telegram to say he was ill. I couldn't believe it. I told the backing group to go on and do two numbers, then I'd take over as the DJ for the evening. My younger brother, Paul, was the regular DJ at Rockafella's. He was known as Paul 'Mr Nice Guy' Stringfellow for the simple reason that he was, and still is, a nice guy, and because he played the kind of easy-listening music I thought the Rockafella's crowd wanted. The club was packed that night because everyone had come to see Matt Monro. I apologised and sent champagne round to all the tables. To my surprise everyone wanted to dance. For nine months I'd been forcing cabaret on them and the only chance they got to dance was after the show. That night we had the best night ever in the club. Not only did everyone have a fantastic time, but I didn't have to pay a performer.

As I commuted between the two clubs, I knew for the first time that our cabaret days were over. The solution was simple: don't confuse what you think they want with what they really want. Rockafella's was so opulent and luxurious it frightened off the type of people who came to Cinderella's. It was like walking from Tesco into Fortnum & Mason. Every Saturday night I'd have to get the door takings from Cinderella's to pay the cabaret act at Rockafella's, yet the answer had been there all along.

Instead of closing Rockafella's we took out the first two rows of tables and chairs and extended the dance floor. We put in a bigger sound system and made a proper entrance to serve both clubs. Instead of playing Frank Sinatra-type finger-clicking music at Rockafella's, we put on smoochy numbers which fitted in with the romantic feel of the place. We removed the stage and put up a huge sepia photograph of a *Gone With the Wind*-style Clark Gable lookalike. It was in stark contrast to the mural I had painted next door: Cinderella's had life-sized St Trinian's-style schoolgirls painted on the wall. They were all lifting up their skirts to reveal stockings and suspenders. It was outrageous, but it worked like a dream. It also set a precedent for the racy, sexy image I've maintained ever since.

I advertised Cinderella's–Rockafella's together as a 'super-scene' and packed both clubs from the opening night. It was a concept which worked brilliantly. Neither club lost its identity because of the contrasting decor, one all raunchy purples and the other subtle browns. The anthem to Cinderella's was 'Leap Up And Down (Wave Your Knickers In The Air)'. Every time I played it, I'd get dozens of panties thrown at me. I pinned them to the top of my DJ box. Rockafella's was more laid back. It was still an incredibly sexy club, but the sex was more subtle. Admission to each club was still kept separate, which created a complication. If you paid to go into Rockafella's you could automatically get into Cinderella's, but it didn't necessarily work the other way round. The Rockafella's crowd were slightly older, and we had a doorman to vet people moving over from Cinderella's. If he thought they were too young and dressed too raunchily he wouldn't let them in. This worked in my favour from a personal point of view because I'd get young girls coming up to me saying, 'Peter, Peter, I want to go to Rockafella's but the doorman won't let me in.'

'Never mind, darling. Come with me.'

'But this isn't Rockafella's . . .'

'No, baby, it's a dressing room. We'll go into Rockafella's in a minute.'

I literally had a ball at Cinderella's–Rockafella's. I was financially secure for the first time in my life. I bought a house for £7,500, detached with its own rose garden. Yet even though I had money going into the bank, it was almost impossible for me to get a mortgage. I was turned down by three different mortgage brokers and laughed at in the Leeds Building Society. Eventually I found a Sheffield mortgage broker who was willing to lend me the money. I changed my red E-type Jaguar for a black and white Jensen Interceptor Marque III, which quickly became a boudoir on wheels. The E-type had been a little cramped for extra-marital sex, though of course I was not put off by that. If the girl was tall I'd open the windows and put her legs through them. The Interceptor, however, had front seats which fell back.

Around this time we retired Dad from the steelworks. The four Stringfellow brothers hired a Rolls-Royce and met him after his last day at work with a bottle of champagne. Geoffrey and I bought my parents a bungalow near Leeds and promised to look after them in their retirement. On reflection it wasn't such a great idea. The steelworks had been Dad's life. Retiring at the age of fifty-three left him with a lot of time on his hands and a lot more time to listen to Mum shouting. Dad's early retirement was more my dream than his. I was a successful working-class boy, doing what all successful working-class boys do: looking after their parents.

Even though the seventies was a blur of blondes, my marriage to Coral was still strong. By the time Cinderella's–Rockafella's was in full swing, she'd come round to the fact that I liked the idea of two girls together. We'd talk about it during our own love-making and she knew it turned me on. I'd often slept with two girls together during the sixties, but now I wanted my wife to join in. On reflection, I think Coral agreed more to make me happy and to keep us together than because she particularly wanted to do it herself. I began finding girls and introducing them to her. If she liked them, we'd play together. The first time she watched me make love to another girl, she said, 'I can't believe my imagination has made me so miserable all these years.' It was nothing like she'd thought it would be. In a way it made her feel better, because she knew our love-making was very different. I'm certainly not advocating that everyone should start getting involved in threesomes because it doesn't always work. Eventually it did become too much for Coral – but not before we'd seduced all her girlfriends. One of them was Carol, a voluptuous girl Coral had met at a hair salon. One night, while Karen and Scott were in bed, we invited Carol over for a drink. After we'd drunk lots of wine, I put on a video of two girls making love. Coral made the first move on Carol and eventually, with Coral's consent, I made love to Carol. It was a beautiful night, not at all sleazy. We all ended up in the rose garden dancing naked. We were having a wonderful time until we looked up to see Scott and Karen in the bedroom window, clapping along to the music. To this day they remember seeing Mummy, Daddy and Carol dancing naked in the garden. Now they know what we'd been doing!

Coral, Carol and I kept our threesome for quite a while. Unfortunately for me, it didn't happen on a nightly basis – it didn't always happen on a weekly basis – but when it did happen it was wonderful. One night Coral wasn't in the mood to play, but I pushed anyway. All three of us were in the house drinking and listening to music. I should have noticed that Coral wasn't drinking the same amount as Carol and I but I got carried away with Carol. Instead of realising that Coral wasn't into the scene, my greed took over and I began making love to Carol on the floor. The next thing I knew there was a stiletto heel in my temple and the pressure was mounting. Coral was standing over me, pressing harder and harder. Of course, as any man will verify, pain and erections are not compatible, so that was the end of that. Coral said, 'You do this when I say so, and never before.' It ruined the evening, but it made me realise that Coral was in control, not me. I've found that in every situation since then: the girl always has to be in charge. Coral had drawn the line: when she wanted to, she did it; when she didn't, we didn't do it. I knew from that night that we weren't always going to make love as a threesome. I was disappointed, but I had other things on my mind.

Cinderella's–Rockafella's was such a huge success that I wanted another nightclub. Geoffrey and I looked around Bradford and very nearly leased a place, but the deal fell through. The next city we looked at was Manchester. We drove into the centre of town and saw a TO LET sign for a basement off West Moseley Street. It looked perfect, so I went to see the landlord about leasing it. I had £50,000 in the bank, which was enough to get started, and I got a brewery to put in some money.

I wouldn't dream of building a club in a flooded concrete basement today, but the only way to learn is from your mistakes. The basement was not only flooded, but it didn't have any electricity or gas. Underneath the basement, where I'd planned to put all my services, was a vault. The building contractor estimated that it would cost £5,000 to take out the vault. Four diamond-tipped drill-bits later, the cost had escalated to £35,000 and he was on the verge of bankruptcy.

I wanted the new club to be a combination of Cinderella's and Rockafella's. It was going to be brass and honey-browns, because I liked the warmth the similar colour scheme had given Rockafella's. On one side there was to be a restaurant and on the other a bistro, with the dance floor between them.

While the new club was being built, Coral and I went to Benidorm for our first Spanish holiday. I could see that the clubs in Benidorm were miles ahead of anything we had in Britain. Their music policy was rubbish, but the atmosphere and effects surpassed anything I'd seen before. One club had a circus big top inside it, with a helicopter hanging from a ceiling covered in spotlights. Up to then I'd only seen lights that would give a flooded effect. In Spain they had lights which produced a narrow beam. Every twenty minutes they'd blow dry ice on to the dance floor, which would swirl around these beams of light. The effect was fantastic.

The moment I got back to Leeds I booked another flight to Madrid for myself and Geoffrey. We went from there to

Benidorm, only to be told by the club's manager that the lights came from Madrid, so back we drove to Madrid and checked into the Hilton. While we were waiting for a room at the bar, I noticed the most beautiful Bardot lookalike reading a magazine in the corner. She caught me looking at her and smiled. Geoffrey told me to go over, but by then we'd been given the key to our room.

We were getting ready to go out when Geoffrey decided we needed to find a couple of girls for the night. The only time I'd come across a prostitute was as a sixteen-year-old in the merchant navy, and I wasn't at all keen. I told Geoffrey he could find a girl and I'd be happy to have a drink with them both. He called the concierge, who said he'd organise an escort. Ten minutes later the concierge rang back to tell Geoffrey that his 'date' was waiting downstairs. When we got to the bar, he said, 'Mr Stringfellow, may I introduce you to Consuela.' I nearly collapsed. Consuela was the Bardot lookalike I'd seen at the bar. Geoffrey knew I liked her, so he suggested that we found another girl for him. Consuela said she had a nineteen-year-old friend. 'I am nothing. My friend is . . .' She went on to describe this vision of great beauty. My sexual greed immediately took over. I told Geoffrey that he could have Consuela and I'd wait for the friend.

When the 'vision of beauty' arrived she had big boobs all right, but everything else about her was big as well. She wasn't in the same league as Consuela, but I didn't have the heart to turn her down, so we all ended up going out for the night. We arrived back at the Hilton smashed. Geoffrey disappeared with Consuela, leaving me with the big girl. We went to the room and I uttered the words I never thought I'd hear myself say. 'I'm sorry, I'm happily married.' But she wouldn't accept a refusal and began taking off her clothes. She said, 'Peter, you like me.' Then she used a passion-killing word. 'You like my titties.' That was it. They are breasts, boobs even, but never 'titties'. I told her I'd pay her for her time, but I couldn't have sex.

Within twenty minutes Consuela was knocking on the door. The two girls chatted in Spanish, and then Consuela said, 'Peter, you should have told me you were homosexual. We would have understood.' I tried to explain that I simply didn't fancy the friend, but neither of them knew what I was talking about.

If there are any prostitutes reading this book, I hope they don't take it personally, but I just can't pay for sex. It might sound hypocritical in someone who will pay a girl £10, £20, even £100 to dance for him, but it's not the same as paying for sex. I'll buy a girl jewellery *after* we've made love; I'll court her with beautiful flowers and the best champagne, but I cannot pay for sex. The thought of it just turns me off.

We eventually bought the spotlights for the new club, but neither of us had thought about the difference in voltage. The lights were made for use in Spain which works on 120 volts. In Britain we use 240 volts, so we ended up having to buy transformers to make them work. Before we left Madrid, Geoffrey and I were sitting in a restaurant thinking about a name for the new club. We wanted it to be the best nightclub Manchester had ever seen. We wanted to be proud to own it. We wanted people to feel good about coming there. We wanted it to be the Rolls-Royce of nightclubs. 'There's only one name for it,' said Geoffrey. 'The Millionaire.'

It sounded perfect. Today it would be gauche, but in 1976 it *was* perfect. Here we were, two working-class kids on their way up, about to open a nightclub called the Millionaire. We needed a new image. We needed Rolls-Royce. But we were about to find out that Rolls-Royce didn't need us.

10

WHO WANTS TO BE
A MILLIONAIRE?

The Millionaire cost £350,000 to build, which put us wildly into debt. A week before it opened, Geoffrey and I rolled into Manchester in our twin Rolls-Royces, his silver, mine gold. We drove straight to Piccadilly Radio, where I went on air and announced that the best nightclub in Great Britain was about to open. The logo for the Millionaire was the Rolls-Royce grille. We even advertised the place as the Rolls-Royce of nightclubs.

Three days before the opening, Rolls-Royce's solicitors sent us a letter threatening to sue if we didn't stop using their name. We pulled the adverts, but we were damned if we were going to lose the association altogether. In the end we got two Rolls-Royce grilles and put one above the bar and the other above the cash box. Rolls-Royce were seething, but they couldn't make us take them down because we'd bought them.

The Rolls-Royces were a great idea. They set a precedent for the kind of vehicles we wanted outside the club, which made two car dealers in Manchester very happy: Lawrence Bower and Chris Miller sold more flashy cars in 1976 than in any other year. Forget BMWs – you couldn't park anything less than a Ferrari outside the Millionaire.

On the opening weekend we took £8,000. Cinderella's and Rockafella's took £8,000 a week between them, which shows what a difference another city can make. But the following week disaster struck. I could have envisaged a host of awful scenarios, but none quite so bizarre as me lying in hospital with my leg in traction. It might sound macho to say I fell off a motorbike, but the motorbike was barely two feet high and powered by a 10cc engine – it was one of a miniature pair I'd bought for Karen and Scott. I'd invited the staff from Cinderella's and Rockafella's to a barbecue at our house and while everyone was lying around in the sun, drinking wine, I got the kids to get the bikes out. They started riding around, jumping over a hump between two trees at the side of the garden. Although I was dressed only in a thong, I decided I'd have a go on one of the bikes. I hurtled off towards the trees, and just as I was about to jump, with the bike, over the hump, someone jumped on the back of the bike. We never made the trees. The bike came crashing down and the handlebars swivelled around, along with my left leg. I was laughing until I noticed that it was at right angles to my body. In my drunken haze, I pulled it round and then watched as it grew to twice its normal size. At first I was in too much shock to feel any pain. Coral laughed when I told her to call an ambulance. I said, 'Look at me!' and in that split-second she saw that I was deadly serious. Before the ambulance arrived the pain started. It was so bad that I cannot describe it. I'd snapped all the tendons in my leg and dislocated my knee joint.

The hospital strapped up my leg and told me to come back the following week, but the pain was so unbearable Coral called them that night and managed to track down a consultant at his home. He came out in the middle of the night and examined my leg. He told me I had two choices: either I saw him the following Wednesday and went on the NHS waiting list, by which time my leg would have set in its current position and I'd have a limp for life, or he could take me on privately and I could have an operation the next day. It was like saying to a man who is dying of thirst, 'If you give me everything, you can have this glass of water.' I didn't have private health insurance, but I didn't care – I wanted my leg fixed, whatever it cost.

Three weeks later, I was still in hospital with my leg in traction. I was in so much pain the nurses pumped me full of morphine. Up until then I hadn't ever taken a hallucinogenic drug of any description, other than laughing gas when I had a tooth pulled out. When I finally came out of hospital I was as high as a kite. I sat down and wrote a waltz, which I called the Royal Waltz. Now bear in mind that I have no musical talent

128 / PETER STRINGFELLOW

whatsoever – I have no idea where all this musical theory came from. When I finished the waltz I started writing stories, songs and poetry. By the end of the first week Coral managed to get me in the bath. I had hardly got in the bath before I was demanding that Coral bring me a tape-recorder because I felt a new song coming on. Then I started singing about God and how the world was so sad. Michael Jackson's 'Earth Song' had nothing on this. Coral thought I'd lost it. I had lost it – totally. When the effects of the morphine wore off I was back to my talentless self.

Eventually I was allowed to hobble around on crutches. Coral loved it. For the first time since 1963, she knew exactly where I was every hour of the day and night. Talk about mothering – she had to do everything for me. She was mother, nurse and wife, and even though I was sleeping downstairs because the bed was too soft, we carried on making love. After a couple of weeks, I was bored witless. One afternoon while Coral was out shopping, I called Linda, one of my regular girlfriends, and asked her to meet me. My leg was in plaster from thigh to ankle, but I managed to hobble to the Rolls-Royce. I stuck my leg out of the passenger window, put the automatic gears in drive and drove to Linda's using one leg. We ended up making love in the car down a country lane. Coral went berserk when I got home. Scott was laughing because I'd escaped, but Coral didn't see the funny side and immediately took the car keys off me.

The Millionaire began to suffer in my absence. Although I had Peter Tyler, Chris Crossley and Brett Paul playing the music, I'd built the club to wrap around me. Cinderella's was doing fine because it was established, and the regulars knew I'd had an accident, but business was foundering in Manchester. After six weeks I couldn't stay away any longer and went back to the decks on crutches. Then I got a stick, which was great for pointing at people. I had a whole collection of them with different tops – gold, silver, brass. One night a girl told me she'd really fancy me if I didn't have the stick, so I gave up playing the invalid and stopped using them. By then I had a cast around my leg which I would take off before bed, then bandage back on in the morning. Sex was too uncomfortable in the car, so I started booking hotel rooms. I would do a deal with the night porter.

For £5 he'd let me use a room for as long as I wanted. I'd take girls there, unwrap my leg, make love and then wrap it back up again. You might well wonder what kind of girls let me do that in my condition, but they were all gorgeous. I met a girl called Elaine during this period. I introduced her to someone else while I was in plaster, but the moment I got the cast off I made a play for her and she became one of my regular girlfriends.

The constant travelling between Leeds and Manchester put a strain on my extra-marital activities. Some nights I'd DJ at Cinderella's–Rockafella's, but my heart was now in Manchester.

During this period, Peter Smith, an executive from Mecca, asked if I was interested in selling Cinderella's–Rockafella's. He said if I could give him a price he'd bring Eric Morley to see me. Eric was very famous in the seventies. He was the managing director of Mecca Locarno, but he was best known as the organiser of the Miss World competitions. Cinderella's had cost £65,000, Rockafella's £95,000, and we owed a further £200,000 on the Millionaire. Geoffrey and I agreed to sell the Leeds clubs for £500,000.

Eric Morley came to the club and spent an evening sitting in one of the booths. Towards the end of the night he said: '£500,000 is a lot of money. We can build clubs for less.' I explained that he was buying our business as well as the premises and that we'd built up both clubs from scratch. Eric Morley had another look around then said, 'OK,' and put out his hand. He never reneged on a single penny. He bought the clubs on a handshake, without even seeing the figures, which were around £100,000 a year before tax. Of course, we got solicitors to draw up the necessary legal documents, but essentially the deal was done that evening.

Geoffrey and I paid off our debts and bought detached houses near Manchester. His was in Wilmslow, mine in Cheadle Hulme. I sold my house in Leeds for £27,000 to my poker friend, Asga. I made £20,000 on the sale. In the six years I'd owned the house, I'd built a conservatory on the back and stolen a piece of the adjoining farmland – one of my mottos in life is if you want it, do it with attitude. There was a raised piece of land adjacent to my garden. The farmer thought it was too dangerous for his cows and horses to graze on, so one day I got my fence moved to incorporate it. I put a gate on to his land – not for him, but so that my two Great Danes could go out for a run. The farmer came storming round, saying the land was his. I told him to check his deeds, because on my deeds the land belonged to me. He demanded to see my deeds, so I said, 'No problem,' but advised him to check his own in the meantime. Once I'd put up the fence he couldn't take it down without proving that the property belonged to him. This turned out to be difficult: he didn't have all the right documents and his predecessor at the farm had left the country. Of course, my deeds never mentioned anything about the three-quarters-of-an-acre plot next to the garden, but I cultivated the land anyway. My solicitor said it was about as bare-faced as you could get, but he told me that if I could hang on to it for five years without the farmer taking me to court, the land would be mine. By the time I sold it, it was legally mine to sell.

The Millionaire Club introduced me to another very different clientele. They were a mixture of Jews, Iranians, Lebanese and Turks. The Middle Eastern crowd were mainly students at the engineering college in Manchester. They weren't your archetypal impecunious undergraduates; they were sons of oil sheiks and rich businessmen. At the other extreme was the rich Jewish set, who were dominated by incredibly powerful ladies. In my typically Libran way, I loved both communities, and became friends with them all. I wasn't aware of any racial tension until one of the Jewish group called me over one night and told me I was letting in too many Iranians. I said, 'Where are they? I don't know what you mean.' He pointed to a group of good-looking guys sitting in a corner. Up until then I'd thought they were French. To me, they were just smart, sophisticated young men with a slight accent. I'd never encountered racism before I went to Manchester. The closest I'd got to tribal tension was the rivalry between the miners and the steelworkers back in Sheffield.

The nationality of my customers was immaterial to me. I'd never seen spending power like it. I became surrounded by people who had money to burn – when they weren't drinking it away in champagne, that is. One week I'd be invited to an Israeli Independence Day party by my Jewish friends and the next I'd be having dinner with Amer Medani, a relation of the Saudi Arabian royal family, whose father owned a big construction company in Manchester. Amer and his brother, Imad, were both honorary princes and incredibly generous people. In Manchester my affection for Middle Eastern people developed. In my experience, they are generous to a fault and have impeccable manners.

Of course, this view wasn't shared by everyone at the Millionaire, and I began to notice a strain building up between the Jewish set and the Middle Eastern crowd. Not only that, there was political tension between different Middle Eastern factions. One evening a group of them started telling me about the impending revolution in Iran. The struggles in the Middle East had not become headline news around the world in the late 1970s so I'd no idea what they were talking about. Not long afterwards a few cars belonging to one group were vandalised by extremist students. There was nothing I could do about fighting in the Middle East, but I did try my best to create racial harmony in Manchester. I decided to have special nights for each of the different countries. I knew I couldn't start off with an Israeli night, because this would upset the Iranians, and vice versa. I decided to introduce the idea slowly and to start off with a Gypsy night. There was a small problem in that I didn't know any Gypsies, except for a car dealer called Tom Hartley. He was a multi-millionaire because he only ever dealt in top-of-the-range cars, like Rolls-Royces and Ferraris. Despite his wealth, he was proud that he came from a Gypsy background. Tom was our token Gypsy and king for the night. I booked a Gypsy dancing team and we had a fabulous evening.

The next 'theme' night was for the French, even though, once again, I didn't know any French people. We had traditional French music, which went down well. Now it was time for the serious stuff. When I organised our first Israeli night, the whole of the Middle Eastern lot turned up. I got the Turks, Lebanese, Iranians and Jews all dancing to 'Hava Nagila' by the Spotnicks.

From where I was standing on the decks, it looked like the United Nations. When it came to Turkish night, the Turks had to outdo the Israelis. They ordered sheeps' heads for the restaurant; the Iranians followed this by ordering a whole sheep with couscous. The only failure was English night. I booked some good Morris dancers, but the club was half empty and nobody liked them.

While the theme nights were keeping my international crowd happy, a new disco phenomenon was enthralling my Saturday-night regulars. It was 1977, the year *Saturday Night Fever* was released. John Travolta was sensational, the music fantastic, the dancing out of sight. The film did wonders for the disco industry. Overnight everyone became a John Travolta. Out came the white suits and fingers in the air. I would get the whole of the Millionaire Club lining up and dancing to the Bee Gees' hits, 'Stayin' Alive' and 'Night Fever'. I found to my amazement that I could lift a girl and twirl her around above my head. If she put her hands up straight and went very stiff, it was easy. *Saturday Night Fever* was followed by *Grease*, the film which made me fall in love with Olivia Newton-John. I eventually met her face to face at the film premiere of *Xanadu* a few years later.

The Millionaire was doing brilliantly; I had a lovely house, a great wife and two wonderful children, who were now at private schools; I had as many girlfriends as I needed, one of whom was now my wife's best friend (I had introduced Elaine to Coral) and we were all playing together. What more could a man want? The answer had been on my mind for quite some time.

I wanted London and international fame.

I was so wrapped up in my mad ambition that I failed to notice the beginnings of what was about to become one of the saddest and most difficult problems of my life. I had failed to recognise that somewhere along the line Geoffrey's heavy drinking had turned into alcoholism. It was a tragedy that would eventually tear me apart. Towards the end of the seventies he was drinking a great deal and going missing for days at a time. Some evenings we couldn't get him out of the club and had to leave him with the keys. This wasn't a problem until he went missing with the keys. We then gave the keys to Roger Howe, who had become manager of the Millionaire, but he was just as bad – he'd lose them within two days. There is something about Roger and keys: the two just don't go together.

Whereas I'm happy in drink, Geoffrey was nasty. Drinkers have drinking friends. One of Geoffrey's drinking partners was 'Shaky' Les, who eventually committed suicide. He was a nice guy, but he couldn't pick a glass up without shaking. There wasn't the same compassion then for alcoholics as there is today. We made jokes about Les's shaking because we just weren't aware that alcoholism is a chronic disease. It took me years to realise that Geoffrey was an alcoholic, and many more years for he himself to accept that he was ill. Like me, he was in denial. Sure, Geoffrey drank too much, but I thought he could stop it. After he'd been on a drinking spree for a few days, I'd have a chat with him and he'd say, 'You're absolutely right. I'll stop.' I soon got to know the pattern.

When I started making regular trips to London to look for premises, Geoffrey was sometimes with me, sometimes not. I found a site near Marble Arch, but the deal fell through. Then I found a new club which had only recently opened. It was called Dial 9, though I didn't know why (if you're in a hotel you dial 9 to get an outside line, but I hadn't stayed in enough hotels for that to mean anything to me). The owner, Nicky Kerman, often spoke about selling it to me and I seriously considered buying it. In the end, it only lasted a year. I also thought about buying Le Valbonne from Louis Brown. He knew I was having difficulties finding premises and offered me his club for £1 million. At the time it seemed a lot of money: I was hoping to build a new club for £300,000. In fact, Le Valbonne would have been a bargain, but I didn't realise that then.

London was never going to be easy. The more I visited the capital, the more aware I became of the chasm between north and south. Perhaps it was my accent; perhaps it was my green velvet suits with the flower in the lapel. Maybe it was my long permed hair. Whatever it was, I was invariably made to feel like an outsider. Even though I owned the best nightclub in Manchester, some London clubs wouldn't let me through their doors. Tramp was one of them.

I'd been refused admission to Tramp on several occasions but one evening I was determined to get in. I went to the door with an advert I'd put in the *Manchester Quick Guide*. It read something like: 'When in Paris, Régines, when in New York, Studio 54, when in London, Tramp, when in Manchester, the Millionaire.' I explained who I was to the doorman and asked him to show the owner, Johnny Gold, the ad. A few minutes later he came back and said, 'I'm sorry, it's members only.' I was livid. Being refused by Tramp was like the whole of London saying no to me.

The next time I tried to get in was when Buddy Greco and his wife, Jackie, invited Coral and me to dinner with them there. I'd met Buddy at the Millionaire. On quiet nights, usually Tuesdays, I'd play obscure songs and talk about the music, rather like a radio DJ. I played music from the forties and fifties and often ended up playing Buddy Greco songs. One night the waiter came over and said, 'There's a gentleman in the restaurant called Buddy Greco. He wants to know why you're playing his mother's favourite song.' I couldn't believe it. It was pure coincidence. I went over to chat to him and from that evening we became great friends. By the time we arranged to meet at Tramp I knew him well enough to be aware that unless he was on stage, he had no idea of time. Coral and I arrived at Tramp at 9p.m. as agreed. I told the doorman that we were guests of Buddy Greco's. The doorman confirmed that he'd booked a table so I said that Coral and I would wait in the bar until he arrived. The doorman refused to let us in unless we were accompanied by Buddy. I was so angry. I said, 'We either walk in now, or I'll come nowhere near the place and you can deal with Buddy Greco later.' He was adamant, so I left a message that we'd gone to Morton's in Berkeley Square, where I knew I was welcome. When Buddy called Morton's, I told him that I wouldn't set foot in Tramp unless Johnny Gold apologised to me personally. After much cajoling I relented. I'm glad I did: it was at Tramp that Coral decided she fancied Buddy's wife, Jackie, and all four of us ended up sharing a room at the Savoy later that night.

Buddy and I made a pact that he wouldn't make love to my wife and I wouldn't make love to his. The girls played together while we watched, then we played with the girls. I hasten to add that Buddy and I did not play together. I'd broken the rules once, with Roger and his wife, Janine, and it upset Roger. Although he was happy for me to make love to Janine while he watched, it was different when Coral joined in. One night when the four of us were rolling around on the carpet in front of the fire, Roger turned round to see Janine and me making love. It upset the balance. Unbeknown to Roger, I once tried to break the absolute golden rule of foursomes with him. While he was managing the club one evening, I phoned Janine and asked if she'd come out to play. I picked her up and we headed off into the country. I was so nervous and excited that I lost control of the Jensen and we skidded into a hedge. By the time we got the car back on the road my libido had died. I took her straight home and nothing happened between us.

If you introduce a third or fourth person into your sex life, you're asking for trouble. You can bet your bottom dollar that someone is going to make a date on the side. I know this for a fact, because I've always done it. One of you might like the idea of three, but the other two might prefer one to one. Three is a good game, but the best sex is one to one.

Although it infuriated me that I couldn't get into Tramp, they were absolutely right to stick to their club rules. I was less bothered about not getting into Annabel's because the membership was more exclusive there anyway. It didn't stop me trying, though. The previous summer in Tunisia, Coral and I had met a couple from London. Every evening we had all made an effort to dress for dinner, even Scott and Karen, and we looked immaculate. On the fourth night of our holiday, this couple came over and remarked on how lovely the family looked. They introduced themselves as Tony and Hilly Marshall. We kept in touch and a few months later they invited us to stay with them in London. It was Hilly's birthday, so she wanted to go somewhere special, like Annabel's. They thought I would know how to get them in: after all, I did own a nightclub in Manchester. Tony worked as a jobber in the city, which wasn't any help, except for the fact that one of the partners in his firm of stockbrokers was a member. His name was Lord Spencer

Churchill, and, according to Tony, he was out of the country on business.

I telephoned Annabel's and told the maitre d' that I found myself in a very embarrassing situation. That when Lord Spencer Churchill had visited Leeds recently, he'd invited the mayor and his wife to have dinner at the club. The mayor was with me and was expecting to dine at Annabel's that evening along with a couple of his friends. The maitre d' was hesitant. I mumbled something about a big charity affair and waited. He thought about it for a second. Of course, I had no idea I was talking to Louis Emmanuelli, the most influential maitre d'/restaurant manager in the whole of London. After a pause he said, 'In that case, sir, we'll expect you later.'

Tony and Hilly were understandably nervous when we got to the door of Annabel's. Tony was supposed to be the mayor of Leeds, yet he talked like a London hooray. At least I had a northern accent, long, permed hair and was dressed in one of my velvet numbers. The moment the maitre d' saw us, I could see him thinking, 'Oh, fuck!' He knew he'd made a mistake, but it was too late, we'd already got through the door.

After a fabulous meal, two bottles of wine and several glasses of port, I decided it was time I became a member of Annabel's. I was using the maitre d's first name by this time, so I called Louis over and told him I'd like to join the club. Before he could say anything, I pressed £100 into the palm of his hand and reiterated what a great club it was. I could feel him desperately trying to uncurl his fingers and pull away. In the end he gave me a withering look and said, 'That won't be necessary, sir. The membership has been closed for many years.' With that, he dropped the money back into my hand and hurried off. I still cringe at the memory of it. Only too much drink could have made me attempt to bribe the most insouciant maitre d' in London. The embarrassment didn't end there. When Hilly and Coral saw Prince Charles on the dance floor, we had to go and dance. I was considering inviting the prince up to Leeds. I can still hear Tony saying, 'Don't, Peter, please don't.' I wasn't quite that drunk, thank God.

The only other club worth visiting, apart from Annabel's,

Tramp, Le Valbonne and Dial 9, was Wedges, which was fronted by Dai Llewellyn. Dai always let me in. He saw beyond the velvet suit and we eventually became very good friends. One evening I was there with Elaine, trying to create the most expensive cocktail possible. It was a mixture of champagne, brandy and fruit which we dubbed the Butterfly Ball. Dai couldn't take his eyes off Elaine. Towards the end of the night, he offered her membership and gave her a form to fill in. I said, 'What about me?'

'Oh, you can just ring up, Peter,' said Dai.

I told Elaine to write down the Millionaire's address and telephone number, because I'd sussed what Dai was about. She gave him back the form and he said, 'Lovely, darling. Is this your phone number?'

'No, Dai,' I replied. 'It's mine. Call me any time.'

After months of searching, I eventually found some premises through an estate agent called Alan Joseph. Geoffrey had done one of his disappearing acts, so I went down to London to look at the property with Roger. It was on Upper St Martin's Lane, a place known as the Little Theatre. Understandably, I'd been expecting to see a theatre; instead we were confronted by a filthy old office block which had been partially boarded up at the front. I couldn't believe anyone would put on plays in a place like that. The agent said that actors paid a nominal rent of £2 a week to use the building for rehearsals. London Transport, who owned the property, were desperate to lease it out. As has been the case with all my club premises, no one else wanted it. London Transport were asking £40,000 a year, which was a monster amount of money. But I had to stop thinking with a Manchester mind: this was London, and it was bound to be more expensive than any other city.

I could see that Roger wasn't keen. He wanted to be more central. This was Covent Garden when it was just a sketch in the planners' minds. The plans were fantastic: one day there would be bars, boutiques and restaurants, but in 1978, it looked like the old vegetable market it still was. With the exception of the Neal Street Restaurant, there was nothing open. There were the beginnings of Peppermint Park, which was going to be an

American-style eatery, and a couple of scruffy, run-down pubs.
I said to Roger, 'What do you think?'

'It's a great site for a club,' he replied, 'but you're going to be
very lonely.'

In other words, it was at the wrong end of town. Of course,
I've spent the last eighteen years throwing his words back in his
face at every opportunity. I had a gut feeling that day. The plans
for Covent Garden fired my imagination and I wanted the
building.

Leasing it from London Transport was not a problem, but
everything else became a monumental saga. We started to apply
for licences and planning permission only to be thwarted at
every turn. The local residents' association opposed planning
permission because they wanted Covent Garden to be kept as a
fruit market for flower-sellers and – and I quote – 'cobblers and
saddlers'. When we finally got permission we had to fight tooth
and nail for our drink and dancing licences. We had to take
menus and prospective chefs and references from breweries and
the police in Manchester to the court. I wouldn't have been
surprised if they'd wanted to hear from my mum and dad. The
magistrates insisted on a minimum entrance charge of £3, which
was a lot of money, considering that the wealthy Manchester
crowd paid only £2 admission to the Millionaire.

When we finally got a licence to sell drinks until 3a.m. and a
dancing licence to 3.30a.m., the chairwoman of the residents'
association said, 'So you think you've won, do you? Why don't
you check your planning consent?' Geoffrey was with me, and
sober, on this occasion. He confirmed that we already had our
planning consent. But when our solicitor checked the documents
they stipulated that we had to close at 1a.m. The following week
we received a letter from the residents' association saying,
'Beware – we know about your planning permission.' To this
day I don't know what happened, but whatever it was, it smelt
funny to me. Between being granted our planning permission
and going to court for our drink and dancing licences, someone
had put a 1a.m. restriction on the premises.

The planning appeal took nine months. I'm sure anyone else
would have thrown in the towel and walked away. We'd spent

thousands on legal fees and travelling to London, Geoffrey was drinking himself into an early grave and the Millionaire was suffering in my absence. It was like living with your wife when she knows you're going to leave her for someone else. The Manchester crowd sensed that I'd be going. Sure, I loved Manchester, but I was waiting to move in with my new girlfriend, London, and nine months was a long time to wait. In the meantime, I was about to fall in love with America. That love affair would cost Roger his marriage and take Geoffrey into the depths of alcoholic oblivion.

11

SAN FRANCISCO
(YOU'VE GOT ME)

Two months into my nine-month wait to open the London club, I decided to take Coral and the kids to the States. I had an open invitation to stay with Buddy Greco in Los Angeles, so I booked a flight and rooms for us at the Beverly Wilshire Hotel for the first few days. It was twenty-two years since I'd stood gazing wide-eyed and awestruck at the Manhattan skyline – this time I was going to see LA, but in very different circumstances. As a seventeen-year-old galley boy in the merchant navy I'd struggled to find a nickel for a sandwich; at thirty-nine, I was a wealthy nightclub owner. Even better, the exchange rate was at an all-time high. We were getting $2.60 to every pound, so hiring the finest Cadillac was not going to be a problem.

I arrived in Los Angeles with New York on my mind. If you've seen one city before the other, this isn't something I'd recommend. I was expecting skyscrapers, neon lights and the hustle and bustle of a busy American city, but I couldn't see anything that resembled my dream. I asked the hotel receptionist where LA was. He looked at me incredulously and said, 'This is LA.' But where? I'm still asking myself the same question today. This place called Beverly Hills turned out to be nothing more than a road called Rodeo Drive. There were no cabs around, and the Beverly Wilshire was like a tomb in those days. It was like the lost city of America without the glamour. I remember sitting in the hotel reception feeling very unhappy. Eleven years later, history would repeat itself when I opened a nightclub across the street. If I'd remembered then what I remember now, I would never have made that mistake.

I called Buddy only to find that he was on tour and wouldn't be back for a week. Coral and the kids looked at me as if to say, 'What next, Dad?' In the hotel magazine I saw that the *Queen Mary* was berthed at New Port, California, about thirty miles away. I told the kids we were checking out of the hotel and going to stay on a fabulous ocean liner, and we all piled in the Cadillac and headed off to New Port. The closer we got to the docks, the more depressing it all became, especially when the kids went silent in the back. When we finally arrived at the ship, it was the most pathetic sight I'd seen, floating in rubbish and in desperate need of a paint job. The porter carried our bags up the rusting gangway and showed us our cabins, which were supposed to be the king-and-queen's suites. Talk about hype. Coral and I stood staring open-mouthed at two of the smallest single beds I'd ever seen. We didn't even discuss it. I paid the porter for the cabins, picked up our bags and left the ship.

We spent the next four hours driving around looking for somewhere to stay. For some unknown reason LA was like Bethlehem that night and everywhere was full. The later it got, the more excited the kids became. Eventually we pulled up outside the Stardust Motel. The owner was too busy smoking his cigarette to hold a polite conversation.

'Cash now.'

'Can we see the rooms first?'

'No. Cash now. You want it by the hour, or the night?'

Clearly this was where the local hookers took their clients, but we were so desperate that I paid the guy and we went to find our rooms. The first smelled like someone had peed in every corner; the one next door was even worse. There was no way we could stay there so once again I got the bags and we all filed out to the car.

By now it must have been around midnight, though none of us had the correct time. There was no one to ask except the girls on Sunset Strip with their mini-skirts and thigh-high boots. Eventually I pulled up and asked Coral to wind down the window. One of the girls peered into the car and exclaimed, 'Gee, surely not with your wife and kids!' I asked her if she could tell me the time. 'You're kidding,' she said. 'I'll tell you this for free, you're wasting mine.' And she walked off.

I was beginning to panic. There was no way we could sleep in the car. I found the telephone number of a guy I'd met in Manchester who'd been rash enough to utter the immortal words, 'If you're ever in LA . . .' and I called him. He was surprised to hear I was in town. 'Hey, we must get together,' he said.

'Yeah,' I agreed. 'How about tonight?'

I explained what had happened, and with typical American generosity, he invited us over to stay at his parents' house for the night. The next day we checked into the Hyatt Hotel. It was on the Strip, a more exciting part of town than the area around Beverly Wilshire, and had the added bonus that the Bee Gees were staying there at the time. The kids were in their element, which meant I was a hero after all.

When Buddy Greco got back from his tour, we went to stay with him and had the most fantastic time. One night, after we'd all had a few drinks, Buddy got out his movie camera and suggested that the four of us had some fun. He wanted me to hold the camera while he played around with Coral and Jackie, then he'd film me. I insisted on going first. When it came to his turn, the film ran out. It still amuses me that he tried to pull a fast one on me.

After spending a few days with Buddy, we left LA for Las Vegas. I booked into the MGM Hotel near Caesar's Palace, but in fact we ended up staying with Fred, an American property developer I had met at the Millionaire. Fred had built a miniature housing estate called the Coventry Estate. Each Hansel-and-Gretel-style house had its own moat with blue water running through it. It was the flashiest, tackiest thing I'd ever seen. This was beyond Disney. I was half expecting Lady Godiva to ride by on a multi-coloured horse at any second. He'd built the estate with a storybook image of Coventry in mind, and it won't surprise you to learn that he'd never been there. 'Whaddya think?' he asked.

I said the only word I could think of: 'Fantastic!'

After a few days' gambling in Las Vegas, we set off for San Francisco. Whereas LA had been a miserable disappointment, San Francisco was everything I wanted America to be, glamorous and fun. Our hotel was on top of Snow Hill, overlooking the city. Coral and I left the kids behind and set off to see the nightlife. We found a small nightclub on Snow Hill called Dance Your Ass Off, which seemed to us a vulgar title for a club. Americans use the word 'ass' all the time. I couldn't imagine there ever being a club at home called Dance Your Arse Off.

I showed the doorman my business card and explained that I owned a nightclub in England. When we got inside there were only half a dozen other people there. It was a great club, but it was empty. The owner looked nothing like a club owner. He was slightly balding and wearing jeans and a T-shirt. This was in the glamorous seventies, remember, when I was wearing velvet suits and sequins to go on the decks at the Millionaire. We started talking and it turned out he'd been in the circus before buying the nightclub. He not only hated the business; he hated his club, the people and the music. He was completely wrong for the job, yet he had a fantastic club with huge potential. As we were leaving that night, he took a run at the wall, did two somersaults and landed back on his feet again. It was obvious this guy belonged in the circus.

By the end of our stay, I'd talked the owner into selling me the club. I'd seen the whole of San Francisco under blue skies and fallen madly in love with the place. London had turned into a bureaucratic nightmare and I just couldn't see the club there ever opening.

When I got back to Manchester I told Geoffrey I wanted him to come to San Francisco and see this new club. He wasn't keen; he hadn't even been keen on the idea of London. I saw London and international fame as the ultimate, but it wasn't the same for Geoffrey. He had the same trappings as me – the big house, lovely wife, great kids at private school and a regular girlfriend – but he didn't have the fun of going on the microphone every night, playing the superstar. His job was to deal with the financial side, and it was boring him. He surrounded himself with people who weren't fun, but serious drinkers. After he'd finished his work he'd sit in one of the booths with his cronies. He was becoming progressively unhappier with his life, but I didn't realise quite how bad things were until I spoke to his wife Carol about it.

I was staying in London with Coral, Geoffrey and Carol. We had a good lunch at Langan's then went back to the Grosvenor Hotel to have a rest and get ready for the evening. At about 8p.m. Carol called our room and asked us if we'd seen Geoffrey. Apparently he'd disappeared after lunch. We didn't see him for two days. On the train back to Manchester Carol burst into tears. She told me that Geoffrey had been coming home from the club after drinking there all night and then drinking a bottle of red wine before going to bed. This was shocking news to me. I had a word with him, and once again he said he'd stop. When he was sober, as he is today, he was brilliant.

On another occasion Carol phoned to say he'd been stopped for drink-driving and was in the police cells in Leeds. It still didn't register that he was an alcoholic, even though he looked terrible when Dad and I went to collect him. They wouldn't give Geoffrey his car keys. Instead they handed them to Dad, and Geoffrey was so annoyed he spat in the policeman's face. I was horrified. This just wasn't the Geoffrey I knew and loved.

At other times he'd be his normal, sober self. He came with me to court when we finally got our appeal date for the London club moved forward to six months instead of nine. We went before the inspector of planning to get the time on the agreement moved from 1a.m. to 3.30a.m., which was the time on our dancing licence. The inspector listened to the evidence, then closed his book and walked out of the room. I asked our solicitor, John Neilson, what he was doing.

'He's going to deliberate.'

'What do you mean, "deliberate"?'

'He's going to make a report and pass it on to the minister of planning.'

'What does that mean?'

'It means we have to wait until he's read it.'

'When will that be?'

'I don't know, Peter.'

'Give me an idea.'

'Two months? Four months? Who knows? You're on a pile.'

Geoffrey wasn't as concerned as I was because, as I said, he didn't want London anyway. On the train back home he got off at the stop before Manchester and I didn't see him again for another two days. We'd been partners for a long time, yet it was always me who chose the city and the design of the club, while Geoffrey backed me up. When I started thinking seriously about San Francisco, I knew in my heart that he wouldn't be interested. But I wanted him to see San Francisco so that we could consider selling the Millionaire and our interests in London, where we had the premises and the licences but where someone would need to take on the problem of the planning. In spite of Geoffrey's lack of enthusiasm, once again I was going to steamroller him into it, as I'd done from Sheffield to Leeds, Leeds to Manchester and Manchester to London.

We were all set to fly to the States when I got a message that Geoffrey was already at the airport. I was feeling hopeful – until I saw him. He was drinking in the bar with one of his girlfriends, a big blonde girl from Liverpool with massive boobs. She liked a drink as well. I could see that he was drunk, but he was still capable of holding a conversation. The plane was leaving in an hour. Geoffrey said he'd stay in the bar for a bit and join me later. I knew he wouldn't come, and by then I didn't actually care.

On the plane I ended up sitting next to a tall guy in a cowboy hat. I was wearing a velvet cap pulled down over one side of my head, so our hats were the conversation-starter. By the end of the flight we were friends. He knew all about my business plans and I knew that he collected ornamental giraffes and that he was in his thirties and semi-retired. He insisted that I stayed with him and his girlfriend, even though I'd booked a suite at the Hilton Hotel. His girlfriend was waiting for him at the airport. The first thing she did when we got into the car was light up a joint. I know it sounds silly, but I was shocked. Flower power had started in San Francisco, but the Mojo Club version hadn't involved marijuana. I felt very uncomfortable. They both carried on smoking joints when we got to the house, so I made my excuses and went to the hotel instead. The girlfriend insisted on giving me a lift, even though she was stoned out of her brain.

I was put in the Chinese suite, overlooking the Golden Gate Bridge, and felt very happy. I sat down and wrote a note to Mum and Dad, thanking them for everything they'd done for me and promising them that, whatever happened, one day I was going to bring them to San Francisco. That night, I went out on my own and met two girls, a pretty American girl and a not-so-pretty French girl who had lots of money. They invited me back to the French girl's penthouse for a drink, and it certainly was a penthouse, huge and opulent. The bathroom had gold swan-necked taps, a marble floor and huge mirrors.

The French girl then took me into the bedroom. I panicked for a moment because I didn't fancy her at all; I had my eye on the blonde American girl. In the centre of the bedroom was a four-poster bed with curtains closed around it. To my surprise, she opened the curtains and said, 'Darling, I want to introduce you to our new friend.' Darling lifted his head from the pillow and gave me a wave. It was her husband, stoned out of his mind. The two girls then rolled a joint. I told them I didn't smoke. The American girl said, 'Try some of this,' and broke a phial of poppers under my nose. I felt as if I was going about twenty feet into the air, then floated back down. It was pleasant, but frightening. The girls thought this was hilarious and started doing the stuff themselves. I felt very uneasy and I didn't like the smell from the poppers, it was too much like chlorine. The druggy atmosphere just didn't appeal to me, but I did fancy the blonde. After they'd smoked another joint, I took her into the bathroom and we ended up making love in the shower. I came out, said, 'Thank you very much,' and went back to spend the night at the Hilton. It seemed as if everybody I met in San Francisco was taking drugs. It didn't put me off, though – I loved the city and I'd made four new friends.

I called Geoffrey, Roger and my DJ, Peter Tyler, and told them to get on the next plane over. I desperately wanted them to see Dance Your Ass Off. The owner was only asking $250,000 for it, and in my view the Millionaire was worth £500,000. Geoffrey flew in first. He arrived with Phil Wayman, a writer, producer and the manager of a band called the Sweet. Phil had flown in from New York and bumped into Geoffrey at the airport. I'd known him since 1969, when he used to come around the clubs pushing various records. He was one of the first people outside the family to mention Geoffrey's drinking. 'Your brother's got a drink problem,' he told me, but I didn't want to believe him. I still thought Geoffrey could snap his fingers and stop. In fact I thought he was deliberately drinking to annoy me. He came to see the club in a drunken haze and didn't really comment. When Roger and Peter arrived, they loved it.

I now had my team with me and a very drunk Geoffrey. We would take him around with us, though sometimes we'd lose him on the way and pick him up later, but more often than not he wanted to stay in the hotel bar. When he was straight, he contributed, although he wasn't wildly enthusiastic. Roger and Peter thought San Francisco was as exciting as I did. It was a mixture of all types and ten times more interesting than Manchester. It was also more glamorous than London and everyone was much more helpful. I'd brought with me the Millionaire menu and the club's graphics, which showed a guy with a top hat and the Rolls-Royce grille. In my naïveté I rang the local paper and asked one of the reporters if he'd write about my menu. He said, 'Just the menu? What about the food?' I suggested he flew over to Manchester to taste it, but he didn't think his editor would allow it. He said the moment we opened in San Francisco he'd be happy to review the club restaurant. I was getting positive responses from everyone. It all looked so easy. The club only needed redecorating, as opposed to building from scratch like London.

Before everyone flew home, I booked a private room at a restaurant called Le Fleur-de-Lys and invited my four San Francisco friends to join us, plus the American girl's husband, whom I suspected might be gay. He was incredibly good looking. She wasn't good looking, but she was rich and she was nice. The blonde girl came, but I wasn't interested in her any more. I'd been with her once and that was enough – it's a pattern I've repeated throughout my life. Towards the end of the night we were all given rainbow cocktails, a mixture of six different liqueurs topped up with sambucca. The waiter went around the table lighting all the glasses. I warned everyone to blow out the flames in case the glass stuck to anyone's lips. Within seconds the table was covered in blue flames and we were all screaming with laughter. It looked like Dante's Inferno. I looked towards Geoffrey at the opposite end of the table. Above his head was a huge picture of a fleur-de-lys. In the light of the flames, I swear I saw a picture of the Devil.

When everyone else went back to Manchester, I stayed on in San Francisco. The sun hadn't stopped shining and I'd fallen in love with a waitress called Kate. The affair lasted two days. When I flew into London I picked up a message from my solicitor. He had good news: the planning appeal had gone through and we could go ahead and build the London club.

Now I didn't know what to do. I didn't really want London any more – I was besotted with San Francisco. But we'd put a lot of effort and time into London, and now we'd finally got the OK. I agonised all the way back to Manchester. I didn't have a house in London, and the money to build the club would have to come from the sale of the Millionaire. Perhaps if I went to San Francisco, I could become famous over there and then move to London. By the time I reached Manchester, I'd made up my mind to do it the other way round: London, then San Francisco. I knew Geoffrey wouldn't come to San Francisco, and half the Millionaire was his. I couldn't buy a business and build it up on £250,000.

The hardest part was breaking the news to Roger and Peter Tyler. Their wives had been very excited about the move and they took it very badly. Peter's marriage survived the disappointment, but Janine filed for divorce. She'd wanted America to be a new start, a place to rebuild their rocky marriage, and now the dream was over. Geoffrey didn't care whether we were going to San Francisco or Timbuctoo.

Getting the go-ahead for London was the end of one nightmare and the beginning of another. I'd got beautiful designs, all the licences, and now all I had to do was build the club. It seemed so simple, except for one thing: I didn't have any money. John Franks, the designer, put the building contract out to tender. The best price was £500,000, which came from a building firm owned by the electrical giants Dixon's. This was for building the shell only – it didn't include furniture, carpets, fixtures, lights and sound. Once again the cavalier side of my character took over. I dragged Geoffrey to London to meet the contractor at the Grosvenor Hotel. He put the contract in front of me and I signed it. Then I started laughing. The contractor asked, 'Why are you laughing?'

'In truth,' I said, 'I'm happy.' I was still laughing when he left the room. John Franks asked me what was so funny. 'Nothing, John. I'm just happy.' When John left, Geoffrey and I looked at each other and screamed with laughter. We weren't happy, we were frightened. I'd just signed a contract to pay £500,000 and we didn't have £100 between us outside the Millionaire's cashflow.

I knew I would have to sell the Millionaire to finance London, which meant we couldn't call London the Millionaire, as we'd planned. I thought about King Edward's, or Bertie's, because they conjured up an image of affluence and style. My Rock-afella's logo had been a figure with a moustache and top hat, the Millionaire's was a top hat and the Rolls-Royce grille and I wanted something along those lines. I commissioned an artist to draw me a string man with a top hat, monocle and a glass of champagne in his hand. I thought it would look a bit like the Saint. It turned out looking like something you might see outside a Soho strip joint. I scrapped that one.

The name was proving a problem too, but not as big a problem as trying to sell the Millionaire Club. I'd thought it would be easy; I'd thought I could call up Mecca and offer them Manchester. They'd bought Cinderella's–Rockafella's in Leeds, so why not the Millionaire as well? But Eric Morley didn't want to know. Mecca already had Tiffany's in Manchester, and they didn't need another club. The real reason didn't come out until many years later, when I bumped into Peter Smith from Mecca. The real reason they didn't want the Millionaire was because they'd learned a big lesson with Cinderella's–Rockafella's. The moment they stopped doing crazy things, like giving away champagne by the bucketful and having complimentary admission for girls on certain nights, they started losing money. You can't buy a club from Peter Stringfellow and obliterate the man. George Hendry discovered this when he bought the Penthouse.

My clubs are created by me, for me and around me. It was a double-edged sword, but I didn't realise this until an executive from Forte came to look at the Millionaire.

By now I was asking £600,000 for the club. In fact, I'd told the building contractors in London that I expected Forte to pay that much as they were thinking about starting a nightclub empire. The Forte executive was impressed with the name, although no one at that stage had seen the books. Geoffrey had always kept the books straight, but because of his drink problem they weren't as good as they should have been. When Forte came to look at them, Geoffrey was on one of his walkabouts and the nicest thing I can say about the guy he left in charge was that he was incompetent. The Forte executive spent three weeks looking at the finances while I wined and dined him at the club. The more he looked, the more he realised that we weren't making any money. The trips to America and legal bills in London had cost us dear, and because the Manchester crowd knew I was leaving, the takings were down from £13,000, to £9,000 a week. Not only that, we'd built up a substantial trading debt from spending the cashflow. Forte could see that the books were a mess, and the more I tried to mpress their guy, the more he realised that *I* was the Millionaire.

I should have taken a back seat, but instead I was on the decks every night with the microphone getting everyone tap-dancing. The previous week I'd seen Lionel Blair in the restaurant and, without asking him, I said to my crowd, 'You're terrible. I'll show you how to tap-dance. Mr Lionel Blair, would you come to the stage, please!' Lionel's version of the story is that he was halfway through his meal when he heard his name and went rigid. Apparently, he looked at his companion and said, 'I don't believe this.' But being a true professional he came over and said 'Hi' as if we'd been bosom friends for years. He took the microphone and showed everyone how to tap-dance. When he handed it back he gave me such a hard look that it frightened me. I felt ashamed about what I'd done, and I would never dream of doing anything like that today. I went over to his table later and apologised. He picked up the bill and tore it up in front of me. I said, 'No problem, it was good value,' and sent over

1. With my brother Geoffrey in 1945.

3. Desperate to be a star: doing the twist at the Black Cat Club in 1962.

2. With my first wife Norma on our wedding day in December 1960.

4. Two posters from the early days, including the one that started it all (Dig this Daddy'O), and another, now worth about £3,000, for the Beatles gig at the Azena Ballroom.

5. The Kinks in the dressing room I built at the Blue Moon, 1963.

7. Programme for 'another great show' featuring the Hollies and Wayne Fontana, among others – but this time I made myself and Geoff top of the bill.

6. More posters: after my success with the Beatles, I wanted to be a big-time promoter.

The original Yardbirds line-up, with Keith Relf on vocals
Eric Clapton on lead guitar, at the Mojo in 1964.

With Sonny Boy Williamson in the first days of the Mojo.

11. With Georgie Fame at the first all-nighter.

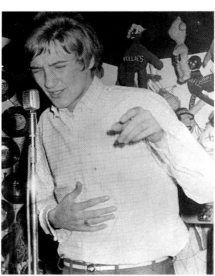

10. Rod the Mod: Rod Stewart at the Mojo in about 1964.

12. Geno Washington, star of the Georgie Fame tour which I compered.

13. Attempting to sing with Ben E. King and Clyde McPhatter, two of the legendary Drifters.

. The first 'rave', 1966. Note the
rthcoming attraction of 'little'
evie Wonder.

14. A piece of rock history: the original Small Faces at the Mojo in the mid-1960s.

16. Flower power in
the summer of love:
Coral and me on our
wedding day in
August 1967.

17. Paul, me, Geoff and Terry: a rare shot of the Stringfellow brothers together, at Cinderella's–Rockafella's in the early 1970s.

18. Marvin Gaye and Stevie Wonder on the night they jammed at Stringfellow's in the early '80s.

19. The fantastic Hippodrome light show: years ahead of its time in the early '80s.

20. The Princess of Wales on her first visit to a nightclub, telling me to tuck my shirt in.

21. My daughter Karen looks on as I show off my seal of approval from William Hickey to his then arch-rival Nigel Dempster.

22. One of my closest friends, Les Dawson, with the beautiful Frizzby Fox at Stringfellow's.

24. Just my luck: the worst photo of me ever taken had to be with Mel Gibson, one of the best-looking men in the world.

23. Bernie and Ziggy Winters with Lionel Blair: Stringfellow's regulars and close friends from the mid-1980s.

25. With Rod Stewart and Rachel Hunter. Rod always introduced me to his latest girlfriend – little did I know this was the next Mrs Stewart.

26. With Lisa-Marie Presley, before her marri to Michael Jackson. I must have been a hard act to follow!

27. An incredibly happy Eddie Murphy leaving Stringfellow's, with equally ecstatic minder.

28. New York: with the owner of the legendary Studio 54, Steve Rubell.

29. With my best friend in America, Robin Leach, who helped me through the minefield of New York.

30. Another legend in the New York club: Andy Warhol, taking a photo of an empty chair. And who said the guy was weir

Karen and Prince Albert of Monaco: proof that I was a hair's breadth away from being a member of a royal family!

32. With Don Johnson and Melanie Griffith at the *Miami Vice* wrap party. Believe it or not, I thought this jacket was fantastic.

33. With Roger Howe, looking pure Miami.

34. With Larry Adler, Charles Althorp and Joanna
Lumley at the Hippodrome.

. With Ronnie Wood, having a serious drinking session.
izzby and Jo, his wife, remain unimpressed.

36. Just keep on smiling: training my grandson Taylor for the paparazzi.

37. Beautiful dreamer ... and Christine!

38. Mum and Dad in the club, at a party during the last Christmas they had together.

39. With my son Scott, obsessed as ever by racing cars – even on his birthday.

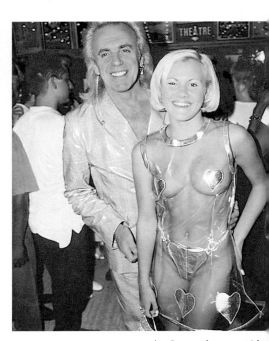

40. Out on the town with latest girlfriend, Hel

another bottle of champagne. We've been friends ever since.

Without Peter Stringfellow the Millionaire wasn't a normal nightclub. I was a one-man show supported by Peter Tyler and Brett Paul. The Forte executive was wise not to buy it. On his last day with me he said, 'This isn't the Millionaire Club, it's Peter Stringfellow's club.' He was absolutely right. He'd inadvertently solved one problem, but he'd also created an even bigger one. I had every intention of being up front in London, but I couldn't call the club Peter Stringfellow's because it wouldn't have been fair on Geoffrey.

Stringfellow's was the obvious name. The fact that Forte didn't want to buy the Millionaire left me in serious financial difficulties. The builders had assumed I would be getting £600,000 from the sale and had already started work on London. Before I parted company with the Forte executive I asked him to write me a letter. It read:

> Dear Mr Stringfellow
> In our opinion, the Millionaire Club is worth every penny of £600,000. Unfortunately, we will not be going ahead with the deal as Forte have made a business decision not to go into the nightclub business.

This letter was going to be my lifeline for the next six months. I carried it like a seaman's caul. I showed it to every debtor and investor until it finally disintegrated, along with my hopes of building Stringfellow's.

12

LONDON CALLING

In my imagination I could see a fantastic club; in real life I was surrounded by irate builders demanding money and the shell of a derelict building. Every penny of the Millionaire's cashflow was going straight into London, and the trading debt was growing out of all proportion to the speed at which the club was being built. On one hand it was keeping Stringfellow's going; on the other, it was devaluing my only asset, the Millionaire. I was giving out £2,000 to £3,000 at a time to the contractor, knowing that I needed at least £700,000 to complete the club. As the figures escalated, I mentally blocked them out.

My first major crisis was when the contractor demanded £350,000 in order to carry on with work. I'd already given him £60,000 from the Millionaire's cashflow and was struggling to pay the wages, rent and rates in Manchester. I went to Lloyds Bank in Sheffield and asked for a £300,000 overdraft. I told Ted Younger, the manager, that I'd pay back the loan from the sale of the Millionaire. Its trading debt was now £125,000, and I needed £600,000 in order to pay the builders and my debtors. He said, 'Where's your business plan?'

'What's a business plan?' I asked incredulously.

I was thirty-nine years old; I'd built, bought and sold seven nightclubs, yet in all that time, I'd never once been asked for a business plan. He wanted 'projections', 'profit forecasts' and reams of paper. It didn't matter that I told him Stringfellow's would open on such-and-such a date and that we expected to take £30,000 a week – he wanted something in writing. In the meantime, he said, he'd help me with the debtors. If it came to it, he would draft a letter saying I always had money in the bank and that I was a trustworthy person.

I was beginning to smell like a desperate man. I encountered this again, many years later in America. When you're in financial trouble, you have an odour about you that people can detect. Peter Scott could definitely smell it. He'd sold his business in the early seventies and put his money in gold. In 1979 the price of gold went from $385 an ounce to $880, and made him a multi-millionaire overnight. He was interested in buying the Millionaire, but, as it turned out, he was more interested in Stringfellow's. When he smelled my desperation he put together a deal which not only gave him the Millionaire, but made him a major shareholder in Stringfellow's as well. I arranged a meeting with Ted Younger and Peter Scott, who had by now produced a business plan. Ted was delighted when he saw it. Bankers are all the same: the more paper you give them, the happier they become. I could see Ted and Peter falling in love. Peter had 'collateral', which was a word I'd never come across before. I wrote it down, because whatever it was, it put a smile on Ted's face. He was happy to see me sold down the river. In his opinion, Peter's idea was the best thing that could have happened. His plan gave me share options in Stringfellow's and a salary. When I heard the word 'salary', I said, 'Hold it.' I wasn't bothered about share options, but there was no way I was going to work for someone else. I stopped the meeting and said no there and then. Peter looked aghast; Ted looked like he'd gone out to lunch. I told Ted categorically that I didn't care how I did it, but when Stringfellow's opened, it was going to be mine.

A week later I called Ted and reminded him that he'd said he'd help me out with my debtors. He was less enthusiastic now, but he agreed to see me. The following week I sat down with him and he asked me what I wanted. 'You remember you said you'd help me with all the people I owe money to?'

'Yes, I will.'

'Great, because they're all outside.' I'd arranged for six major debtors to meet me at Lloyds Bank in Sheffield. Ted went white. He looked out of his office and saw a sea of faces waiting in reception. I told Ted that I needed him to back me up because a letter wasn't good enough.

He looked at me. In that second, his bank manager persona slipped and Ted Younger became my friend. He took all six debtors into a room and negotiated on my behalf. They were demanding £700,000 to finish building Stringfellow's. They'd seen the letter from Forte, and thought I was getting £600,000 from the sale of the Millionaire. It was like the 1954 film *The Million Pound Note*, in which Gregory Peck never has to cash his million-pound note because the more he waves it the more credit he is given. Of course, the million-pound note wasn't real, and neither was my £600,000 from Forte.

By the end of the meeting with the debtors, Ted had agreed to pay them £75,000. At last the bank's legs were in. It saved the day and gave me space to find a buyer for the Millionaire. I went to meet another candidate, a man called Joe Bolan, at his house on Bishops Avenue in north London, a.k.a. Millionaires' Row. By now, all the financial pressures were beginning to take their toll on my health, and I could barely talk. At one time I would have been impressed with his fabulous mansion, but I no longer cared about such things. Did he want the club or not? He said he wanted to send John Okam, his right-hand man, up to Manchester. If, at the end of three weeks, John thought the club was OK, he'd give me £400,000. He wanted his teenage son to be the DJ at the Millionaire and asked if I would teach him. I said I couldn't give him talent, but I'd certainly show him the basics. Before I left he said, 'Hey, you ought to get your throat checked out. It sounds really bad.'

It turned out that I had polyps in my throat. The doctor said I needed to have them surgically removed and would have to stay in hospital for two days. In the end I had them removed under a local anaesthetic. It wasn't because I was brave – I simply didn't have the time to do it any other way. Within three days I was talking again. I still had an incredibly sore throat, but I managed to get back to Manchester in an attempt to lift the Millionaire from its lethargy. Joe's son joined me at the club. I liked the guy but I could see he would never make a superstar DJ. I told John Okam to tell anyone who asked that he was on a management course, not that he was there to buy the club. It was a pathetic, tissue-thin excuse, but I didn't want to arouse suspicion. Neither did I want to repeat the mistake I'd made with the Forte executive. It was difficult to keep away from the decks. People kept coming up to me saying, 'Peter, it's my birthday ...' 'Peter, when are you going up there?' 'Peter, will you play ...' I was terrified that this guy would suss me out.

Eventually I did an hour, which built up the atmosphere, and then sat and had dinner with John. 'You're good on the microphone.'

'Oh, cheers. It's just a bit of fun now and again.'

I then went into a monologue on the brilliance of Peter Tyler and Brett Paul.

Over the next three weeks I began to think I'd wrapped up the sale. John seemed happy with the club, so it was just a question of when I'd get the cheque from Joe. London was coming along slowly, thanks to the £75,000 loan from the bank, and things were looking up. My son Scott kept telling me to buy a new car to cheer myself up. He was talking about a Porsche, which I couldn't pronounce properly. Posh, Push, what's that? Scott was always mad about cars. After days of being pestered, I went to look at this very snub-nosed car. Scott convinced me that it was the best car in the world, so I traded in my Stingray and bought a £30,000 bright red Porsche Turbo. Hire purchase was out of the question as by this time I'd been blacklisted, so I ended up paying cash. The first thing I did was to take it to a vacant airfield and let Scott drive it. I sat him on two cushions and gave him his first driving lesson at the age of thirteen. I then drove down to London and found it could do 150 mph. I've only done that speed twice in my life. The second time was in a borrowed Aston Martin Ventura which I was reviewing for the *Daily Express*. In fact I did 160 mph, but I didn't mention that in the write-up.

The Porsche was great fun while it lasted, which wasn't long – I was about to have a crunch meeting with the designers and contractors in London. To cut down on the costs I told John Franks not to buy carpet for downstairs. I wanted the whole area for dancing. John Franks vetoed this idea, claiming that the fire brigade would insist on a designated dance area, even though I knew from experience that people dance anywhere and everywhere in a nightclub. Nothing has happened in this business that I haven't foreseen. My idea was later to come to fruition in the form of the rave, where there were huge spaces with no specific dancing areas. Rather than upset the fire brigade, my planners and the licensing boards, however, I went ahead with carpets.

The contractor called to say that they wouldn't lift another tool until they received some more money. I passed on a message via John Franks that Joe Bolan was about to buy the Millionaire and that in two weeks' time they could have all the money they needed. I called Manchester to check how John Okam and the son were getting along and found that they'd both disappeared halfway through the third week. When I went back to see Joe, he said he wanted to do a deal which would include String-fellow's. He enthused about giving me share options and said that in return he'd fund the rest of the building work. This was beginning to sound familiar. I was desperate, but I knew I'd rather sink the club than let it be taken away from me.

I was beginning to toughen up under the pressure. People around me were noticing the change. I'd always been the DJ, with Geoffrey looking after the financial deals, and now I was having to do both jobs. Being praised for my business acumen didn't make me feel good, I would have given everything to have had Geoffrey sober and back supporting me. I was missing his input more and more. Occasionally he'd pull round, but his sobriety rarely lasted longer than a day.

With Joe Bolan out of the picture I went to see another guy, Gerald Summers. He owned a club called Pips in Manchester, which was trendy, rather than glamorous like the Millionaire. My pride didn't want a local to buy it unless he was going to pay big money, like £500,000. Gerald Summers had just opened another club in Manchester called Romanov's. It had a large sound system and a big dance floor with flashy decor. I remember thinking that he'd nearly got it right, but the decor was wrong. In fact the seeds of the Hippodrome were sown when I looked at his club, but at that stage, and with the way things were going, I didn't think I'd ever own one club in London, let alone two. I'd known of Gerald Summers for some years, but we'd never been friends because we were in competition with each other. It was the same with George Best, who opened a club in Manchester called Slack Alice. He closed just as I was opening the Millionaire, which was great, because the last person I wanted to compete with was the greatest footballer Britain has ever produced.

Gerald Summers wanted to see figures. I don't know how I arrived at the sum, but I showed him a £75,000 profit on the Millionaire. Gerald, various directors and me all sat around a big table at Romanov's to discuss them. Two people stayed outside the room, a financial director called Mike Lester, and the accountant, Brian Smith. I didn't know them then, but they were both to become principal players in Stringfellow's. I bluffed my way through the meeting. By now everyone knew that the club revolved around me, so I told them I was prepared to go back to the Millionaire and work part-time on the decks. My proposal didn't impress them, however. In a matter of days, the answer was no.

A few days later I got a call from Mike Lester. He said he liked my ideas, but I needed help with the presentation. Within forty-eight hours he had drawn up a new set of figures for the Millionaire and a business plan for Stringfellow's. In return for his help, he wanted to be the financial director of Stringfellow's. I was impressed. The following week he came with me to see Ted Younger at Lloyds Bank. Ted didn't bother to read Mike's five-year projection, he simply flicked through the document admiring its thickness and presentation. Once again, I saw the power of paper. By the end of that meeting the bank had loaned me a further £200,000.

My next step was to take Mike and his magic papers and show them to the board of directors at Dixon's, who owned the contracting firm which was building the London club. All work on Stringfellow's had stopped, so I had to be straight with them. They either built the club, or I'd go bankrupt. Dixon's board was very conservative, full of old guys with whiskers. I stood before them and put on my finest performance. I showed them the business plan and told them that I was building the best nightclub in Great Britain; that it was going to cost £900,000, including the sound and lighting, and that I would pay them back over a period of five years. I was totally honest with them. I told them I needed the £200,000 loan from the bank to buy plates, knives and forks and to pay a PR company to help launch the club. After I'd finished my speech one of the directors stood up and said: 'Mr Stringfellow, let me get this correct. You are not only asking us to build your club, buy your carpets, your furniture, your sound system and your lights, but you're asking us to wait five years for the money?'

I looked him straight in the eye and replied, 'Well, at least you're going to get the money. If you stop now, all the money I owe will be lost when my company goes bankrupt.'

I didn't care any more. I was facing the wall. Mike and I left the room and let the directors discuss my proposition. After ten minutes they called me back and said they'd agree to build the club.

And that, ladies and gentlemen, is how you get from renting a church hall to owning a £1 million nightclub. It was nothing short of a miracle. I'd set out to impress the board with my total honesty and to convince them that Stringfellow's was going to be brilliant, and I'd succeeded. All I had to do now was to make everything I believed come true.

By now word had got around London that a new club was being built. I no longer felt like an outsider and knew that my days of being turned away at the door of Tramp were over. The next time I went there, it was with Harold Tilman, an old friend I'd met in Manchester and Leeds. Harold was the first man to give me a present. He gave me two suits, a red one and a gold one, big, baggy linen suits which I wore to death. Harold was friendly with Johnny Gold, who owned Tramp. The night he took me to the club, he introduced me, at long last, to Johnny. 'I've been hearing about you – you're building a new club,' said Johnny.

'It's OK, Johnny, he's not after your crowd. He's going mainly for the people at Le Valbonne,' Harold butted in hastily.

I looked around the club. 'No, I'm not. I'm coming for this crowd.'

Johnny went visibly stiff. 'Well, get on with it,' he said, and walked away from the table.

Johnny Gold and I eventually became friends, although we've never been close. We have a mutual respect for one another.

While building continued in London, I tried to build up the Millionaire in the vain hope of selling it before Stringfellow's opened. It was now 1980, and the only place being written about outside London was Studio 54 in New York. If your club wasn't south of Watford, there was no way you could get a mention in the national press. I'd had one write-up in the *Manchester Evening News*, and they said they couldn't do another piece on the club. 'What about all the stars?' I asked.

'What stars?' they said.

Well, there was Pat Phoenix from *Coronation Street*, Buddy Greco and, er, Tom Jones had popped in, though I couldn't call him a regular. Although *Coronation Street* was filmed in Manchester, none of the stars were real ravers. Then one day a producer from Granada Television came to the club and introduced me to Chris Quinten, who was about to join the soap opera as Brian Tilsley. I liked Chris immediately. He shook my hand and looked over my shoulder at the dance floor. The first girl he spotted was Elaine; then he started eyeing up my waitresses. I wasn't too keen on that. Elaine was my regular girlfriend and I was sleeping with half the waitresses. After he'd been in a couple of times we sat down with a bottle of champagne and I explained the situation to him. 'She's mine, she's mine, and you see those two waitresses over there, they're mine, and Elaine is mine, and when you meet my wife, she's mine, and Peter Tyler thinks that girl over there is his, but she's really mine as well. After that it's open house.' From that day on, that's exactly how it was for Chris. People make a joke out of Chris Quinten, but I give him a lot of credibility. He left *Coronation Street* after ten years and went to America because he wanted to become a film star. He met and married Leeza Gibbons, who was a famous television presenter in Los Angeles. He didn't make it in America, and his wife left him after he began drinking, taking drugs and womanising. He ended up back in London trying to get work as an actor. There is a very unsavoury trait in the British: they like to kick a man when he's down. Chris was a sitting duck for the British media, and they drove his name into the ground. It didn't matter how hard he tried to fight back, he didn't stand a chance. Eventually he came to work for me at Stringfellow's, but that's another story.

In 1979 I was struggling to get a mention in the national press. One day I saw an item in Nigel Dempster's gossip column about the owner of Studio 54 in New York, who claimed he'd turned away a sheik. I rang Nigel Dempster and told one of his staff that I'd turned away Arab princes at the Millionaire – it wasn't any big deal. In my naïveté I thought Dempster would write whatever I told him. I was wrong. But whatever minor incident happened at Studio 54, it ended up in the gossip columns. I simply had to see the club for myself. I booked a flight to New York and saw red ropes outside a nightclub for the first time – ropes that I couldn't get through. I also saw something I thought could only happen in America: people standing outside shouting, 'Me, me, me,' and pleading with the doormen to let them in. I had too much pride to stoop that low, so I went to the door and pretended to be Peter Frampton.

I'd been mistaken for Peter Frampton ever since the Mojo Club days. It used to irritate the hell out of me, but now it could be put to some useful purpose. Peter Frampton was ten years younger than me, but with my red suit and long, curly hair, I could have been his double. In fact the whole of New York thought I *was* Peter Frampton. People were hanging out of taxis shouting, 'Hey, Peter, howya doin'?' At first I didn't realise their mistake. I thought, 'Yeah, it's quite reasonable that I should be known in New York; after all, I do own a great nightclub in Manchester.' To add to my credibility as a rock star I went into Studio 54 with the journalist Robin Leach, who presented *Lifestyles of the Rich and Famous* on television. I'd only been in the club about ten minutes when a cocaine dealer came up and asked me for the $4,000 I owed him. I told this guy I'd never seen him before in my life and that I never touched drugs. He looked at me as if I was insane. He kept on and on, until in the end I had to get Robin to convince him that I wasn't Peter Frampton, but Peter Stringfellow, from London. A similar thing happened in Xenon, another trendy nightclub in New York. The owner came up and asked me to settle my bar bill, which was several thousand dollars. Once again Robin Leach came to the rescue. I didn't mind attracting girls by pretending to be Peter Frampton, but I had enough debts of my own without being asked to pay off his.

At Studio 54 I heard the death knell of my career as a talking DJ. They played constant music all night, and no matter how hard I tried to convince myself that it needed linking, I knew deep down that the days of introducing records were over. Not only was the sound brilliant, they had lights which moved in time with the music.

I went back to Manchester and told everyone that the talking DJ was finished and that we'd have to start mixing the records. Peter Tyler could do it because he was a musician, but I couldn't mix two records to save my life. When I managed to make them sound reasonable, everyone clapped.

Although I'd been impressed by Studio 54, I was still convinced that the Millionaire was a nightclub worth writing about, even though being in the middle of Manchester was apparently akin to being in the Outer Hebrides. I gave up trying to get hold of Nigel Dempster and decided to write to all the monthly magazines instead to see if they would review the club's restaurant. A couple of them had run reviews of the Boxtree, a small restaurant on the outskirts of Leeds. I'd eaten at the Boxtree and thought the food was excellent, but it was incredibly pretentious, and I thought my food was equally as good, if not better. I couldn't understand why everyone was raving about the place. I'd overlooked the fact that the Boxtree had about six chefs and I had only one, Nicky Szardis, who was Greek, as was everything he cooked. He had only two helpers, Nigel and Milly, who washed the dishes. By my standards, the Millionaire did have an excellent menu. It was certainly the most advanced of my clubs to date. I'd started off selling chips at the all-nighters, which nobody wanted because they were all taking pep pills to keep awake. Then I'd progressed to steak and chips at the Penthouse, which was OK because you can't go wrong with a steak. At Cinderella's I'd employed my first maitre d',

Bernardo, who introduced flambé to the menu. By the time I opened Cinderella's–Rockafella's, we'd moved on to scampi and chicken in baskets. Compared with my previous restaurants, the Millionaire was at the cutting edge of taste. OK, so the menu was limited and the food was provincial Greek-inspired, but it had to be worthy of a review.

My letter, which I sent to all the top magazines, including *Tatler*, *Vanity Fair* and *Harpers & Queen*, read something like this:

> Dear Sir,
> I'm sick to death of reading restaurant reviews about mediocre, middle-class restaurants in the south of England. Isn't it about time you came out of London? You could start by reviewing my restaurant at the Millionaire Club in Manchester. I have an excellent chef, who makes excellent food and an excellent army of staff ...

I also had an excellent maitre d' called Alfearo. He was like a reincarnated Caesar. He wore big, sparkly jackets and screamed like a queen at all the waiters. The ones he wasn't sleeping with, he'd fire. He had a peculiar habit of never looking anyone in the eye. If he thought someone was important, he'd hand them the menu while staring at the ceiling.

About a month after I sent out my letters, I had a call from Quentin Crewe, the restaurant reviewer for *Harpers & Queen*. He said he was up in Manchester and that it was his wife's birthday. Could they come and have dinner at the club? My immediate thought was 'Fantastic!' followed a split-second later by 'Aaaargh!' when I remembered that Nicky Szardis was on holiday. I immediately told Roger to get him back, which was impossible because he'd flown to Cyprus the previous day. To make matters worse, Quentin Crewe decided to come on one of the crappiest nights of the year, a May bank holiday. When I say nobody was in Manchester, I mean *nobody*, except my staff, Quentin and his wife.

Instead of cancelling, I thought we'd make the most of the night and let Nigel do the cooking. Although Nigel was allegedly

Nicky's trainee, he was really nothing more than a helper. We told Nigel before Quentin arrived that grouse was off the menu, because we only had one grouse and it had been cooked the night before. Quentin's wife ordered a steak, but Quentin ordered the grouse. Alfearo, whom I thought would save the day, turned from Caesar into a blubbering, obsequious mess and didn't dare tell Quentin that the grouse was off.

Nigel and Alfearo thought they could resurrect the grouse and make something edible out of it. Nigel picked the flesh off the bones and heated it in a pan. Alfearo served it along with one of Nigel's own creations – leeks in a cheese sauce, a dish that was so solid you could have stood a spade in it. I hadn't realised that Quentin Crewe was in a wheelchair, which wasn't a problem, except that there was no room for me to get around the table to talk to him. I couldn't cook for him and I couldn't fawn over him, so I got on the decks and played music for him. I couldn't hide the fact that there was no one else in the club, so I played and talked over the microphone for an hour and a half.

After they'd eaten their meal, the Crewes thanked me and left. My heart sank. I went to see Alfearo. 'Mr Stringfellow,' he said, looking up at the ceiling. 'What did you expect me to do? Tell Mr Crewe the grouse was off? This is the *Millionaire Club*.' There was little point in saying anything to Nigel; he couldn't speak and spent the next two weeks bumping into walls.

When the review came out, it began with something like, 'The nicest thing I can say is that the whole thing was such a waste of time . . .' I laughed when I read it. I laughed even more when I was taken along to review Quentin Crewe's own restaurant a few years later, but by then he'd forgotten the dreadful meal I'd served him.

At the same time as I was trying to generate publicity for the Millionaire, I was intermittently rushing down to London to check on the building work at Stringfellow's. A month before we opened, in August 1980, I was forced to sell the Porsche for £27,000. The Millionaire had been cashflowed to death and I needed the money to find staff for the new club and a public-relations company to help launch it. I only knew a handful of people in London. I knew the stars who had played at the Mojo, but I hadn't seen most of them for fifteen years. I knew Elton John, but we weren't exactly mates. I was friendly with Rod Stewart, but he wasn't in town. The only celebrity who promised to come was Robert Powell. Three weeks before opening, the PR company sent telegrams to the press. They followed this up with another the next week and in the third week everyone received their invitations.

Everything looked set to go, except that I didn't have a car. I couldn't use my 1976 Eldorado Cadillac because I couldn't afford the petrol to get to London in it. Mike Lester, who owned shares in a garage in Manchester, said he'd swap my Cadillac for a BMW 301. At least that would give me a little bit of status. At the same time he offered to swap Roger's old Range Rover for a brand-new one, on the condition that he could keep the insurance for his old car. Roger was a bit concerned by this, but I dismissed the idea. A couple of days later, Coral rang to say that the whole of south Manchester was blocked off because of a fire at Mike's garage. I immediately called Mike and told him I wouldn't have anything to do with him if he'd been involved with the fire. As much as I needed his help, I couldn't risk being associated with anything criminal. He convinced me that he was innocent and I accepted his explanation. After all, I had enough problems of my own without worrying about his.

I was about to open a nightclub in the middle of a recession – unemployment figures had reached two million for the first time since 1935 – and I was £1 million in debt. Whether or not Mike Lester burned down his garage was of little importance to me, but I was about to discover the truth anyway.

13
FROM A JACK TO A KING

My opening night was going to be Thursday 7 August 1980. The reason I like Thursdays is that I know everything is going to be given away free and we can get straight into business on the Friday and Saturday. The three most important elements were all in place: the sound system, the lights and the food. I'd bought my sound system and lights at a disco convention in New York. The lights were on huge chrome wheels with multiple prongs. They were made to order by a Canadian company who sent them by post a fortnight before we opened. I told everyone they'd come from New York because it sounded more glamorous than Canada. They might just as well have come from outer space, because no one, I mean *no one*, could assemble them. In the end I had to get the managing director of the company to fly over from Canada and put them up. At first he refused, until I told him he wouldn't be getting his cheque if the lights weren't up in time. He arrived three days before we opened. The lights and sound were hugely important because we needed them to be better than everyone else's. Legends had opened in London six months before me with exactly the same concept as Stringfellow's. It had a little restaurant upstairs and a disco downstairs. I was as sick as a pig when I saw the place, but I knew my club would be better.

I also knew that our food would be better, because I'd headhunted a chef from a wine bar called Rumours in Covent Garden. Roger and I went to their opening night and were amazed to see the kind of food we'd been eating in San Francisco earlier that year. We hadn't realised at the time that it was

nouvelle cuisine. As far as the people at Rumours were concerned there wasn't enough food on the plate. That night I
recognised the mad chaos which goes with openings: the bar
wasn't organised and there weren't enough glasses. In the
middle of the mayhem, Roger and I ordered a meal, which took
an hour and a half to arrive – significantly slow, as it turned out.
When it finally came it was fantastic. I went back the next day
and offered the chef a job at Stringfellow's. It was a heaven-sent
opportunity for him because he knew that the clientele at
Rumours would never appreciate his carefully arranged steamed
vegetables and his minuscule portions.

My own opening night was similarly chaotic. With all my
clubs I've walked the thin line between disastrous chaos and
raving success. To have a successful opening night, you have to
have some element of disaster, though I didn't know what a real
disaster was until I opened New York. That's when the air-
conditioning unit broke down and the restaurant flooded with
water. With Stringfellow's it was less dramatic – the carpets
were still being laid and the paint was wet, but apart from that,
my only real concern was that I had nothing to wear. I'd bumped
into the hairdresser Billy Shears at the opening of Rumours and
asked him if he could suggest somewhere to buy an outfit. I had
about £50 on me, which was all the money I had in the world.
Billy took me to a trendy shop on the King's Road called
Johnsons. Lo and behold, I saw exactly what I wanted in the
window: two suits, a pale pink and a pale blue, for £22 each. I
splashed out and bought both.

I was now feeling very excited about the opening. I'd gone
beyond feeling nervous. It was like being a fighter pilot going
into battle: you're not nervous because you don't anticipate
what will happen. You might think about the possible consequences of x, y and z happening, but once you've committed
yourself, the outcome is in the lap of the gods. If it all went
wrong I didn't have anything to lose – apart from everything.
I've always looked for parachutes but this time I didn't have one.
A manager of a company can walk away after a collapse, a
public limited company can usually absorb disaster, but I didn't
have any of those luxuries. It had taken two years from the first

time I saw the Little Theatre in Covent Garden to open Stringfellow's. Everything I'd dreamed of and worked for was now on the line. I was pumped full of adrenaline and so super-confident that I was bordering on madness.

When we finally put aside the red ropes, Coral and I stood at the door, ready to shake everyone's hands. Next to Coral was one of our friends, Lesley. Coral had led me to believe that we'd all be sleeping together at the Waldorf Hotel later that night, so even if everything at the opening went wrong, at least I'd have something to look forward to.

One of the first people through the door was John St Clair, a tall, good-looking photographer. John was very eloquent, very gay and knew absolutely everyone in London. I had no idea who half the people the PR company had invited were, but John seemed to know them all. As they came through the door he would tell me their names. He'd say, 'Lady Edith Foxwell,' and I'd take her hand and say, 'Lady Edith, it's a pleasure to meet you.' I greeted all the reporters and top PRs by their first names. It looked as if I'd taken the trouble to find out who they all were. I made a lot of friends that night. Everyone is impressed when you remember their name, including me.

Pat Phoenix, the star of *Coronation Street*, came down from Manchester and Elton John came, not to see the club, but to meet Pat Phoenix. Patrick Mower and Suzanne Danielle were there, which was big news because their relationship was always in the gossip columns. The opening night coincided with a star-studded party earlier that evening at the House of Commons. A lot of the stars, like Edward Fox, came to Stringfellow's afterwards.

After I'd greeted everyone, I went on the decks and played my part as the super-DJ. Towards the end of the night Richard Compton Miller arrived. He was the 'man about town' on the London *Evening News*, which was about to close. I knew that if Richard didn't like the club I'd be dead. I ended up getting a big tick from him the following week. I also got a big tick from John Blake in his Ad Lib column in the *Evening Standard*. Nigel Dempster, of course, didn't mention me, but the opening generated a lot of other publicity. I had the centre pages of the

Sunday Mirror and immediately fell in love with my new media image. I loved seeing myself and Coral in the papers. We looked glamorous. This was what I'd come to London for. As far as I was concerned, I was an instant celebrity. It was Peter String-fellow and the rest of us glamorous people in London.

By the end of the opening night I was totally and utterly exhausted. I'd used up all my bar stock and hadn't taken a penny because everything was free. I was expecting a delivery the following day which I needed to sell. I was feeling happy, confused and frightened all at the same time. I now had a new nightclub on my hands and I owed multi-thousands. I could see that the food had taken ages to come out of the kitchen and that we were running out of glasses. Yes, it had been a wonderful success, but I couldn't ignore the problems. The club was filthy and the staff were exhausted too. As I locked up that night I knew I'd have to start all over again tomorrow.

Coral, Lesley and I walked wearily down St Martin's Lane towards the Waldorf Hotel. I was exhausted, but not too exhausted to anticipate what was going to happen between the three of us that night. Coral looked fantastic and Lesley looked gorgeous. Then it happened. Coral informed me that Lesley would be having her own room at the hotel. To this day I don't know whether she said it to deliberately annoy me. She knew me well enough to realise that it would lead to a confrontation. To tell me a few days in advance was one thing; to tell me the night we actually opened the doors of the club would have been OK, but to tell me a matter of yards from the hotel was not something I could pass off lightly. I stopped dead and said with a very low growl, 'If she doesn't sleep with us *tonight* there's going to be big trouble.' With that we started one of our epic shouting matches at the bottom end of St Martin's Lane.

Coral was a good fighter. I don't want anyone reading this to think our volatile relationship was about me beating her up – on the contrary, Coral always got the better of me in any physical encounter. The moment she started pushing, shoving and slapping, I would stop. Once Coral started fighting there was no stopping her. Within seconds we were grappling on the floor and Lesley was trying to separate us. Coral was strangling me when the police pulled up. They had trouble getting her off me. She then began accusing me of starting it all. The police, being wonderful macho men, immediately took Coral's side. I could hardly say, 'She started it. She won't let her friend sleep with us.' After the police had heard enough yelling and screaming they arrested me and tried to put me in the back of the patrol car. With that, Coral switched sides and began pulling the policemen off me. I tried to reason with the police. 'Look, chaps, I've just opened a nightclub and we're all very tired. I've had a bit of an argument with my wife but now we're heading off to the Waldorf to get some sleep.' I remember one of the policemen saying to the other, 'Come on. We don't want anything to do with this.' Thank God they left us to it.

Lesley ended up sleeping in her own room and Coral and I, as always, made up that night. Together we were a dynamite formula – a Scorpio and a Libran. Coral was a typical Scorpio: she'd push, push, push for a reaction. Librans can take a lot of pushing, then they snap and lose control. We'd have huge explosive moments followed by mad passion. Our opening-night fight was by no means our last. We'd had many fights before then, and would have more before our marriage finally collapsed.

When we opened the doors to the public on the Friday night, the club was packed. Saturday was even more successful. We were taking more money than I ever imagined a single club could make. Our first week brought in £30,000, which was staggering compared to the £13,000 we made in our best week ever at the Millionaire.

Although we had the paparazzi at the opening, I didn't talk to them until the following Monday. I thought the club would be packed every night because we were in London, but our first Monday was very quiet. Halfway through the night Eddie Kidd came in with a group of photographers trailing in his wake. Apparently, Eddie had left the Embassy Club, which was one of the trendiest nightclubs in the early eighties and a mini-Studio 54, after a row with his girlfriend. The photographers had followed him to Stringfellow's, which was fine by me. I loved the idea of them taking photographs. While Eddie Kidd drowned his sorrows at the bar, I took Richard Young, Alan Davidson and Alan Grizbrook to one side. Now bear in mind that these three men were, and still are, the most respected paparazzi in London. I told them I would give them £100 for every photograph they got in the papers if the caption mentioned Stringfellow's. They all laughed, Richard Young the hardest. Thank God they didn't take me seriously. If we'd shaken hands on that offer I would be a very poor man by now. No nightclub, before Stringfellow's or since, has had as much publicity. Those three photographers helped my club to become very famous, and no doubt they made themselves some money on the way.

Richard Young did me a big favour after the party following the premiere of the film *Xanadu*. He'd taken a picture of Britt Ekland, Susan George and Olivia Newton-John in which, for some reason, they all looked like budgies. When he showed me the picture I said, 'You can't use that one, Richard.' It was just the worst photograph of three of the most beautiful women in the world. Richard promised and the picture never appeared. I really fawned around Olivia Newton-John that night. I'd been in love with her since *Grease* and couldn't hide the fact that I was flattered to have her in my club.

I learned a big lesson about the press at that party. I watched dozens of journalists eating and drinking their way through the film company's party budget, only to completely pan the film the next day in the papers. I couldn't believe that these people could be so two-faced. They were happy to accept the hospitality knowing full well what they were going to write.

I had no problems with journalists and paparazzi in the early days. After a while I started seeing photographs taken at my club, but with no mention of Stringfellow's. The caption would mention the celebrity's name, then say they were at a 'West End nightclub'. This infuriated me. I told the paparazzi guys that if they didn't mention Stringfellow's they couldn't take any pictures.

They didn't take me seriously until Stevie Wonder turned up one night. I hadn't seen Stevie since the sixties and was amazed when he said he remembered playing at the Mojo. The paparazzi guys knew he was coming in so they all arrived with their cameras. I told them to leave their equipment in the cloakroom because I didn't want any pictures appearing without a mention. The photographers were all sitting at the bar when Marvin Gaye walked in. I took him over to sit with Stevie in the restaurant and left the paparazzi guys. As the night progressed, Stevie said he'd like to play the piano and invited Marvin to sing along. Having the pair of them in my club was fantastic, having them play and sing was unbelievable. The photographers were going crazy. Stevie sat at the piano and said, 'OK, folks. I'm going to play a few tunes with my best buddy Marvin. Let's all keep it cool.' To hear these two guys jamming was like watching history being made. I couldn't contain my excitement. I quietly walked on stage and pressed the record button of the tape machine. As I walked off stage, Stevie stopped playing.

'Ladies and gentlemen, I'm enjoying playing music tonight, but someone's just turned on a tape recorder. If that person would kindly turn it off I'll continue.'

Everyone started looking around: 'Who's done that?' 'Who'd do something like that?' I was horrified.

'Er, it was me,' I said rather sheepishly. I went back on stage, turned off the tape recorder and Stevie started playing again. After about fifteen minutes Richard Young came up to me.

'Peter, let me take a picture. I promise you I'll always get the club a mention.'

'It's not good enough, Richard, I want assurance from all the guys.'

Eventually, Alan Davidson, Alan Grizbrook and Dave Hogan, who was my house photographer in those days, came and promised to mention the club. They all got the picture. Richard Young's photograph went around the world, and from that night onwards my club rarely appeared without a credit.

Those paparazzi guys helped make my club look fantastic. Stringfellow's was undoubtedly gorgeous on the surface, but behind all the glamour, we had problems. The most immediate problem was the food. It tasted wonderful, but the chef could not get it out fast enough. The first lunchtime was a complete disaster. We had fifty diners, out of which thirty bills had to be ripped up because no one got their food on time. Not only was the food incredibly slow, but the lighting was all wrong for dining during the day. Even after I changed it, I knew that lunches were never going to be successful because the restaurant always looked like a nightclub restaurant.

About six weeks after we launched, Liz Brewer, who was one of the PR people at the opening party, contacted me and said she wanted to take over my PR. She said I needed to relaunch the club because I'd pitched it all wrong and made a terrible mistake. She said with her help I could take out the Annabel's crowd. I burst out laughing. Even though we'd been open less than two months, my confidence had grown in that time. I had no intention of going for the Annabel's crowd. I wanted to take out Tramp and Le Valbonne. I eventually did take out Le Valbonne, but as far as Tramp was concerned, I had to be content with sharing their clientele. On my opening night, Louis Brown from Le Valbonne said to me, 'Welcome to London, the new king of clubs.' Louis and I became good friends after that. I was devastated when he died of a heart attack in Paris a few years later.

We were making mountains of money, but we didn't have a system for dealing with it. Mike Lester employed an office girl who immediately got three days behind just counting the money. I trusted Mike implicitly. By nature I trust rather than mistrust, so I let him get on with organising the back-room stuff. I didn't question him too closely, but I began noticing that he was walking around with pockets full of cash. He was paying out money and not keeping any receipts, which was a signal that something was wrong.

Stringfellow's had been open about a month when Mike Lester was arrested for arson. When he came out of prison on bail he came to see me with what he thought was a *fait accompli*. He wanted £70,000 a year, plus bonus, a car and 25 per cent of the company's shares. His deal was very different from the one I had in mind, which was no shares, no car and about £400 a week. There was still a lot of work to be done and the company owed too much money for us to meet his demands. It doesn't matter how far my back is against the wall, I will never accept something if I'm pushed. I can't be blackmailed or pressurised into doing *anything* where business is concerned. If someone presents me with an ultimatum and threatens to leave, then I will let him go. It's not stubbornness, it's a survival mechanism. I told Mike Lester I appreciated everything he'd done for me and that in recognition of this, I'd give him – he was expecting me to say 'a major directorship', but instead I said 'a pay-off'. He was very shocked. He knew he was about to go to prison, so he accepted the £25,000 he was offered.

Before I sacked Mike Lester, however, I'd contacted Brian Smith, the accountant I'd met at Romanov's along with Mike. He was the man Mike telephoned every time I asked about our finances. I told him I was about to get rid of Mike and offered him the job of financial director. He accepted and moved down to London with his wife and children. Brian stayed with me until he died of a heart attack in 1987. He gave me two fantastic pieces of advice: one I took, the other I didn't. The first was that I should start paying into a pension scheme. Next to insurance, pensions are probably the most boring topic of conversation on earth. I could barely sit through accountants' meetings, let alone listen to pension plans. I had no intention of dying before I was ninety, by which time I was going to be a multi-millionaire. Brian nagged and nagged until finally I got a pension. Now I thank him from the bottom of my heart. His second piece of advice will be revealed later.

Under Brian's auspices we found a new cashier, Mary Dawes. The first office girl was so behind with the books that she left in floods of tears. I remember being stunned when Mary came for an interview. She was incredibly raucous and spoke with a broad East End accent. Roger and I liked her immediately, and took her on. She turned out to be a financial wizard. Within days she'd squared up the books. Mary is still with me today, as are Johan and Roberto, my restaurant manager and maitre d', who joined at about the same time. They'd both worked in casinos and were used to long hours.

With Johan and Roberto, I thought I could make lunches work. The chef was good, but as he was the slowest chef in the world, it didn't matter how quick the other staff were, we still couldn't get the food out fast enough. In the end I stopped doing lunches. I also dispensed with the early-evening cocktail period. My drinking licence stipulated that we had to charge an admission fee, but understandably, no one wanted to pay £3.50 on the door of a bar at 6p.m., and there was no way I could get the licence changed.

Johan, Roberto and Mary apart, I had numerous difficulties with my staff in the early days of Stringfellow's. I made the mistake of employing a doorman and a receptionist who were an item. It seemed a good idea at the time, but I soon realised that it was a recipe for holidays in the Bahamas at my expense. I quickly brought in a rule which still stands today: no waiter or waitress goes out with the bar staff, and no doorman goes out with a receptionist.

One of the biggest problems was violence on the door. I'd seen violence in the north, but nothing as frightening as the aggression of the East End gangs. One night someone threw a paving slab through the front door after he'd been turned away from the club. It was on those nights that I yearned to be back in Manchester. I'd left a club where everyone loved me, a great house, my wife, my kids. I'd exchanged my stable, comfortable lifestyle for one ruled by fear and instability. I remember leaving the club one night thinking, 'What have I done?' I was in a deep depression after yet another fight outside. I'd adopt what I call my 'Cliff Richard' mode, where I'd do everything by the book and call the police and expect them to sort things out. They'd take ages to come and would never take our side. I was used to the Manchester police, who didn't argue – they just put the culprits in the back of the van and took them away. In Leeds the police would say, 'Who started this?', which was the most inappropriate question to ask when there was blood and hair and bits of flesh stuck to the walls. During the Cinderella's days I'd get letters from people saying:

Dear Mr Stringfellow,
I was walking past your club with my friend, when out of the blue, one of your doormen dragged me off the street and beat me senseless against the wall.

The letters always failed to mention their authors' own part in the fracas. They'd probably been refused entry and started shouting insults like, 'You big fat bastard, your mother's a whore and you're nothing but a poof anyway.' After they'd followed that up with a swing at a doorman, I don't doubt he would have retaliated.

The Metropolitan Police were different from the Leeds police; they were cold and unsympathetic. I remember feeling very alone and very afraid when I first opened in London. I wanted out, but I couldn't see a way of escaping. I decided the only way to get through this was to treat it like a three-year commission in the army. I decided to keep my head down, work really hard, then sell the club.

The hardest part was hiding these doubts and insecurities from the media. The PR company had done such a good job of promoting me that I was getting interview requests from all over Britain. I had reporters coming from towns and villages I'd never heard of, all wanting the same story. I got sick of repeating myself: no, I wasn't from Manchester, I was from Pitsmoor in Sheffield. I had to maintain this wonderful success story to the outside world when I knew deep down that I was up to my eyes in debt and worried whether the club was going to make it. On the surface everything looked fantastic. The stars were coming in. As always they were super-nice people who liked to have a good time. Bruce Forsyth would occasionally jam on the piano at the end of the evening.

I learned a very important lesson from Bruce in the early seventies. Coral and I went to watch him in cabaret and saw him die a death. He was brilliant until he stopped telling a joke and tried to make fun of some hecklers. He completely lost the thread of his performance and told the audience he was going to leave the stage if the hecklers didn't go. With that, he walked off. I went over to the four hecklers and told them that they ought to do themselves a favour and get out, because the doorman was a huge guy. In fact the doorman was the weediest-looking guy I've ever seen, but the hecklers believed me and took off. But when Bruce came back on stage he couldn't get his audience back. I learned that night that once you lose an audience, you can never get them back.

The next time I met Bruce was in Rockafella's. I went on stage deliberately to try to impress him with my act. After I'd delivered my usual DJ banter and got everyone up dancing, I went to talk to Bruce. I was expecting him to say, 'Bloody hell, you're good, you ought to have your own TV show,' but he didn't say anything. About two hours later, as he was leaving, he said, 'You're pretty good on that microphone.' On reflection, I was pretty raw in those days.

Bruce Forsyth was not the only performer to jam on the Stringfellow's piano. Kenny Lynch would often play at the end of the night and although Lionel Blair didn't jam, he'd bring his friends in to party. Any film star in town would invariably end up at Stringfellow's. We were selling champagne not by the box, but by the lorryload. I also quickly realised that we could put up our prices and no one really cared. It wasn't like the north – no one in London seemed to question what they were paying. Despite all this, I still thought I'd made the wrong move. During this period a director from Forte came in and I asked him if he wanted to buy the club. He said, 'Peter, you're tired. Don't even think about selling it. This is yours, and it's going to be a fantastic success.' He was right, I was tired, more tired than I'd ever felt in my life. Stringfellow's was successful, but the pressure of success is often greater than the pressure of failure. With failure you can put up your hand and walk away; you can turn over on your pillow and say, 'Fuck it, it's gone.' Success you have to deal with.

Every weekend I'd go back to Manchester to see Coral and the children. For the first time ever, I began to appreciate the normality of family life. On Tuesday morning I'd drive back to Roger's cottage in Islington and start the week again. Only Roger could have found a cottage in the middle of London. It was in a magic little area off Upper Street, hidden behind two huge stable doors. I didn't believe him at first. Ivy-covered? Cobbled drive? In *Islington*? £100 a week? No way. Then I saw it. It was the cutest little house I'd seen, with two small bedrooms, a lounge, kitchen and bathroom.

Roger and I moved in when Stringfellow's opened. Correction: Roger, me and his girlfriend, Suzy. Correction: Roger, me,

Suzy and his two kids. Correction: Roger, me, Suzy, two kids and two fucking dogs who became the object of my hatred, like no animals have done before or since. That's not counting a regular invasion of the biggest snails you've ever seen, which came from the derelict building next door. Roger I could live with. His girlfriend was pretty, so she was all right, and the kids were lovely, so they weren't really a problem. Janine had divorced Roger by now, so the only time he got to see them was at weekends. When they came down, I would leave on the Sunday morning and go back to Manchester to allow him to spend some time with them. The dogs, however, were smelly. I wouldn't have them in the house while I was there. I'm a fastidiously tidy person, a legacy of growing up with lino instead of carpets. Mum insisted that we picked up every crumb, otherwise the house looked dirty.

Amid all this, I was regularly bringing girls back to the cottage. I had freedom the like of which I'd never experienced before. I was using the club as my private harem. Of course, I knew I couldn't have anybody I wanted, but I wasn't short of girlfriends. I'd look at the bar and see which blonde was the tallest, then I'd make a beeline for her. It drove Roger crazy because he couldn't do that any more now that he was living with Suzy. Roger was as crazy about women as I was, but he was no longer in the game. Suzy was lovely, but Roger felt trapped. The walls of the bedrooms were so thin that they could hear everything that went on in my room. While it drove Roger mad, Suzy found it exciting.

For the first six months, Roger would reluctantly leave for the club before me. The moment he was gone there would be an electric atmosphere between Suzy and me. One night it got too much and I made a move on her. We quickly rushed upstairs and made love. Roger must have been telepathically linked to us that night, because he rang Suzy shortly after I left for the club. We both knew how to trick girls into telling the truth. Roger just pretended I'd told him what happened and Suzy burst into tears and begged his forgiveness. When I got to the club Roger said, 'You bastard. Why did you do that?' I told him I'd spent six months seeing a beautiful girl lying half naked around the house and I couldn't help myself. Roger understood – he'd known me long enough. I never tried anything with Suzy after that and we all stayed friends.

While I was enjoying my freedom, I knew it couldn't last. Coral was about to give me an ultimatum I couldn't ignore: she either came to London or had an affair. Separating from Coral was the last thing on my mind. I was about to make one of the most painful separations of my life, and I needed her support.

14

MIXED EMOTIONS

Every so often we read about a superstar's brother or sister who struggles in poverty while their sibling has millions. I've never understood that. Sure, I haven't been able to look after all my cousins, but at least I've never forgotten my parents and brothers. I've always tried to involve them in my clubs. Geoffrey started at the Black Cat with me; Paul joined straight from school and Terry worked for me for a while, but then decided to do his own thing. I often wonder whether Geoffrey and Paul would have been happier if they hadn't got involved in the nightclub business at all. With hindsight I don't think they really had a choice. I just assumed they would work for me. I was big brother, the leader of the pack. Geoffrey had never wanted to go to London. Although he'd occasionally sobered up while we were building the club, he didn't make it to the launch. I desperately wanted to help him, but there was very little I could do.

One day I took him to an alcoholic unit in Manchester, which was one of the best in the country. I held his hand and wouldn't even let him go to the loo on his own – I knew if I did he'd get through a window and escape. Geoffrey was drunk at the time. By then he was permanently drunk. The consultant asked what I wanted to do. I told him I wanted him to take Geoffrey into the rehabilitation unit and dry him out. The consultant said: 'I'll do that when Geoffrey wants me to.'

'But *I* want you to do it.' I looked at Geoffrey, who was sitting with a glazed expression on his face. I said, 'Geoffrey you've got to do it, it's your last chance.'

'I'll make an appointment,' sighed the consultant, 'but I'm telling you now he won't come. You won't, will you, Geoffrey?'

I really felt for Geoffrey. If he'd been diagnosed with cancer, I could have put my arm around him, offered to get him the best help money could buy and he would have taken it. As an alcoholic he didn't want anything. He didn't want to be cured.

The consultant was right. Geoffrey failed to turn up for the appointment. When I went back to ask his advice he said, 'Mr Stringfellow, you are wasting your time. Until Geoffrey is ready, you may as well throw your money through the window.'

One night when Geoffrey was sober, I took him into Stringfellow's and introduced him as my brother and partner. He promised me he'd only drink orange juice that night, but I could see he was getting drunk at the bar. People were buying him vodka and he was mixing it with his orange. I was so angry with the people around him that I had one of them thrown out. It was wrong of me. Only a few weeks before I'd done the same thing myself when an executive from Warner Brothers had come into the club. I offered him a drink and he asked for a Coca-Cola. While he wasn't listening I said to the barman, 'Put a whisky in that,' which was a very stupid thing to do. When the guy tasted it, he spat the drink out on the bar. He was a recovering alcoholic. I've never forced a drink on anyone since.

You can help someone dying of cancer; you can hold their hand, show them love, spend time with them. You can't do that with alcoholics. It's a killer disease: it kills family, friends, business and it eventually kills the alcoholic himself. Geoffrey lost everything, including me for a while. I got sick of the lies. 'No, I won't drink any more,' and he did. 'No, this isn't alcohol,' and it was. I was working under enormous pressure and trying to cope with mounting debts while Geoffrey drowned himself in alcohol. He had no choice, of course: he was addicted. There was nothing I could do for him, except let him go from the business.

I went to his house in Manchester and told him I wanted to buy him out. I'd had enough. I could have carried on giving him money, and he could have carried on going on benders. The drink would eventually have killed him and someone else would have owned his share of the business. I wasn't prepared to let his alcoholism do that. I'd put my life and soul into the business, and I wanted it to work. There was no saving Geoffrey at that time. The Millionaire was worth nothing because of the debts and I didn't know whether Stringfellow's was going to go bankrupt. What I did know was that I couldn't go on with him in that state. Even then he opened a bottle of red wine and began drinking it, which infuriated me even more. I was trying to talk some sense to him and his wife, Carol, and all he wanted to do was drink.

I knew I'd have to sell my house in Manchester to pay off Geoffrey. I offered him the profits from the sale and a substantial deal that remained private. I left his house that day not knowing what would become of him. I won't say I didn't care, because I did. It was one of the saddest days of my life. We'd been together from the very beginning, but now the partnership was over.

In the following year, Geoffrey would come to me and tell me he'd stopped drinking. On one occasion he said he was going to build a club in Manchester and asked me to help him arrange a financial deal with the bank and a brewery. He built a club called the Number 1 for around £300,000. He told me later he'd built it drunk, run it drunk and bankrupted it drunk. Even though I was left with some of the debt, I was amazed and impressed that he'd managed to carry it off. Each time I met him, he promised me he'd stopped drinking, but he never had. One day he rang to say he'd read about some treatment George Best had tried, which involved having some pellets put in your stomach. He tried that, and although it didn't work, I knew that at least he was making an effort. There was a glimmer of hope. But he hadn't reached the gutter yet. He would eventually get that low and come back, but not for a few more years.

Coral was incredibly supportive throughout the split with Geoffrey. She never once argued about selling the house and giving him the profits from the sale. She'd seen me under pressure, she'd seen me ill, she'd seen me trying to sell the Millionaire and she'd seen me lose my brother to alcohol. She didn't question where we were going to live, she just accepted that she would come to London and live in the cottage. Selling the house meant losing our last piece of financial security. It also meant losing my only refuge from the pressures of London. I've often wondered what made me give up my cars, my house – everything, in fact – for London. It seems to be a thread running through my life: whatever it took, I did it. Whatever happened I knew at least we could eat. I also knew the club could look after me if I looked after it. If it came to it, I could always sack my DJs and work full-time on the decks myself. Even if it ended up being just a disco, I knew it would make some money.

In fact Coral was relieved to be leaving Manchester. I hadn't taken her threat to have an affair literally, but nevertheless it was very out of character for Coral to even mention anything so drastic. I'd only ever once doubted her fidelity. We were at Rockafella's one night having dinner with Dean Marshall, who'd played with the Deputies during the Mojo days. He was now using his real name, Barry, and was lead singer with the group Bitter Sweet. After we'd finished eating, I left the table to make love to a girl in one of the emergency exits. I came back after about twenty minutes and saw that Coral and Barry both had their hands under the table. I looked under the tablecloth and saw that they were holding hands. I was totally shocked. *'You're holding hands with my wife!'* I shouted. *'How dare you hold hands with my wife?'* Barry was very apologetic. Coral looked sheepish. It didn't matter that I'd just been making love to some girl, I was outraged that my wife should show affection to another man. Apart from that one occasion, I never thought it possible that Coral would look at another man, so to hear her threatening to have an affair was a bit alarming. I told her to come to London the moment she got a sale. We took the first offer, which was £70,000. The buyer had only just left the house when Coral jumped on a train to London.

Roger had managed to keep some money from his divorce settlement, so he bought a cottage in Chiswick. Coral and I didn't have any money, so we took on the place in Islington for another six months. I'd given up hope of getting any money from the sale of the Millionaire. The debt factor was massive and the club was very run down. It had had the same carpet for four years, the furniture was shabby and the takings had slipped to £8,000 a week. It had cost £340,000 to build in 1976, and I eventually sold it to Granada for £320,000 in 1981. On reflection I was lucky to get that, given the condition of the place and the sliding profits.

There was certainly not enough money to pay off the Stringfellow's debts, but there was enough to assist with some of them. Brian Smith was a wizard with the books and eventually he cashflowed us out of problems. By the end of the first year we were still open, and according to the media, we were London's star attraction. We still had fights on the door, but the good side far outweighed the bad and I began to relax a little.

When Coral and I left Islington we leased an apartment on the Marylebone Road, where we stayed for the next eight years. We'd gone to look at a house in Chelsea and got the shock of our lives. It was the pokiest little house, but it was for sale at four times the amount we'd got for our mansion in Manchester. It was obvious that we couldn't afford to buy a house in London that we'd want to live in, so we decided to rent instead.

The moment Coral came to London, she wanted to take an active part in Stringfellow's. I had all the staff I needed for the evenings, so I decided to start doing lunches again. From the first day it was obvious that Coral had a strong, easy rapport with businessmen. I went on LBC Radio to advertise the lunches and made the mistake of writing my own advertising copy. I said something like: 'Here's a message to all secretaries. Ladies, tell your bosses that you know somewhere he doesn't know ...' It caused an absolute furore. People rang up the radio station in disgust. How dare I assume that all bosses were male, and that all secretaries were female? Someone had to explain to me what it was I'd done wrong. It never crossed my mind that there might be a female executive out there with a male secretary. For the first time I was introduced to the concept of 'sexism'. Sex I knew about, but sexism was alien to me. Eventually I made amends by going back on air with a parody of the first advert.

Nevertheless, the executives who turned up for lunch were all male, without exception. The prestige of executive lunches in the early eighties was defined by their length. After copious amounts of wine had been drunk, people wanted to move on to large brandies. I was so paranoid about losing my licence that I wouldn't let anyone drink after 3p.m. A lot of restaurants would stay open on a wink and a nod, but my Cliff Richard mentality prevailed. Of course, I soon realised the hypocrisy of our licensing laws. They are a joke. Everyone knows of places all over London who will serve drinks until any hour you like. Magistrates pretend to be a breed apart from the rest of society. They treat club owners and publicans like children. At the time it seemed ridiculous that we couldn't serve alcohol all afternoon. Of course, the law was eventually changed, and surprise, surprise, it didn't turn us into a nation of drunks. It's a little-known fact that one square mile in the West End of London can get drinks licences until 3a.m., whereas everywhere else in London it's 2a.m. In New York they can drink until 4a.m., Miami 6a.m., and then there is ludicrous LA, where drinking stops at 1.45a.m. My attitude is how dare the legislators make drinking illegal? It infuriates me that our tastes and desires are censored by faceless bureaucrats, the same bureaucrats who know exactly where to go themselves for an after-hours drink.

Having to take our customers' drinks away at 3p.m. didn't make us popular, and the slow service with the food didn't help. Coral was more successful in selling £600 memberships than she was in getting rebookings for lunch. I knew I'd have to stop the lunches again, but they meant a great deal to Coral, and I didn't know how to tell her. I decided the best way to break the news was to take her on holiday. Before we flew off to Greece, Coral telephoned all her special customers and told them she would be away for ten days. Then she sat down with the chef and made sure the menu was arranged for the next two weeks. When we got on the plane I put my arm around her and said, 'Darling, I've got something to tell you. I've closed lunches.' It was a strained plane journey, to say the least. In the years that followed she never missed an opportunity to bring up the fact that I stopped the lunches behind her back. If she accused me of being deceitful, it was never about sleeping with other women. No, it was the low-down, sneaky way I'd finished the lunches.

The restaurant continued to expand in the evenings, however, even though we were still slow in getting the food out. Fay

Maschler, the *Evening Standard*'s food critic, gave us our first review. While she didn't recommend any Michelin stars, she was complimentary about the food. I liked Fay enormously. Not long afterwards, she took me to the opening of Quentin Crewe's restaurant in Knightsbridge. Fay quoted me as 'her companion' and gave him a brilliant review. Quentin might have slated my food at the Millionaire, but damn it, I liked his. Fay and I drank a lot of wine that lunchtime. There was certainly an attraction between us. I still had my long, permed hair and certainly didn't look like Fay's kind of person. Nigel Dempster's wife, Lady Camilla, was in the restaurant at the same time. She looked me up and down and said in a very plummy voice, 'Well, Fay, he looks jolly good news to me.' I wouldn't go as far as saying I was a bit of rough, but I certainly looked different from the regular London lunching set. After lunch Fay and I went back to her house for coffee. We were getting along very well until her daughter came home from school. Had I known that she and her husband, the publisher Tom Maschler, were about to separate, I would certainly have made more of a play for her. She's a very attractive lady and still a great friend of mine, as is her new husband.

I've been in some weird situations in my life, but that lunch had to be one of the weirdest. I'd been in awe of Quentin Crewe coming to my club in Manchester, and two years later, there I was, sitting alongside one of the most respected restaurant critics, reviewing *his* restaurant. At the time I didn't appreciate the irony of it. A lot of hard work had got me there, but only my huge ego and supreme confidence stopped me thinking, 'What the fuck am I *doing* here?'

No matter what bizarre situation I've found myself in – and they haven't all been pleasant – I've somehow managed to escape with my self-confidence intact. There are few things I really regret doing, but a lot of things I cringe at when I look back. Like the first time I appeared in front of the camera in the sixties. Vicki Wickham from *Ready Steady Go* must have been sick of me pestering her for a chance to present the programme, so to divert me she put me forward to appear on a game show hosted by Hughie Green. The questions were simple, things like:

'Who is missing from this line-up? Paul, George, John and ...?' During rehearsals Hughie Green ran through his script and told everyone what to say and where to walk off. When it came to the live programme he asked me what I did for a living. I told him I was a DJ of soul music. He then asked me what soul music was. Instead of explaining, as I'd done in the rehearsals, I told Hughie I'd sing something for him. I launched into the only song which came to mind, a number Malcolm Townsend had written for Johnny Tempest and the Cadillacs. By the second line, the studio band had joined in and I sounded brilliant. I could see Hughie was desperate to get rid of me. The idea was to get on Hughie's Treasure Trail, but by the time I'd answered all five questions, the trail was full so I had to leave. Hughie thanked me for playing and went to hand me the £35 I'd won. I said, 'No, Hughie, I'd like you to give this money to charity.'

I cringe when I think about it, but not as much as Hughie Green cringed when I said it. He said, 'Peter, that's very good of you, but *you* keep the money and give it to charity.'

The charity happened to be Charlie Chester's casino, because that's where Johnny Hall and I lost it after the show. We barely had enough petrol in the Triumph Herald to get back to Sheffield. Before we left the casino I said to Johnny, 'Give me the money.'

'What money?'

I knew that Johnny always carried half a crown in his top pocket to buy cigarettes. Anything could happen to Johnny as long as he had something to smoke. Eventually, after a great struggle, he gave me the half-crown. I put it on the roulette table and of course I lost it. Not only did we have no money and not enough petrol to get back home, but Johnny had to go all the way without a cigarette.

I sometimes wish I could have been a singer, because singing is a clearly defined talent, like being able to play the guitar or paint. My talent, if you can call it that, had always been my personality. I had a way of communicating with people. I had confidence. I could pick up a microphone and create an atmosphere. At Stringfellow's it was different. I began to get a mixed reaction from the crowd. I'd open my hour-long spot with a few smoochy numbers, then go into party time and play things like 'Rock Around The Clock'. At that point the 'cool' London crowd would retire from the dance floor. One night I came off the decks thinking I'd done a brilliant spot. This young guy came over and asked me if I owned the club. I told him I did. He said, 'Have you just been up there playing the records?' I was waiting for him to say how good I was, but instead he said, 'Why do you do that? If I owned the club, I wouldn't go up there and do that.'

'I do that because that's what I'm good at,' I explained.

'I don't think you're very good,' he said.

It was the first time that anyone had ever criticised my talents as a DJ. I realised then that the showman DJ was dead as far as London was concerned. I knew I couldn't mix two records to save my life, so I quickly withdrew from the decks. From then on, the restaurant became my stage.

I was still bringing my personality to the club, but I missed going on the decks. We'd been open about a year when I heard that the Copacabana in New York was for sale for $1 million. I'd been there with Peter Tyler when we went to New York to buy disco lights, so I knew the club. It was similar to String-fellow's, built on two floors, with a restaurant bar upstairs and a dance floor downstairs. I remember liking the layout, but not the crowd: compared to our affluent set at Stringfellow's, the Copacabana set were very downmarket. In its favour, the Copacabana had a long and illustrious history – Frank Sinatra, Sammy Davis Jr and Dean Martin had all made their names there.

Within days Roger and I were in New York looking at the club. People have often asked me why I didn't go to the Continent, or buy another club in the north of England. The answer is simple: I'd come from the north and didn't want to go back there. Once I'd seen the spending power in London, I knew I could never make the same amount of money anywhere in the north. As for the Continent, it never really interested me. New York was different, however. My attitude at the time was America or nowhere.

I immediately started negotiating with the owners of the

Copacabana. There was only one problem: I didn't have $1 million. I didn't actually have any money, but that had never stopped me before. First and foremost I wanted to get a price out of these guys. The $1 million asking price had been wildly underestimated. The owners wanted $2 million or nothing. I finally bartered them down to $1.5 million and told them I'd give them the money in stage payments. I was ready to sign a deal with Stringfellow's as my collateral, even though I still owed thousands on the club. Then it transpired that the Copacabana only had one year of its lease left. I was amazed that these guys thought they could get so much money when they didn't actually have anything to sell. Their landlord would renew the lease, they said. I went straight to the landlord, who told me he had no intention of renewing their lease, but that he'd do a deal with me. He wanted $250,000 as a down payment, and then we'd arrange the rest of the money when the lease ran out. I knew I had nine months to wait, which gave me time to clear up some of the debts on Stringfellow's.

Three months later, the landlord changed his mind, signed another ten-year lease with the club owners and the price went back up to $2 million. I was hugely disappointed, but the experience had not been wasted. I'd got the taste of America back in my mouth. I'd also got sick of being mistaken for Peter Frampton on the streets of New York. I'd had enough. I wanted to be Peter Stringfellow, not some lookalike musician. I decided to go blond.

The following week I walked into Billy Shears' hair salon and saw the most peculiar-looking girl. She had pink hair, green make-up and was wearing what I can only describe as a nappy from which her bum was hanging out. Her name was Frizzby Fox. My first thought was, 'Weirdo head, great bum.' She was twenty-one years old and one of Billy's colour experts. If I'd been Joe Public, as opposed to Billy's friend Peter Stringfellow, Frizzby would have coloured my hair. But because it was me, Billy decided to do it himself. For four hours I sat with tinfoil on my head. When the time came to remove the foil I was so excited. The salon went quiet as he removed the last piece. 'OK, OK, don't look yet,' said Billy. He gelled and blow-dried my hair. 'It's different, but I think you might like it.' He swivelled the chair round to face the mirror. My first words were, '*Fucking hell!*' My hair was fluorescent orange. I wanted to go blond, not orange. Billy had seriously screwed up. I didn't make a scene, because, being me, I convinced myself that it was wild and wonderful. The girl standing next to me had pink hair, so maybe orange hair wasn't that bad after all. Before I left, I paid Billy and gave Frizzby an open invitation to Stringfellow's. When I got home, Coral freaked out, I mean totally freaked out. She said I looked like a dandelion.

Five days later Frizzby came into Stringfellow's and told me that I couldn't walk around London with my hair that colour. I took her advice and went back to the salon. This time, Billy stood back and let Frizzby colour my hair blond. By the time she'd finished, I fancied the pants off her and my hair looked brilliant. She agreed to have dinner with me the next evening. I had to take her to the outskirts of London because she was so noticeable. In fact I took her to as near to Roger's cottage as I could get, although all night I kept wondering whether I could make love to her because she looked so weird. In the end I decided she was sexy, and took her to the cottage. Roger didn't mind me using it, provided I used the second bedroom. But I wanted to impress Frizzby, so I took her to Roger's bedroom. We ended up making love and it was fantastic. Roger was furious. He said it looked as if somebody had been murdered in his bed. The sheets were covered in make-up, hair dye, false tan and God knows what else it took to make Frizzby the spectacle she was.

While my affair with Frizzby was developing, I continued to look for premises in New York. The next possible site was on East Seventeenth Street, between Broadway and Sixth. It was perfect – a huge loft space with a mezzanine floor. This time I went direct to the landlord. He wanted $250,000 as a guarantee for the rent; after that, I could start building. I figured I could build the club for $500,000, which seemed a reasonable sum. When I got back to London and saw Brian Smith, he quite rightly thought I'd gone insane. He said, 'Let me show you some figures,' and went into a blah-blah routine about how much we owed.

'What's this figure, Brian?' I asked.

'That's depreciation.'

'No, Brian. It looks like profit to me.'

He called it depreciation, I called it profit, but it was the same thing. From then on he always did two sets of figures: one showed depreciation, which was our tax allowance against our capital investment; the other showed the same amount as profit. According to Brian's figures, we still owed £500,000 on String-fellow's. This was great news – I'd thought we owed £1,000,000. Brian wanted me to stay in London and concentrate on paying off the debt.

I backed out of East Seventeenth Street because there was no way I could raise $500,000 to build the place. I didn't have any credibility with the American banks and I wasn't in a position to borrow money in London. I'd even planned to make this landlord a partner – 'I'll take your building, I won't pay you any rent; you lend me the money to build the place and I'll give you 25 per cent of the company' – he was such a nice guy. In the end we shook hands and walked away. Someone did eventually build a restaurant there, but it went bankrupt after two years.

Back in Stringfellow's an American came over one night and introduced himself as Randy (only Americans could call their kids Randy). He was slightly effeminate, but a nice chap. He said he worked for Tramel Crow, one of the richest men in Dallas. He'd been sent to Britain to find the best nightclub, which he'd heard was Stringfellow's. Tramel wanted to use the name for a nightclub he was building in his hotel in Dallas. Within days I was flown first-class to Dallas for talks with Tramel. Randy collected me from the airport in a Cadillac with bull horns on the front. In the back were two pretty PR girls who, according to Randy, were 'there to make my life comfort-able'. Oh really? I thought. Thank you, God. Except they weren't staying in my hotel and one of them – the prettier one – had a boyfriend. They took me out that night to a very impressive club. In the middle there was a fish tank with sharks in it. Soft drinks were served in waxed cups with the name 'Tango' written on the side, instead of in glasses. I couldn't understand why they didn't use these cups for all their drinks. The idea stuck in my mind.

The following day I took my plans, photographs and menu to show Tramel Crow. He loved Stringfellow's and suggested we had dinner that night. We ate at 6p.m. and by 7.30 he had left. I couldn't believe I was talking to this guy about a nightclub. His idea of a late night was bed at eight o'clock. I tried to get both girls back to my hotel room that night, but neither of them wanted to be seen there. One of them said her boyfriend would be leaving the next day and I could go back with them then. What she actually said was 'with us', which sounded as if I was being offered the pair of them. I hadn't had sex for two days, so I was feeling a little edgy, to say the least.

The following morning I had another meeting with Tramel. He told me to sit down with his designers and start making plans. I told him I couldn't do that until he'd discussed a deal.

'We'll do that later, son.'

'I'm only here one more night. We'll do the deal today.'

'Well, what do you want?'

'$250,000 as a payment for the name Stringfellow's and 10 per cent of gross.'

I thought he was going to have a heart attack.

'Oh, and my expenses paid when I come over and meet people as Peter Stringfellow.'

He wouldn't take my offer. His idea was no down payment and we'd work out a percentage if the club became successful.

'What on earth could you give me that would be worth $250,000?'

'My name, the design, the colour scheme . . .'

Tramel interrupted me to tell me that he already had the colour scheme, which was green and white.

'Disaster. Absolute disaster.'

Before I shook his hand, I told him I was going to open a Stringfellow's in New York. He said, 'You'll never get one in New York, son.' We parted on good terms. I always remember him telling me about his son. Tramel Jr liked racing cars and spending vast amounts of his father's money. It seems ironic that my son ended up racing cars for a living.

On my last night in Dallas I went back to the PR girls' apartment. Marylou was the pretty one I fancied, and Elle was

OK, but not great. After a couple of minutes, Marylou said, 'OK, I'll leave you guys to it.' She gave us a wink and went off to bed. I didn't fancy Elle at all, but I didn't know what to say to her. Three in a bed would have been wonderful, but Elle on her own didn't feel too good. She told me she'd got rid of her boyfriend for the night and that we had until 10a.m. It was a nightmare. I couldn't fake it. In the morning she was all over me and I still couldn't manage it. I eventually found Marylou's room. Marylou didn't want to know because Elle was in love with me. The whole thing was awful: one girl was crying, the other thought I was rotten, and somewhere in their apartment I'd lost the butterfly earring Frizzby had bought me. She was really annoyed when I told her, but until she reads this book she'll never know where I lost it.

When I returned to London I redoubled my efforts to find a club in New York. All the time I was revaluing the worth of Stringfellow's. In my opinion the London club was worth £1 million. If we got the debt down to £250,000, I would have three-quarters of a million in collateral.

The next premises I looked at were on East Nineteenth and Park Avenue South. It was a whole ground-floor basement in a fantastic gothic-looking building. I loved the building, loved the area and immediately got an attorney to start negotiating on my behalf. As far as I was concerned, I had collateral and was ready to do a deal. I remember sitting in a boardroom with the landlord, various directors, Roger and my attorney. I was about to sign when the attorney asked if we could look again at the zoning documents (zoning codes are the American equivalent of planning permission). It turned out that the premises were zoned for a restaurant only, not for cabaret and dancing. To hire a zoning specialist I would need to pay him $20,000 before he even picked up a pen. I'd been through all that with String-fellow's, and I couldn't face another expensive, lengthy wait. Before the zoning appeal could go through, I would have to get the approval of every resident in the nearby block of flats. My attorney said I had a fifty-fifty chance of getting the zoning changed, but he didn't seem able to give me a single example of anyone who had succeeded. It was impossible.

I was desperately depressed. Yet again I'd spent money on attorneys and got nowhere. I got off the plane from New York feeling deflated. As the cab drove into the centre of London I sat in the back deep in thought. I knew that Brian Smith was right: I should forget about New York and put my efforts into Stringfellow's. The cab turned into Charing Cross Road and crept slowly in the traffic towards Leicester Square. As I pondered my situation, my eyes automatically registered all the familiar sights: the second-hand bookshops, the Italian café, the Talk of the Town ... I turned to look again. The sign I'd passed a thousand times was now hanging in pieces.

The Talk of the Town had closed in my absence. I tried to ignore it; I certainly didn't want it, but then I didn't want anyone else to have it, either. But it held the answer to my quandary. It took a premonition, £3.5 million and my sanity to realise the Hippodrome.

15
TOGETHER IN ELECTRIC DREAMS

The Talk of the Town screamed at me every time I saw the building. I was hoping someone would take it for a theatre or a cabaret club. I didn't care what it became, as long as it wasn't a disco. The problem was that the Talk of the Town was too big and too empty to ignore. After I'd walked past it a dozen or more times, I started to make tentative inquiries. It was owned by Forte, for God's sake, the same people who had refused to buy the Millionaire. I couldn't understand why they didn't want it any more.

I'd been to the Talk of the Town twice in my life. The first time was with Geoffrey in the seventies. We paid £30 for our seats and sat in the balcony watching high-kicking showgirls. The second was in 1980, to see Buddy Greco. Buddy was great, but the place itself was tired and lacked atmosphere. I remember telling him I thought it would make a great place for a disco. Buddy said I ought to approach the owners, but I didn't take him seriously. I was about to open Stringfellow's and up to my eyes in debt.

Two years later I still had debts, but I now had the credibility that went with owning one of the most successful nightclubs in London. The Talk of the Town had definitely seen its heyday. It was damp, smelly and full of bits of 1950s kitsch. Absolutely everything needed renewing. While the estate agent was showing me round, I began making plans: I wanted to clear the downstairs, paint it all black and fill it with lights and sound. The more I looked at the club, the more I wanted it, yet I couldn't make up my mind. Every time the estate agent told me that this or that company was interested in it, I got angry. In my view, no other leisure company knew what they were doing. If I took it on, I knew the place would be a monster success. Even Brian Smith was enthusiastic. His attitude was, 'Thank God it's not in New York.' He was even optimistic about getting the money to develop the place. At that time I was thinking I'd need in the region of £500,000 to £750,000 to clean it up and put in lights and sound.

While I was looking around, I had a telephone call from the theatre director and impresario Trevor Nunn. He explained that he and Andrew Lloyd Webber, who'd written the musical *Cats*, wanted to talk to me about an idea. I'd been to see *Cats*, but I'd fallen asleep halfway through it. (Mind you, to my son's disgust, I'd also fallen asleep during the British Grand Prix at Silverstone, so it was by no means a comment on the quality of the production.)

Andrew and Trevor wanted to rent the venue every night until 10.30p.m. They explained that Andrew had a great idea for a show which involved roller skates. I couldn't understand his idea, although now, of course, I know that what he was describing was what became *Starlight Express*. After a couple of meetings I decided that it wouldn't work. Andrew isn't the most talkative man, and we didn't have any rapport. It sounded like a show for kids to me. I couldn't envisage my nightclub crowd arriving as the musical audience was leaving. In the end I turned down their offer. Just as I was developing my own thoughts for the world's greatest disco, Andrew Lloyd Webber was developing his thoughts for the world's greatest stage show.

The more I looked at the Talk of the Town, the more fascinating it became. Phil Pike, the caretaker, would explain the history as we wandered around. Before the Talk of the Town it had been the Hippodrome, the first indoor circus in Europe. It had warrens of tunnels running beneath the floor, which were known collectively as the elephant walk. Underneath the stage was a huge water tank fed by an underground river called the Cranbourne. In the circus days, the arena had been filled with water to let the polar bears and seals do their acts. The story of its first owner, Horace Edward Moss, was equally fascinating.

He was a music-hall tycoon and wild showman who'd almost bankrupted himself to get the place opened in 1900. He introduced an innovative heating and ventilation system called the 'plenum' system which had never been used before in a place of public entertainment. The Hippodrome's electricity supply came from two different companies in four sections to minimise the chance of failure. Moss's ideas were truly outrageous for the period, yet he never stopped believing in his dreams.

I don't believe in reincarnation, but it is strange how my life echoed that of Edward Moss. Our personalities, our aspirations – even our attempts at innovation – were uncannily similar. Once I knew its history, I wanted the place. I went ahead and signed the lease without consulting anyone.

It turned out that no one else wanted it anyway. They'd seen a story about the Talk of the Town that I'd missed while I was in America. The entire building was infested with every type of cockroach known to man. The London health authorities had been waiting for it to close so that they could exterminate the infestations. Not only that, the building still had asbestos in it from the 1950s, which all had to be stripped out. The fire brigade then came in, clapping. They too had been waiting for it to close so that they could replace all the fire exits.

By the time I'd consulted my designers, John Franks and Paul Roberts, and taken into consideration all the safety aspects, I was looking at £1 million. I then had to add the Theatre Preservation Society to the list of concerned bodies. They immediately started opposing my licence applications because they didn't want this historic building turned into a disco. When we eventually got our licences, the Theatre Preservation Society were instrumental in keeping our numbers down to 1,300, when the place would easily hold up to 2,500.

I knew if I wanted the club to be successful, I'd have to put in the best sound system ever, and turn it into truly the world's greatest disco. I wanted to blast out anything that had been done before, especially Studio 54 in America. I sent out the word that I wanted the best of everything, including the latest laser lights and finest video equipment. I was introduced to two guys, Mark Fisher and Jonathan Park, a pair of whizzkids with excellent credentials. They'd created the collapsing wall used in the Pink Floyd roadshow for the song 'Another Brick In The Wall'. At the time, it was the most technically advanced stage show on earth, so these guys were perfect.

I told them I wanted the best lighting and sound system that had ever been put in a nightclub, one that couldn't be surpassed. I wanted them to create a system for me and close the door behind them. My idea for a video-projection unit had been used only once before, by the BBC. It was a 20ft by 30ft screen which could only be bought in America – for $65,000, a ludicrous amount of money.

Then I was introduced to Tony Gottelier, who knew about the latest water-cooled lasers. I'd seen green lasers, which weren't that impressive; I wanted something different, something that hadn't been tried before. I asked Tony to get me a rainbow effect.

After a few weeks, Fisher–Park brought me a model of the lights and sound. It showed six huge devices with what looked like six petals on each. They'd come down from the ceiling and open up about twenty feet from the ground. Each petal would have its own multiple lighting effect. From the dance floor, four poles would emerge, and on each there would be more lights. Mark and Jonathan told me they'd designed a sound system to work alongside the lights. It was the first multi-directional sound system in the world. It would come down from the roof and face the dance floor for the disco, then swivel towards the stage when we had an act on. As far as I was concerned, it looked perfect. The cost, not including the sound, would be £1 million. By now I was looking at £2 million to refurbish the club and get the lights and sound installed.

Brian Smith told me we had a fighting fund of £350,000. He also told me that the bank thought I was fantastic and the brewery believed I walked on water. Between the two we could raise £1 million. By taking the profit from Stringfellow's cashflow, rather than using the cashflow itself, which had proved so detrimental to the Millionaire, we could just about make up the money. Once again we did deals with everyone. We offered to pay half up front and the rest when the club was up and running.

Yet again I was prepared to gamble everything I had. If the new club didn't work, I'd be left in so much debt I'd have to sell Stringfellow's, or go bankrupt, possibly both. When the building work started, I still didn't have a name. I had two possibilities, Talk II and Space. Talk II retained the old image of the Talk of the Town, which I wasn't too keen on. Space conjured up the universe and the future, which was more the feel I had in mind. I got Peter Tyler's brother John to design me a logo for Space. It was kind of what I wanted, but somehow the name didn't have quite the same impact as my previous club names. I decided to keep it as a working title, and if nothing else suggested itself, then I'd open as Space.

By now the landlord was cleaning up the outside of the old Talk of the Town as part of the leasing agreement. The building was covered in scaffolding and each day I could see it getting better. The more they cleaned, the more it became the Hippodrome. The name was carved in stone on every corner at the front and back. One day I had a call from the builders to say they'd found some old Hippodrome posters behind some railway sleepers in a boarded-up emergency exit. There were loads of them, dating back to 1899, fixed on to the walls. I immediately rang the Theatre Preservation Society, who then called the poster museum people. They were all incredibly excited. They said it would take them six months to take down the posters. I knew it would be at least six months before the club was ready, so I let them start their project.

I had a dream shortly after the Theatre Preservation people started work. In it I was standing in front of the Talk of the Town, looking up at the sign. As I was staring at it, the sign suddenly fell down. Behind it was the word Hippodrome, carved into the stone, as I'd seen it carved in so many places in my waking hours. I woke up in the middle of the night and decided to give the building back its original name. It was obvious – the answer had been staring me in the face for months. The logo for the old Hippodrome was a Greek chariot. In ancient Greek and Roman times a hippodrome was an open-air course for horse and chariot races. In more recent history the word came to be used for music halls or circuses.

I called John Tyler and told him to scrap the Space logo and start again with a new one. I wanted to keep the chariot theme, but instead of an ancient chariot driver, I wanted a Darth Vader-type spaceman with wild horses. Instead of a lance, he would be holding a laser gun.

Tony Gottelier convinced me that we needed a lighting synthesiser computer to go with the Fisher–Park lights. He told me he could design one, along with another fantastic device which would involve two spaceships coming out on tramlines from the back of the club. When the spaceships reached the middle of the dance floor, they would turn round and flood the place with even more lights. I could see them in my mind's eye and I loved the idea. I told him to go ahead and build these things. Every time Tony described them I had no problem in visualising his concept, but I should have realised that there is a big difference between being able to picture something and monitoring its transformation into something concrete. At least what Fisher–Park were doing was tangible. I went to the factory and saw these huge satellite contraptions, which were, I hoped, going to become my main lights. Fisher–Park introduced me to the word 'prototype'. In my experience, it means 'this might not work'. 'Off the shelf', on the other hand, means it's tried and tested. Everything that went into the Hippodrome was a prototype, and, I was about to discover, everything didn't quite work.

The excitement of watching the club being built quickly turned to despair. Where my lights should have been, I could see only scaffolding; the elephant walk, which was going to house all the electrical equipment, was so chaotic that I stopped going down there in an attempt to preserve my sanity. I love watching a new club taking shape, but I hate the disorder and mess that goes with it. I'm like that at home: if someone wants to redecorate my house, I have to move out rather than live with the disturbance.

When we finally got the light system in place, I found that the speakers wouldn't turn round properly. Then we discovered that although the lights would come down from the ceiling, they would not go back up again. We could have built a jumbo jet more easily than the light system at the Hippodrome.

Once I'd got the idea of prototypes in my head, I wanted everything to be a prototype. I wasn't content with having black leather seats in the club, I wanted black and *silver* leather. There was no such thing as silver leather, for a very good reason, but as always I learned the hard way and insisted on having some made. Then I had another 'great' idea about glasses. I knew we were spending as much as £1,000 a month on replacing broken glasses at Stringfellow's, and knew it would be at least three times that at the Hippodrome, so I thought I'd have some made in plastic. I'd been impressed by the ones I'd seen in Dallas and decided to design the ultimate nightclub 'glass' in black and white.

Research has never been one of my strong points, but plastic 'glasses' sounded a brilliant idea to me. I found a firm in Leeds who were prepared to make them with the club's new logo imprinted on the side. Unfortunately, they would have to have the mould specially made in Portugal, which would cost £30,000. I didn't care about the price. They were going to be sensational.

By now I'd passed the £2 million mark and was quite unconcerned about how much I was spending. In my mind, the more the club cost, the more money it would make. Brian Smith was scarcely able to catch his breath. He called me into his office one day and said, 'If you stop spending now, this is what you're going to make.' Then he drew a zero on a piece of paper.

'No, Brian,' I replied. I took the piece of paper and wrote a 1 in front of his zero, then added another five circles.

'No way on earth,' said Brian.

Financial directors, accountants and solicitors are brilliant, but any entrepreneur who listens to them will never go into business. If I'd taken advice from any of those people in the beginning, I would not be a multi-millionaire today.

I celebrated my financial predictions by buying a 1972 Rolls-Royce Corniche for £17,500. It was black with a cream hood and absolutely gorgeous. One of my loveliest memories is of driving around London in it with a girlfriend naked in the passenger seat. I'd bought her a fur coat – cliché, I know, but it was nice – and she got into the Roller wearing it with nothing on underneath. We drove around Buckingham Palace and up and down the Mall having a lot of fun in the front seats. Unfortunately, I had retained one bad old northern habit – drinking and driving – and the Rolls-Royce didn't last too long.

One night I'd been drinking in Stringfellow's with Mark Knopfler from Dire Straits and the comedian Russ Abbott. It was Mark's birthday and we were all totally smashed. As a precaution I'd given one of my drivers the car keys. When we closed the club, he took me to my apartment, gave me back the keys and took a taxi home. I crawled into bed next to Coral and fell asleep. About an hour later the telephone rang. It was one of the technicians from the Hippodrome with an urgent problem. I thought I'd sobered up enough to drive, so I jumped into the Rolls-Royce and headed for Leicester Square. As I turned into Chinatown I saw a policeman standing in the middle of the road with his hand up. He asked me if the car was mine. I said, 'Yeshoffisher.' It was like something from a *Carry On* film. It was a waste of time me blowing into the breathalyser because I could barely stand up. I was driven to the police station and given the option of a urine test or a blood test. The difference, I thought, would be about twenty minutes, the time it would take for a doctor to arrive. So I chose the blood test, thinking it would give me time to sober up, but I'd only been in the cell a minute when the doctor knocked on the door. He'd been in the cell down the corridor testing someone else. I ended up in court with a fine and a one-year ban. They did me a big favour: I've never driven a car after having a drink since that day.

Luckily, Stringfellow's and the Hippodrome are within walking distance of each other, so I could pop over to the new club most nights. Every time I went there, there would be thirty men working on the lights. One night I asked Mark Fisher why we needed so many electricians. 'They're not electricians, they're technicians,' he explained. The difference between the two was about £100 an hour. By that stage I didn't care how much it was costing – I just wanted the club finished.

About three weeks before we opened, the video screen went up, and to my delight it worked. The laser could still put out only one colour, which was infuriating in view of the fact that I was paying for a rainbow effect. I called in Tony Gottelier and asked him how he was getting along with the computer deck to work the lights. Instead of giving me a sensible reply, he stood there open-mouthed and went into a trance. 'Tony?' I said. *'Tony?'*

I'd given the guy too much credibility. I knew from that moment that he hadn't even started work on the computer deck. Mark Fisher stepped in and told me he could wire up a regular panel board to work the lights. Aaargh! I couldn't stand the thought of having the most advanced lighting system in the world wired up to a common-or-garden deck. I was having two DJ stations at the Hippodrome and wanted the computer deck to sit between them. The idea was for the DJs to blend the music together. I'd put a Roland synthesiser on one of the decks so that Peter Tyler could add to the music. It was a visionary idea in 1982, before dubbing became commonplace.

The whole thing was turning into another nightmare. Tony Gottelier was in a trance, the lights weren't working properly, and what about these bleeding spaceships? Surprise, surprise, the spaceships had been built, but the machinery to make them move was nowhere in sight. Thank God I hadn't listened to all of Tony's 'brilliant' ideas. He'd also wanted me to get a laser video, which sounded fantastic at the time. I just thank God I didn't commit myself to that one. To this day no such thing exists.

To go with the futuristic image of the Hippodrome, I employed a 'hip' team to attract the 'alternative' London crowd. I got Frizzby to join the team, along with a gay compere who I employed as my MC. Bradley Cornwallis-White was good looking and had a great rapport with people. I brought in Steve Blacknell to join Peter Tyler on the decks, because he too had the kind of image I wanted for the club.

One week before opening I began to have palpitations. I knew that the lights didn't work and the brilliant silver leather I'd ordered was coming off on everyone's clothes. We couldn't stack the plastic glasses because they were getting scratched and we couldn't put them in a normal glass-washer because they kept flying off the brushes. The chaos was mounting, and to top it all, everyone had 'flu. I called Barry Grimaldi, my private doctor, and asked him to come and have a look at the staff. He examined everyone and said that we all had influenza and were all overdoing things. I told him about my lightheadedness and palpitations. 'Are you taking medication?' he asked. I said that I wasn't, then I remembered I'd been regularly sniffing a Vicks sinus spray for the whole of the previous week. Barry told me never to use it again. It was causing the palpitations. If I could get hooked and overdose on a Vicks sinus spray, I knew I could never try cocaine.

Two days before we officially opened, a City bank booked the entire club for a dinner dance. It gave us the chance to see all the equipment working. We put tables and chairs on the dance floor and brought in silver-service waitresses. I didn't want to check on the food; I didn't want to know. These guys had paid a fortune for the booking, but I didn't care whether it was edible or not. I was more concerned about the entertainment. Halfway through the evening, Sarah Vaughan was going to come up through the middle stage and start playing the piano. I stood on the balcony and waited. The spotlight hit the stage, and the middle part began to rise up from the elephant-walk area beneath. I'd been warned that the mechanism which operated the middle stage was a bit wonky, but I'd spent so much bloody money already that I'd drawn the line at buying a new one. My technicians had said it would just about work, but they hadn't bargained for Sarah Vaughan *and* a piano. So the lights came on, the band started playing and, just as Sarah Vaughan's head appeared above the middle stage, the mechanism stuck. I could just see the top of her boobs from the balcony. Everybody else had to be content with her head. She played the whole set like that. Thank God she was only on for twenty minutes.

It took four weeks for a new motor to arrive, so we had no middle stage on the opening night. I know now I'll never die of a heart attack, because if I was ever going to have one I'd have had it then. Coral realised that the Hippodrome was taking over my life. She tried to help me, but I cut her out. It was my baby, and I was possessive about it. I even kept Roger's input to a minimum. I would call him in at the last minute to sort out the catering. Johnny Hacket was looking after the bar, but everything else was just me and the designer, Paul Roberts, who took over after John Franks returned to Leeds.

I sent out 1,500 invitations and estimated that about 2,000 people would come to the opening. I knew I couldn't go over my numbers because the police were watching me. Even the Greater London Council was on standby to check that my lasers were operating at the right height. On the big night Coral and I had a screaming argument just as we were leaving the house. It was a warning signal of what was to come. She'd seen Frizzby around the place and sensed that there was something dangerous about her. Coral treated her with absolute disdain. As far as she was concerned, Frizzby was a dummy. Frizzby didn't help matters, because the moment Coral appeared, she'd become tongue-tied. Frizzby was actually very quiet and shy beneath all her pink hair. I wanted her to go on stage and front the hip team, but she was too frightened even to hold the microphone. Bradley, my MC, had no problem and Steve, the DJ, was brilliant, but Frizzby couldn't do it.

We opened the Hippodrome on 17 November 1983 and packed the place out. It was champagne all round, but people wanted to drink it out of a proper champagne flute, not from an imitation plastic one. I had to go around pointing out the beauty of the plastic flutes. I said, 'Don't see it as plastic, see it as something new and high-tech.' The 'glasses' did look stunning, but that's because they were brand new. By the third night they were scratched and grubby and looked pretty disgusting. I gave up on them after a week and told all the customers to take them home. They did – every last one disappeared.

I was so nervous on the opening night that I drank too much, too fast. Everyone was waiting for the big crescendo, when the lights would come down, open up and dance up and down in time to the music. They came down all right, but that was it. They didn't move again all night, and they wouldn't go back up, either. I was mortified. The Hippodrome had cost £3.5 million and nothing worked properly. Brian Smith was ready for a mental hospital, and so was I. Once again we were £2 million in debt – and that was not counting the money we'd taken from the cashflow of Stringfellow's. I decided to save the night by going on stage and explaining what had happened.

I stopped everyone dancing and tried to explain what should have happened. 'They come down, this turns, that turns, they close, then these things over here come out and up there, the laser, which is green, should really be a rainbow, and, and ...' I was simply rambling on and on. When I finally finished the crowd gave me a round of applause and just carried on dancing.

The first review we got was from the *Evening Standard*. It read something like this: 'At a spectacular opening at the Hippodrome, the magnificent £1 million lights dazzled us all. The only baffling part of the evening was when a tired and emotional Peter Stringfellow went on stage and started telling us about some new lights he was going to bring in.' I was amazed that the reviewer thought the lights were sensational – he'd only seen a tenth of what they could do.

Every night the technicians would come back and work after the club closed, and each night the lights got a little bit better. The moment the lasers started working in full colour, the GLC stepped in. They allotted me my own inspector, who would come in on a nightly basis to check that the lasers were directed above eye-level. They were powerful, but they weren't dangerous. It was yet another stupid rule to which I was forced to adhere. I told the inspector that the Hippodrome opened at 8p.m., even though we never opened the doors until 9p.m. He'd sit on the balcony with a cup of tea and wait until 8p.m., which was the time the staff arrived. I'd shout, 'We're open now!' and put the lasers on half-power for twenty minutes. Every night the inspector and I had the same conversation.

'Well, you've seen them working. Would you like another cup of tea?'

'No, Mr Stringfellow. Thank you very much.'

'No, thank *you* very much.'

'I hope you have a good night.'

'Thank you. Bye.'

'Bye.'

'Bye.'

Then we'd open the doors to the public and let rip with the lasers. Either the inspector never realised the people in the club were my staff, or he was a super-nice guy who didn't care.

The lasers were, as I've said, water-cooled, and incredibly expensive. I had to have my own water meter fitted, which cost a fortune. But they were magnificent. When the lights finally worked properly, they were out of this world too. Peter Tyler was a genius with them. He'd bring them down and make them dance in time to the music. People were coming from all over the world just to see the light show.

My imagination ran wild at the Hippodrome. I spent most of my time looking for weird acts to put on stage during the evenings. I had one guy who would come up through the middle stage and erect his own gallows. We'd put the spotlight on him and watch him hang himself. The stage would then go down with him still hanging there from his neck. It sounds gruesome, but believe me, it was funny.

The Hippodrome gave me back my showmanship, the part of my character which had been stifled at Stringfellow's. It also gave my son, Scott, a new career. As much as I wanted him to join the business, he had other plans. He wanted to be a racing driver. It was largely my fault. I once bid for a day's racing tuition for him at a charity auction, and from that day onwards he was hooked. The Hippodrome bought Scott two Formula Ford cars and sponsored his team. Having our name on the side of a racing car was perfect for the club's image, but I hated watching him race. I was always relieved when he had a problem with one of the cars and couldn't go on the track. By the second year Scott had started to win cups and moved up to Formula 3. In three years, the club spent over half a million on sponsoring him, but we got a lot of publicity in return. Scott is obsessive, like his father, but while I put all my energy into nightclubs, he puts his into cars and racing.

The Hippodrome was a wonderful, high-tech place – so high-tech, of course, that nothing worked at first. Never, ever again, I decided, would I have another prototype. In the year it took to build and in the following years I was totally absorbed. Coral sensed that my life had changed. She wasn't at ease with the cross-over from Stringfellow's to the Hippodrome, and knew that the place was a big threat to her. I was sexually besotted with Frizzby, even though at that stage Coral didn't know, for sure, that I was having an affair.

My next innovation involved closing the Hippodrome to the general public on Monday evenings. I had a brilliant new plan. I was going to introduce the first all-gay night. It was to change the face of the London gay scene and bring some of the straightest men out of the closet.

16
I Am What I Am

Everyone thought the Hippodrome would destroy String-fellow's. I was probably the only person in the world who didn't believe that. I knew the clubs would complement each other. My very straight upmarket crowd loved the idea of me owning London's most outrageous nightclub. I would regularly have dinner at Stringfellow's then take a group of people over to the Hippodrome and show them the other side of London night-life.

During the first year, Bradley and Frizzby and I were invited on to breakfast television to talk about the club. We decided to stay up all night and go straight to the studio, even though we were all pretty drunk. While I was sitting on the sofa being interviewed, Bradley and Frizzby wandered over to the weather chart and stood on either side of the weatherman. It was live television, so the producer didn't have time to move them before the camera turned to the weather chart. The weatherman was in the middle of announcing that it was going to be cloudy on the south coast when Bradley piped up, 'Oh, no, we can't have rain in Brighton. My mum's going to Brighton today.' With that, he removed the clouds from the south coast and swapped them with the sun on the west coast. The whole thing was hilarious.

It hadn't occurred to me that Coral might be watching at home. She knew that the show finished at 9.30a.m., so by eleven o'clock I should have been back home. But Frizzby and I went straight back to the Hippodrome and made love in the office. I thought we were safe, but as usual super-clever Coral had read my mind. All of a sudden there was a banging on the door.

Thump! Thump! Thump! I knew by the urgency of the hammering that it was Coral. Believe me, no one banged on a door like Coral. Instant fear is the only way to describe what I felt. Frizzby, on the other hand, didn't panic. She was the type of person who could stay calm in any situation. She told me later that she turned to ice inside, but it didn't look that way to me. While I desperately tried to get dressed, she coolly composed herself. The moment I opened the door, Coral came crashing into the room and went straight for Frizzby. I had to pull her off because Frizzby wasn't fighting back. Coral was yelling abuse at Frizzby – she used to call her the 'weirdo witch' because of all the theatrical make-up she wore. Frizzby had beautiful skin underneath it all, but it was years before I saw her without her make-up.

Every man and woman is capable of deluding him or herself, and Coral was no exception. But this time the evidence spoke for itself. Frizzby was wearing a black mini-skirt and boots, and the door was locked. I wouldn't have been in there if I hadn't been playing. Coral was prepared to see this one out. She knew that London had changed me. My celebrity status had grown, and although Coral shared some of that, the focus of attention was directed at me.

I'd always loved Coral but her strength was sapping me. Whereas Frizzby was happy to stand beside me, Coral wanted to stand in front. I remember the first time I told Frizzby I was falling in love with her. She had checked that Coral wasn't in Stringfellow's and then came over from the Hippodrome to see me. I told her then that I was going to fall in love. It wasn't something that happened unconsciously: I actually made up my mind to fall in love with Frizzby. She drew me in. She never argued with me – in fact, she agreed with everything I said. She looked up to me. With Coral, on the other hand, everything was always a battle. She challenged everything I said and did. Whereas Frizzby was relaxing, Coral was exhausting. And Coral didn't understand the Hippodrome.

From the moment I opened the club, I wanted to have a gay night. The only gay club I'd been to was the Trocadora in San Francisco. I loved it. There was something about the gay atmosphere that I really enjoyed. I knew instinctively that if I wanted the Hippodrome to be a success, I had to get the gay market on my side. The only gay club in London in the early eighties was Heaven. It was owned by Richard Branson, although he didn't advertise the fact: homosexuality was more hush-hush then. Apart from Bradley, who was as camp as a row of tents, I knew only one other gay man, John St Clair, the photographer who knew absolutely everyone and who had identified the guests for me at the opening night at String-fellow's. It was John who helped me to start up the gay night at the Hippodrome. He went through his address book and invited all the gay people he knew. He advised me to send out the invitations in brown envelopes, because a lot of them kept their homosexuality hidden.

The first gay night was a revelation to me. While the majority of men were archetypal queens, I was also introduced to a very different type of homosexual: the 'straight' gay. To my astonish-ment, these were married men with pin-striped suits – and boyfriends. One of them said to me, 'Peter, I hope you won't think any less of me, but I'd like to keep my wife for Stringfellow's and my boyfriend for the Hippodrome.' Obviously his wife didn't know, and I certainly wasn't going to tell her.

There was a lord, who shall remain nameless, who regularly sat in the company of transvestites. He was rather drunken, with rancid breath, but he was never short of homosexual company. The sight of 'straight' men with boyfriends shocked me. Up to then, I'd thought all gay men were either effeminate or out-rageously camp.

I think the confusion was mutual when I turned up one night in a see-through orange jumpsuit. I'm not exaggerating – it was a real come-on. It left a lot of guys wondering whether I might be gay. Why else would Peter Stringfellow, Lothario and womaniser, be wearing a gossamer-thin outfit on gay night? Frizzby got worried. She said, 'Either stop drinking on gay nights or don't go near Graham, because you're flirting with him.' I knew Graham was a guy, but after a few drinks he looked like a stunning blonde in his dress slit up to the thigh. He was very seductive.

We had two sets of waitresses at the Hippodrome on gay night: one group wore black tutus, the others white. I made the boys wear the black tutus and the girls the white ones to prevent any confusion. The boy waitresses were better looking than a lot of the girls, so it was easy to make a mistake after a few drinks. Graham was the only guy I allowed to wear a dress, because he was part of my hip team and he always looked gorgeous. One night he came up to Frizzby and me on the balcony.

'Peter, Peter, I've got a problem.'

'What's that, Gra*ham*?' He always insisted we stressed the 'ham' in his name – he didn't want to be bracketed with all the other ordinary Grahams.

'I've been flirting with a straight guy at the bar and he wants to take me home.'

'So?'

'Well, he doesn't know I'm really a boy. I think he thinks I'm a girl. But I really like him.'

'Leave it to me.'

I didn't want any trouble. I decided to explain the situation to the guy at the bar. If he got angry, Graham wouldn't be around. The object of Graham's affections was a very straight-looking City type. He had an air of affluence about him – good suit, Rolex watch, gold cufflinks.

'Hi, I'm Peter Stringfellow. I believe you're waiting for one of my waitresses.'

'Yes, I'm waiting for Gra*ham*.'

'Look, I'm going to be straight with you. Gra*ham* is a boy.'

'You think I didn't know?'

'Well, if you're happy with that, fine.'

'Yeah. How long is he going to be?'

'Five minutes.'

I went back to Graham and said, 'Everything's fine, but keep your dress on.'

'Oh Peter, I told you he didn't know.'

'Of course he bloody knows. He's waiting for you.'

Graham disappeared into the night. I can't begin to imagine what they did together.

Paul was another waitress who caused confusion among the

customers. Without doubt, he was the most stunning. People would come up to him and say, 'My God, Marilyn Monroe personified!' I'd reply, 'No, that's a boy in suspenders.' One afternoon, Paul, or Paula, as he liked to be known, came into the office, very tearful.

'Peter, I'm sorry, I can't wear the black tutu any more. I'm a *girl!*'

'No, Paul, you're a boy.'

'Please let me wear the white tutu. Please. I never get any trouble.'

'Paul, I'm telling you to wear the black tutu.'

The following week I saw Paul strutting round the club in a white tutu. I called him into my office and told him I'd sack him if he didn't take it off and put the black one on. He went down on his knees and pleaded with me. 'Please, please, Peter. I'm a girl.'

'Paul, you've got a cock between your legs.'

'I know, but I won't have it for long. I'm saving up to get rid of it.'

I made him wear the black tutu until he had his sex change a year later. It wasn't the colour that offended him – it was what it represented that he didn't like. Paul and another waitress, Nicky, who also had a sex change, both became beautiful, happy young girls. They told me afterwards that the fantastic tips from the Hippodrome had helped them pay for their operations.

The gay crowd at the Hippodrome were a blasé bunch when it came to celebrities. There were certain people to whom they paid homage, but on the whole they were hard to impress. Eartha Kitt was one of their icons. She came on stage at the Hippodrome, sang one number and spent the rest of the evening verbally abusing them. They loved her to death. They liked Tina Turner, too, although she didn't create quite the same excitement. Tina sat on my knee that night, which I found very exciting, but as far as the gays were concerned she wasn't in the same league as Eartha. There was only one celebrity apart from Divine who could top Eartha, and that was Freddie Mercury.

One night the doorman told me that Freddie was coming into the club and he wanted to know where I was sitting. I got the DJ to put a spot on him as he came through the back exit. Freddie's entrance was awesome. The moment the light hit him, everyone stopped dancing and began clapping. It was as if the Queen had come to the Hippodrome. In fact Freddie *was* the queen of the gay scene, the king and the queen. Nobody danced for about ten minutes, they just stood there in silence and watched him. After he'd sat down at my table, I sent word to the DJ to turn the spotlight off him. He was wearing all white and looked every inch a star. He wasn't unapproachable, just very aware that he was on show. It was like sitting with royalty – even Princess Diana didn't create that much attention when she finally came to the Hippodrome. After about half an hour he joined some friends on another table. He could have joined any table that night – they were all his people, they all adored him.

Freddie only came to the Hippodrome that once. He preferred private parties, as did a lot of the celebrity gays. Phil Pike, who became my stage manager, would organise private parties in a back room for people like Kenny Everett and Wayne Sleep. I was never invited to these soirées, although Bradley, my MC, would regale me with the details afterwards.

The first New Year's Eve at the Hippodrome was brilliant. I spent most of the night on the decks playing to a packed club. We had the lights dancing in time to the music, dry-ice whirling around the lasers, streamers exploding from the ceiling – every kind of special effect. I remember standing on stage thinking, 'Wow, I did all this.' When I eventually had nightclubs around the world, people would ask me if I ever stood back and said, 'Wow, this is all mine.' I can honestly say that that night at the Hippodrome was the only time I ever stood back in admiration of my own achievements.

Within the first year of the gay nights at the Hippodrome, some of the customers were beginning to talk about a disease which was affecting their community. HV something or other. I didn't know what they were talking about. It was John St Clair who explained to me how AIDS was killing gay men, especially in America, and that everyone was frightened. It was John's idea to throw a fund-raising party for the AIDS charity the Terrence Higgins Trust. Not long after that charity evening, a lot of what

I called the 'straight' gays stopped coming to the club. The gay crowd at the Hippodrome were by far the most promiscuous bunch of people I'd ever come across. They chased each other like crazy. Even though I was straight, I could sense the sexual charge in the place on a Monday night. The only exceptions were the established pairs who sat like married couples in the restaurant.

The success of the Hippodrome made me hungry for more. The club had only been open four months when I started Hippodrome Records. One of the main reasons for launching the record company was to involve Coral. Up until then, she'd been excluded from everything. I decided to make my first record with Bradley, because he was popular on the gay scene. For once, Coral agreed with me. The difference between my record company and the one Richard Branson started was that his first signing was a major success. Branson had launched with Mike Oldfield's *Tubular Bells* and Virgin Records went on to become a multi-million-pound company. Success breeds success; failure merely brings more failure. Bradley sang 'I Am What I Am', a *Cage Aux Folles* song which Gloria Gaynor released in December 1983. I was more interested in finding a new star than in making money, but unfortunately, I ended up with neither. 'I Am What I Am' became the theme song for gay nights at the Hippodrome, and in recent years it has become the anthem for anyone coming out of the closet – Michael Barrymore, for example. But when Bradley made his version in 1984, it was way ahead of its time, because Bradley had never been in the closet in the first place.

With all my business ventures, I've learned the hard way. The record company was no exception. I knew nothing about distribution. I thought EMI's distribution company would flood the shops with Bradley's single. I had no idea that they were only pressing 2,000 copies and waiting for the shops to demand more.

After Bradley, I signed up Paul Inder, the sixteen-year-old son of Lemmy, the lead singer with Motorhead. Paul was incredibly good looking, wonderfully talented and, to my mind, a star waiting in the wings. He sang 'Chelsea Girl', a number he'd written himself. I spent £25,000 on making a video to coincide with the release. The record was an immediate flop.

I knew I had to find a hit, or Hippodrome Records would be in serious trouble. Shortly after my flop with Paul Inder, I bumped into David Martin on a plane going to Marbella. He'd written 'Can't Smile Without You', which had been a hit for Barry Manilow in 1978. David was married to Bruce Forsyth's daughter, Debbie, who was a beautiful, lovely lady. As I knew Bruce from Stringfellow's, we had an immediate rapport. I told David my problems with the record company and he told me, 'Making records is easy. It's like pissing up a wall.' I'll never forget that quote. What he should have said was, 'Losing money on making records is like pissing up a wall.' But David had confidence and charisma, so I took him on. Eventually I found out that he knew nothing about running a record company. In his defence, he was a wonderful songwriter.

We employed Pat Jay as his assistant. She had perfect credentials, having worked for many years at Atlantic Records. I liked her immediately. She's a very attractive lady and incredibly loyal. When my personal assistant left, Pat became my PA and has worked with me ever since. Not only is she a happily married mother, but she's a church-going Catholic. In fact Pat's the perfect assistant for a sex-mad atheist. She's my confidante and my moral adviser. If she ever decides to write a book herself, I'll know I'm in deep shit.

With Pat Jay and David Martin, I decided to bring back Dusty Springfield. She'd had lots of hits in the sixties and I thought it was about time she made a comeback. What I didn't know at that time was that Dusty had retired to Los Angeles in a very 'delicate condition'. To me, she was a superstar who should never have faded. Coral took on the job of finding her in LA and talked her into coming to record with us. I offered her £25,000 up front and paid her expenses. My idea was that wonderful Dusty would be knocked out by my offer, we'd make a smash hit and we'd all live happily ever after. Unfortunately, it didn't work out like that. The moment Dusty met me she took an instant dislike to me. I soon discovered that her 'delicate condition' was a euphemism for a nervous breakdown. I didn't know she was gay at that time, either, so my charm offensive was somewhat lost on her. She liked Coral, but didn't like me or Frizzby. The first thing she said to Frizzby was something disparaging about her pink hair.

It took a few days for the trademarks of Dusty's delicate condition to come out. The moment she got off the plane, she went straight into the studio and sang 'Butterflies', which was one of her favourite songs. We were all impressed. She was jet-lagged, yet she managed to hit the highest note in the song. In the subsequent months, however, she never managed to hit that note again. In fact she never finished one number, with the exception of 'Butterflies'. Neither would she agree to re-release any of her old songs.

In expectation of 'wonderful' Dusty joining my label, I told the BBC that she would star in the first of six live programmes from the Hippodrome. I said she would sing all her old numbers and finish with her new single. When it came to the actual night, she wouldn't sing any old numbers and we didn't have a single. However, she had dyed her hair pink for the television show. Frizzby went berserk. Dusty had been rude about her hair, and then deliberately copied her image for the programme. From then on the dislike was mutual. Right up until thirty seconds before the cameras started rolling, Dusty was refusing to go on. In the end she sang some obscure numbers from one of her least successful albums. It was a complete nightmare. By the end of the night I was ready to join her in her nervous breakdown. She was emotionally distraught for many reasons which I never understood. I thought she was just being awkward.

For six months I paid for her apartment in London and kept a car standing by in case she wanted to go out. I even bought her a cat, because she was missing her cats in LA. However hard I tried, nothing would endear me to her. And boy, did I try.

In fairness to Dusty, she was disappointed that Hippodrome Records wasn't run in a more disciplined fashion. I like to get emotionally involved in business and Dusty wasn't used to that approach. She turned down all the songs I'd commissioned for her, even though they'd been written by top songwriters. One of them was called 'My Love Life Is A Disaster', which I thought was perfect. Needless to say, Dusty wasn't interested. She even refused to work with Edwin Starr, who came into the studio to help her. When I heard Edwin sing 'Butterflies', I wished I'd recorded it with him, because he sounded a million times better than Dusty. Finally I lost patience and screamed that she was an 'ungrateful bitch'. She looked at me and said, 'You don't know what it's like to cry yourself to sleep every night.' I thought she was telling me the name of a new song.

In the end I ripped up her contract. It was obvious that Dusty Springfield was not going to be my Mike Oldfield. By the time we released 'Butterflies', the single had cost me £99,000. Any other person could have launched a record company for that. On reflection, the single cost me a lot more than money: it also marked the beginning of the end of my marriage. Coral thought the song was about me and her. She interpreted the words, 'If you love me, let me go, butterflies need to be free,' as a signal that we should part. The lyrics to 'Butterflies' did turn out to be prophetic, but we had a lot more fighting to do before we eventually separated.

After Dusty Springfield I tried to record with Mary Wilson from the Supremes. Whereas Dusty was moody and introverted, Mary was outgoing and friendly. We liked each other immensely. She came into the studio and recorded a song which had originally been written for Dusty. She sounded fantastic. I was all set to release it when we found out that she was still under contract to an American record company. They were geared up to sue the moment she made another record, so we abandoned the project.

Edwin Starr did eventually make a record with us, a song he wrote himself, called 'It Ain't Fair'. With the help of a £25,000 video, it reached number 56 in the charts on 1 June 1985 and stayed there for four weeks. I was ecstatic. We were planning to follow it with an album, until in the fifth week it disappeared. I phoned EMI and discovered that they hadn't pressed enough copies to keep it in the charts.

Hippodrome Records was a calamity from start to finish. 'It Ain't Fair' summed up my feelings. We made thirteen records, and that was the only one to chart. The last single I made was with Frizzby Fox, and that, too, was a flop. Frizzby was a female version of me when it came to talent, except that I was louder. We had to amplify her voice, which only amplified the fact that she couldn't sing. Once again we made a £25,000 video, which has to be the weirdest video ever made. Frizzby didn't move an inch. She was so shy that she couldn't sing if I was in the room and she couldn't dance in front of the cameraman.

The gays loved Frizzby's flamboyant image. They saw her as the 'ice queen'. But underneath all the make-up she was, as I mentioned earlier, cripplingly shy. One of Frizzby's greatest fans was the late comedian, Les Dawson. Les was a lovely guy, but very lonely, as his first wife, Meg, was dying of cancer at the time. He would often chat quietly with Frizzby. All the girls loved Les: he was an incredibly funny man. After Meg died we didn't see Les for a while. Then one day he turned up. He'd met a beautiful new girlfriend called Tracey and was going to get married. Unfortunately, I never saw Les after he married again. When he died a few years ago, everyone was terribly upset, especially Frizzby. Frizzby had great empathy with people. She could talk quietly with anyone, however famous, yet she couldn't talk into a microphone to save her life.

I remember trying to get her to introduce the singer Divine one night. All she had to say was, 'Ladies and gentlemen, Divine!' That's all. In the end I cut even that down so that Bradley would say, 'Ladies and gentlemen,' and Frizzby would have to say only one word into the microphone. I kept saying, 'One, two, three . . .' but she couldn't speak. Suddenly a voice from the balcony shouted, *'Say "Divine", you stupid bitch!'* We looked up to see Coral. She'd been watching for an hour and couldn't understand where I was getting my patience from.

Coral had no respect for Frizzby. She never understood how I could consider leaving her for a girl she thought was stupid. On another occasion I foolishly invited Frizzby to a dinner party with Coral and some friends. Afterwards we began playing that game where everybody says what they're going to be doing in two years' time. I'd seen the same game break up a marriage once – a friend's wife had stood up and said, 'I will have divorced Robert in two years' time.' Everyone instantly sobered up. For good measure, she then added: 'Of course, by then you'll be living with your lover.' He hadn't known that his wife knew about the mistress. Sure enough, they were divorced within two years.

Frizzby didn't say anything quite as dramatic that night. When it came to her turn, she said, 'In two years' time I want to be happy.' Coral's fingers froze to her wineglass. She looked deprecatingly at Frizzby and said, 'What a pathetic, *pathetic* answer.' Poor Frizzby was no match for Coral verbally. Whereas Coral was formidable, Frizzby was vulnerable. People only saw the weird image; they didn't see the quiet, potent sexuality which I grew to love. Coral could never have made a friend of her. As for a threesome, the very idea was absolutely out of the question. I think Frizzby knew that there was a chance she could end up with me. She hung in there and played all the right cards. She never flirted with anyone; she never made me feel jealous; she never showed any doubt. She did all the things that made me feel relaxed. Very occasionally she'd do something that surprised me.

Among all the weird and wonderful acts at the Hippodrome was an illusionist who threw knives. For the three nights he played the club, Frizzby became his assistant. It was the only time I ever saw her comfortable on stage. He put her in a box and sawed her in half, then he tied her to a spinning wheel and threw knives around her body. That did surprise me. She would let some half-drunk guy throw knives at her, yet she couldn't speak into a microphone. After her performance she made a promise to the magician never to tell anyone how the trick was done. I pleaded with her for many years afterwards, but she never broke her word.

The next time a performer needed an assistant, Frizzby refused, as did Peter Tyler, Roger Howe and my entire staff. No one was prepared to sit on the shoulders of the trapeze artist as he walked across the Hippodrome on a tightrope. I threatened each and every one of them with the sack, but they were all adamant. There were 2,000 people in the club that night, all waiting for a volunteer. The only solution was to get up there myself. I was half cut when I climbed the ladder and sober when

I reached the top. I climbed on to this guy's shoulders and did exactly what he told me to do. I stayed very quiet and didn't move, which was not difficult, considering that we were 80ft in the air without a safety net. Fuck, fuck, fuck, fuck, fuck, fuck, fuck, was the only thing I thought as we crossed the rope. The whole of the Hippodrome froze in silence. Brian Smith went colder than most. Unbeknown to me, he was sitting on the balcony with three bankers who'd invested millions in the club. Afterwards he made me swear never, ever to do anything so stupid again. If I'd fallen, I'd have taken the company with me.

Amid all the madness, Brian Smith was the voice of reason. About a year after the Hippodrome opened, a very shaky Geoffrey turned up. A lot had happened in the previous four years, but I'd never given up hope that he'd sober up. I told him that if he'd truly stopped drinking he could come to work in the office with Brian Smith. Brian and I were in agreement that it was better to have Geoffrey where we could see him, rather than to keep sending him money to get him out of scrapes. He was very weak, so for the first few months he shadowed Brian. It was ages before I really believed he'd stopped drinking and even longer before I could trust him. If he left the office, I would panic. 'Where's Geoffrey?' I expected him to be having a drink somewhere, but he never did.

Eventually he told me how he'd taken the long route back to sobriety. He'd had a fight in some drinking dive and woken up in the gutter covered in blood. For some reason only he knows, it was at this point that he decided he'd had enough. If he ever writes a book he can explain it himself. I do know that he went to an Alcoholics Anonymous meeting and stuck to the programme. No tablets, no medicine, just AA and his own character. I know that it is his character that saved him. You couldn't go further down than Geoffrey was. For four years, I'd been waiting for a call to say that he'd been found dead somewhere. I would have been devastated, but not surprised. I'd tried everything, but in the end, the doctor in Manchester had been right. It was something he had to do himself.

With Geoffrey back on board, my life became easier and I began to relax. The Hippodrome was in its infancy. It was about to mature into a headline-grabbing monster with a life of its own.

17

THE CIRCUS

The Hippodrome held a unique fascination for me. I loved the building, its history, the characters, everything about the place. It had spanned the Edwardian and Victorian periods, first as the world's biggest indoor circus in 1899, then as a fabulous music hall in 1909. I'd now taken it into the twentieth century and made it the world's greatest disco. I had some of the best times of my life at the Hippodrome, because I could let my imagination run wild there.

On the first gay Easter Monday I decided to pay homage to the old days by bringing back the circus. I booked a lion, a dancing bear, an alligator and a snake. I didn't know anything about licences for wild animals, and needless to say I didn't check. As usual I got carried away with the excitement of it all. I went to a theatrical shop and hired myself a ringmaster's costume. I told all the staff to dress up as appropriate, which they all did, except for Bradley. For some reason best known to himself he decided to come as an angel. He couldn't have got further away from the theme, but Bradley, being Bradley, said he 'simply had to wear wings'.

I made the arrangements for all the animals, with a very big man who worked for a travelling circus. He told me that the lion would happily walk on a lead, even though they'd never tried it before; that the alligator would open its mouth so that someone could put his head in it and that the bear would dance merrily on stage. He even offered me a pair of dogs which would jump over each other. It all sounded great. The trapeze artist who had balanced me on his shoulders offered to bring in his snake. I closed the back bar for the night so that we could keep the lion in the emergency exit at the back of the club. I wanted it to come on stage, for everyone to gasp in amazement, then for it to roar and be led off again.

On Easter Monday night I went to check on the lion. I'd only ever seen lions in zoos and on television, so I had no idea what they looked like face to face. I was half expecting it to be the size of a Great Dane. It turned out to be big, very big. It fitted in with my nightmare image of a lion. Throughout my life I've always had, and still have, when I'm under stress, a recurrent dream that I'm being chased by a lion. My gut reaction on seeing one in real life was sheer terror. And something wasn't right. The lion was pacing the floor and the only thing between me and it was a couple of chairs. Not only that: the very big man from the circus has been replaced by a very little man. The big man apparently owned the circus and the little thin man in front of me was the lion trainer. While the trainer tried to reassure me, the emergency doors suddenly flew open and in bounced Bradley in his angel's costume, along with a blast of music from the sound system. The lion took one look at Bradley, who probably seemed to her to be the biggest, most edible bird she'd ever seen, and let out a roar. A really big, terrifying *rrrroooaaaarrr!* that shook every bone in my body. Bradley literally vanished in a cloud of wings and dust. I should have cancelled the show there and then. I didn't. I wanted it to go on. The trainer told me the lion would calm down again and I believed him.

I went on stage and told my crowd of 2,000-plus gays that I was about to bring on 'the queen of queens'. 'Gentlemen and ladies,' I said (that was how I introduced every act on gay night), 'we at the Hippodrome are proud to present, for the first time in eighty-four years ...' As I was speaking, I could hear the lion roaring in the background. When I finally said, 'Queen Bluey!' the fanfare started and the spotlight hit the emergency exit. Nothing happened. 'Well, as everyone knows, queens can be a bit touchy, so for the second time this evening, let me introduce Queen Bluey!' The crowd loved the ad-lib, but there was still no sign of the lion. From behind the emergency-exit doors we could hear a thumping, then a banging, then a knocking and a crashing. Suddenly the doors flew open and the lion charged out. By the time she reached the stage, the trainer was horizontal on the other end of the lead. I froze to the spot. I thought she was coming for me, but instead, she pounced off the stage on to the dance floor. I've never seen a nightclub clear so fast. Two things were in my mind: first, that someone was going to get eaten, and secondly, that I was going to be bankrupt. Unbeknown to me, the circus had people standing by with nets – if I'd known they needed nets, I wouldn't have gone ahead with the show. As the lion charged towards the far emergency exit, the trainers managed to cover her with the nets.

You could have heard a pin drop. There was complete silence except for the panting of the lion. Then the booing started. That was a bit confusing. Were they booing because no one had been eaten? No, they were booing because they thought we were being cruel to the lion. I immediately switched on to automatic pilot. I picked up the microphone and walked towards the lion, talking very quietly, asking everyone to stay calm. The big man had appeared again and was now lying over the lion to keep her down. As I moved closer I asked him what I could do to help. 'Stroke her tongue,' he said. Stroke her *tongue*? My God, it looked about two feet long. But in situations like that, you don't think about the consequences, you do whatever is necessary. As I stroked the lion's tongue I carried on talking very softly into the microphone, explaining to the crowd that any minute the lion would be taken out through the back. The moment I stopped stroking its tongue, the lion caught my eye. I knew I had to back off very quickly because she was about to jump up. Sure enough, she leapt to her feet and careered towards the exit, with both trainers still attached to the net. She jumped straight into the circus van and back to safety.

I was so relieved that no one had been fatally mauled that stupidly, I decided to carry on. I was about to learn something very important about wild animals. They can smell fear. By the time the dancing bear came on stage, he had turned from a benign cuddly beast into a rampant, grizzly monster. Instead of dancing, he got his owner in a bear hug. The crowd thought they were smooching, but I could see from the look on the guy's face that the bear was squeezing the life out of him. They quickly shuffled off the stage.

The alligator came on next. He'd been asleep all afternoon, so soundly asleep I'd been worried he wouldn't wake up for the show. Now, however, he was wide awake and totally animated. The idea was to open the alligator's mouth and stretch his jaw to a point where he couldn't close it. Then I was going to put my head in his mouth. But every time the trainer tried to open its jaw, the alligator snapped it shut again. He tried for a few more minutes, but I could see it wasn't going to work. In fact I'd seen enough for one night. The trainer asked if I wanted the dogs and the snake brought on. I said, 'No way.' Poodles or not, they'd probably have turned into rabid killer canines, and the sleepy old snake was no doubt waiting in the wings ready to spit venom at everyone.

A photograph of the escaped lion went around the world and even made the papers in Japan. Not long afterwards I had a call from the Greater London Council. They wanted to know what I was doing with uncaged wild animals. They ended up suing the circus owner, which put him out of business. The last time I brought an animal into the Hippodrome was when Divine came down from the roof on a baby elephant. I didn't get a licence for that one, either. After that I gave animals a wide berth. When Gary Glitter slid down from the roof, he did so covered in roses. However, we did manage to stage a motorbike stunt with Eddie Kidd in the club.

The Hippodrome certainly lived up to its reputation as the world's greatest disco, and in turn, I became known as the world's greatest disco owner. Well, I did up to a point. I was the world's greatest disco owner everywhere except in Britain. An American television company once came over to interview myself, Paul McCartney, Phil Collins, Bob Geldof and Roger Daltrey at the Hippodrome. The programme named the five of us as the most famous people in the world. While they were there, the British press came down and took pictures of us all. When the photographs finally appeared in print here, I'd been mysteriously airbrushed out of them all.

When Paul McCartney came to film his video for *Give My*

Regards to Broad Street at the club, I mentioned to him that we'd met in 1963, in Sheffield. He told me he remembered the gig, but I think it was just Paul being nice. He'd been around the world many times since then, so either he has a brilliant memory, or the Azena Ballroom was more impressive than I'd thought.

What happened at the Hippodrome could not have happened in any other nightclub anywhere in the world. We not only had the space, but we had the kind of clientele who liked the alternative. They were a real mixed bunch. Although the gay crowd generated the most publicity, the majority of them only came in on Mondays. The rest of the week it was open house. We attracted people from across the social spectrum, from punks on the dole to affluent hoorays.

It was during the Hippodrome period that I met Charles Althorp, now Earl Spencer, the brother of Princess Diana. One day Roger showed me a newspaper cutting of Charlie in some nightclub and I wondered why he'd never been to either of mine. By coincidence, he came to Stringfellow's with a crazy male friend that very evening. I joined them for a drink and liked them both immensely. With Charlie's permission, Keith Butcher, our house photographer, took his picture. When it appeared a couple of days later, I noticed that Charlie was scowling. The next time he came into the club I told him he really had to start smiling for photographs. I had a theory that if he smiled in every picture the newspapers would have so many happy ones they'd stop printing them. From that day onwards he took my advice. I deliberately made a point of not mentioning his sister – for a start, it would have been too crass, even for me, and in any case, I liked him for himself. He was a fun guy who liked champagne, my kind of guy.

Not long after Charlie started coming to the club, I invited him to stay in my apartment in Marbella, a glamorous, one-bedroomed flat just outside Puerto Banús. I'd bought it as a retreat, a place where I could get away from the partying in London, but I hardly ever found the time to go there. Although I'd seen him regularly in the nightclub environment, it wasn't until he walked into my apartment that it dawned on me that I had the brother of the future Queen of England as my guest.

That afternoon he joined me and three of my waitresses who were sunbathing topless by the pool. We all got on very well together. He particularly liked Joey, who was gorgeous with small boobs. That night we went out to dinner at the local Indian restaurant. I decided to let the manager know in advance who I was bringing, partly to impress him, and partly to ensure that we got a decent table. But the waiter on the telephone completely misunderstood me. He thought Prince Charles was coming in that night, not Charles Althorp, the brother of the princess. The moment we walked through the door they started bowing and scraping and calling him Your Royal Highness. Thank God, he found the whole thing hilarious. It could have been excruciating, but Charlie managed to turn it all into a big joke.

Charlie and I became great friends after that. He would come to Stringfellow's for dinner then we'd head off to the Hippodrome. After the club had closed Charlie would join a group of us in the Sun Luck Chinese restaurant, which illegally served drinks after 3.30a.m. He loved the transvestite crowd, although there was never any hint of him being gay. Like me, he adored their theatrical side. Bradley, Ruby Venesuala, Ebony and *Graham* made up the entourage most evenings, and he loved them all. At that time Charlie had just left school and was thinking about going into public relations. I remember telling him that he'd be much better on radio or television. He was still quite shy in those days, especially with the press. He had a demure way of putting his head down, rather like Diana did. Away from the cameras, though, he was quite different, very charming and great fun to be with. The only time I saw him take an interest in a girl it was in my own daughter, Karen. Unfortunately, she had a boyfriend, Mark Young, at the time. Charlie told me he thought Karen was beautiful so I told her what he'd said. He would have made a great son-in-law, but Karen was far too much in love with Mark then to look at Charlie.

It was through Charlie that I heard about the Business. They were a newly formed band made up almost entirely of aristocrats. The three names I remember are the Marquis of

Worcester, known as Bunter, Lord John Johnson of Somerset and Lady Theresa Manners. Bunter sounded like Joe Cocker and Lady Theresa was beautiful, so I could see their potential. I invited them to make a record and a video on the Hippodrome label. My idea was to film them at a banquet being held in a cave. They would all wear evening dress and drink from goblets. At the end of the video I wanted the camera to drop down to Lady Theresa's feet, where we'd see her dress fall to the floor, revealing a g-string, stockings and suspenders. I was away when the video was made. It was fantastic except for one thing: she didn't drop her dress. I still claim that was the reason their record wasn't a hit.

On the evening of the release, we held a private party for friends and relatives of the group at the Hippodrome. The club became the House of Lords for the night: it was wall-to-wall titles. Lady Theresa's parents came – the Duke and Duchess of Rutland – her grandmother, the Duchess of Argyll, and the Duke of Norfolk, along with a host of other names from *Who's Who*. The Duchess of Argyll had been a party girl in her youth and was now an old lady. Halfway through the evening, the noise got too much for her and she asked me to find some cotton wool for her ears. It was 1.30a.m. and we were in the middle of a nightclub: where on earth was I going to find cotton wool? Karen's boyfriend Mark went in search of something suitable. Twenty minutes later, he came back with a Tampax.

'Where are those cotton plugs?' bellowed the duchess.

'They're coming, they're coming,' I said, desperately trying to pull the cotton wool off the string. I managed to get half of it off before the duchess impatiently took it from me. She stuffed the broken Tampax in her ears, apparently quite oblivious to the string hanging from the left one. 'Thank you, young man, that's much better.'

It wasn't funny at the time. I remember thinking, Jesus Christ, I hope no one realises.

That evening I tried to matchmake Charlie Althorp with Lady Theresa Manners. I thought they'd make the perfect couple: both were attractive and titled. Unfortunately, Charlie told her she had a good voice but a big bum. Lady Theresa took this personally and burst into tears. The *Sun* ran the story the following day.

On Charlie's twenty-first birthday, Frizzby, Karen, Mark, Bradley and I were all invited to Althorp Park for his party. I was introduced to Diana for the first time that evening. She'd heard all about the Hippodrome from her brother, although I'm sure he'd given her judiciously edited highlights. Diana introduced us to Prince Charles, who was, as always, affable and charming. To me they looked like a happy couple. In spite of the stories their subsequent split generated, I would swear they were madly in love that evening. It was at Charlie's party that I prompted Mark to propose to Karen. I thought it would be the best place in the world to announce an engagement. Karen accepted him and everyone, including Prince Charles, offered their congratulations.

Not long after meeting Princess Diana at Althorp Park, I decided to invite the London Festival Ballet to the Hippodrome. I had a brilliant idea: halfway through the evening, the middle stage would come up and we'd stop the disco music so that everyone could watch the dancers. The ballet company sent two of their principal dancers to perform a *pas de deux*, along with a pianist and a cellist. I kept the whole thing a secret until the moment they were due to appear.

They did a few set pieces from *Sleeping Beauty* and *The Nutcracker*, and were absolutely sensational. I'd never been to the ballet, so I was impressed to say the least. After they'd finished and taken their bow, I announced over the microphone that we'd like to see it again. They went into their routine a second time. After the encore, the crowd went wild. I thought everyone wanted to see them perform so I announced them for a third time. I had no idea this was totally unprecedented. It was only then that I noticed the state of the dancers: the ballerina's hair was plastered to her head with perspiration and all her partner's make-up had run down his face. When they finished dancing, for the third time that evening, the male dancer looked at me and said breathlessly, 'Don't say another fucking word.'

I was hooked on the ballet after that. I went to see the London Festival Ballet and met their director, Peter Shaffus. I suggested that he held their hundredth anniversary celebrations at the Hippodrome. He thought it was a great idea. It was more than a great idea, it was ingenious, because the Princess of Wales was, according to her brother, dying to see the Hippodrome, and is a fan and patron of ballet. One night I'd even suggested that she come in a disguise, but Charlie said she would never dare do that. A few years later, however, she did turn up in disguise, with Sarah Ferguson, who was about to become the Duchess of York. They were both dressed in policewomen's uniforms – they'd been to Annabel's to gatecrash the Duke of York's stag night.

The Hippodrome went into top gear for the celebrations. I checked with Buckingham Palace whether there were any special arrangements we needed to make for the princess. We were told that she would sip dry white wine, which was an easy one, and that she liked meat, but wouldn't eat a lot. In those days Princess Diana was still the fairytale princess: it would be a long time before her marital troubles and bulimia came to light.

David Miles, the Hippodrome's chef, created a special dish for Diana which we still have on the menu at Stringfellow's. He prepared fillet steak in the shape of a butterfly and served it with a mushroom and Boursin sauce. The London Festival Ballet were wonderful to me. They let me greet her at the door and take her along a line-up of people waiting to be introduced. She was then to retire to my office, freshen up in the bathroom and join my table on the balcony. The moment she arrived I told her how delighted we all were to have her at the Hippodrome.

'Well, you've tried hard enough,' she said with a smile. 'And tuck your shirt in.'

My shirt was an Issey Miyake, which was meant to hang loose. We both laughed and the ice was broken. She sat between myself and Peter Shaffus at dinner and alternated between the two of us. She was flirtatious, but not in a sexual way, just enough to make us feel relaxed. She was very unlike the other royals I'd met. Princess Anne was rather stiff, Princess Margaret was worldly and Prince Charles was above it all. Diana was altogether more gentle, more beautiful and more sexy than any of her in-laws. While Peter Shaffus talked to her about the ballet, she wanted to know about the fun side of the Hippodrome from me. I was certainly doing most of the talking – and most of the drinking. I found it very difficult to reconcile her two sides: on one hand, she was a beautiful, sexy, flirtatious young woman, and on the other, she was the Princess of Wales, our future Queen. I wanted to ask her to dance later, but after several glasses of wine it didn't quite come out like that. 'I was wondering if I could possibly see you later,' was what I think I said. She gave me a very strange look. 'To see you for a dance – er – I certainly didn't mean—'

'I should think so, too,' said the princess. Several more drinks later I told her about my quandary – that on the one hand she was this, on the other hand that – and asked whether there was something less formal I could call her.

Her advice was crystal clear, although she gave it with a smile: 'Stick with The Princess, Stringfellow.'

There were a lot of celebrity guests at the club that night, including Boy George and his mother. George says in his autobiography that the princess asked to meet him, which isn't quite true. George had just come out of his deep drug addiction and I pointed him out to the princess, who was sitting with me on the balcony. She said she'd seen him on the television, so I asked her if she would like to meet him in person. Then I went and got George and his mother, which delighted the princess and delighted George even more.

When I said that the Hippodrome went into top gear to prepare for the evening, I wasn't exaggerating. I had my Star Bar redecorated for the princess's visit. I had the jukebox taken out and filled the place with beautiful antique furniture and chandeliers. Before she left I asked her if she would like to see the Star Bar. To my absolute chagrin she said she didn't have time. So she never saw the Star Bar, which had cost me £35,000 to refurbish in her honour. Neither did she have time to dance with me. Just as I was about to ask her, the band stopped playing. That aside, it was a truly wonderful evening. Even Nigel Dempster congratulated me. I can't remember his exact words, but they were something like, 'For a guy who's come as far as you have to have dined with the Princess of Wales, I take my hat off to you.' For years I'd chased and courted Dempster. He'd kept his distance until that night, when he finally acknowledged my achievements.

The moment the princess left, everyone relaxed into the party atmosphere of the club. A group of celebrities, including the whole of London's paparazzi, retired to the Star Bar for more champagne and antics. The photographers were keen to get a picture of David Steele, the leader of the Liberal Democrats, with a party girl, Cleo Rocos. David is a lovely guy, but small; Cleo is equally lovely, but very large, especially her boobs. One of the photographers asked David to pick Cleo up in his arms. The moment he tried to lift her off the floor, the two of them toppled over and Cleo's boobs fell out of her dress and all over David. It was like daylight. Twenty-five flashguns went off simultaneously, and twenty-five photographers were very happy. Every newspaper carried the picture of David and a bare-breasted Cleo. That was the main story from the Hippodrome that night. It was typical of the tabloids: look at these boobs – and by the way, the Princess of Wales was there, too.

Not long after the Royal Ballet celebration, Charlie Althorp stopped coming to the Hippodrome. He was difficult to get hold of on the telephone and seemed to have disappeared from the London social scene. I heard from one of his friends (although Charlie himself never confirmed this) that the Queen herself had asked him to cease his nightclubbing activities. His 'Champagne Charlie' image was seen as an embarrassment to his sister. A few years later Charlie brought his wife, Victoria, to the club and thanked me for all the invitations I'd sent him. He'd been busy with the estate and his young children, which explained his disappearance from the club scene.

Perhaps he'd simply grown tired of going to nightclubs every night. If so, he wasn't alone. Even Coral was beginning to relax. She didn't see the need to push for more. In her mind, we had two successful nightclubs, Scott and Karen were grown up, and we didn't need expand. She was ready for us to walk hand in hand into the sunset. I couldn't have disagreed with her more. I still wanted New York.

While all the madness was going on at the Hippodrome, I was still making regular trips to New York. Nearly every trip started with an argument. If it wasn't about Frizzby, it was about some other girl. I didn't mind her complaining about Frizzby because Frizzby was a genuine target. Occasionally, however, she'd accuse me of flirting with some girl I'd never even met, which would really annoy me. There's nothing worse than being accused of something you haven't done. After one particular row, I started getting a terrible buzzing in my head from all the shouting. I remember yelling, 'Christ, Coral, now my head's buzzing.' She shut up after that, but the buzzing didn't stop. My head buzzed all the way to New York and it was still buzzing two days later. At first I thought it was a sympton of the 'flu I'd caught in London, but when the 'flu cleared up and the buzzing didn't, I flew straight back to London to see Barry Grimaldi. He said, 'Is it your head or your ear?' It felt like my head, but the buzzing was actually in my left ear. He examined me and said, 'I've got bad news, Peter. It's tinnitus.' My first reaction was, 'OK, where are the tablets?'

'No tablets.'

'OK, I'll have the injections.'

'No injections.'

'All right, I'll have the operation, then.'

'No operation.'

'What are you telling me, Barry?'

'There's no cure for tinnitus. You'll have to live with that buzz for the rest of your life.'

Barry's words took a long time to sink in. I thought I'd never be able to live with it, but I do live with it, every second of every minute of every day. Over the years I've had every possible test done on my ears, both here and in America. The results are always the same. I've got tinnitus for life, and one day I'll be completely deaf in my left ear, even though the buzz will stay there forever. The specialist told me that I must have trauma-tised my ear at some point in my life. I suspect it happened in 1965, when the Pretty Things played at the Mojo Club and I was pushed up against the lead guitarist's amplifier for three-quarters of an hour. I didn't complain at the time because two very pretty girls were squashed up against me. I couldn't hear a damned thing for two days, but it took twenty-two years for the real damage to show.

New York took my mind off the tinnitus. It gave me a focus. I'd left Lesley Harwood, a young real-estate agent, in charge of finding me premises in the city. She finally telephoned to say she'd found a perfect building on East Twenty-first Street. The address sounded great, so I jumped on the next plane to New York.

There, in all its dilapidated glory, was my nightclub. The building had been an old printing works. It had cracked concrete walls where the machinery had been ripped out, a flooded basement and the charm of a bombsite. In its favour, it had space and a great location. The moment I saw the place, I wanted it. But what I wanted and what I got were two very different things. To me New York was a cool, happening place where comic-book heroes were born. To everyone else, New York was a drug-infested city run by the Mafia. Fiction and fact were about to clash. Big-time.

18

NEW YORK, NEW YORK

I have a big problem when I want something. Instead of being cool and indifferent, I get excited and show interest. With women it works a treat; in business it's a major handicap. Showing honest enthusiasm is never a good way to negotiate. I made precisely that mistake with Peter Catillano, the landlord of East Twenty-first Street, and in spite of the trouble it's brought me it's still one of my failings.

Peter Catillano was a sharp, slim, sophisticated New Yorker with thinning hair and glasses. Behind the cool business exterior was a hint of warmth, enough to make me like him. He told me immediately that he had an offer on the table and was about to sign a lease with the owners of Rascal's. It sounded plausible enough. Rascal's was a disco-cum-café whose gimmick was to throw sawdust on the floor and put a big barrel of free peanuts in the middle of the room. I wanted to convince him that my concept was much more sophisticated. I didn't just show him photographs and menus, I invited him and his wife to London so that he could see my clubs for himself.

In return, he wanted me to give him $10,000 to show my intentions. If he didn't like my clubs, he would return the money, and if I changed my mind, he would keep it. My financial director would have thrown his deal out of the window. In my wild enthusiasm I not only agreed to give him $10,000, but also to pay for flights to London for him and his wife and his hotel bill. All he had to do was to stall the owner of Rascal's.

Luck was definitely on my side the day they arrived in London. That very night the Duchess of Gloucester had booked

Stringfellow's for a private party. There were so many influential people in the club that we had MI5 on the door. Peter Catillano and his wife were most impressed. The whole of the restaurant was jammed with ladies and duchesses. When Viscountess Patricia Rothermere, or Bubbles, as she was better known, turned up with her husband, Viscount Vere Rothermere, the chairman of Associated Newspapers, we couldn't find them a table. She was mortally offended. 'If I don't have a table in ten minutes we're leaving,' she said. After ten minutes she flounced out with her husband in tow. If I could have found them a table, believe me, I would have done – I couldn't even get a table for myself that evening, let alone for Nigel Dempster's boss.

Peter Catillano and his wife and Coral and I ended up eating at the Hippodrome, where by coincidence, another hooray bash was going on. Every London nightclub owner will agree with me that people from Knightsbridge, Kensington and Chelsea are terrible dancers. What they lack in co-ordination, they make up for in enthusiasm. If there's a bunch of them dancing to modern music, it's best to stay clear of the floor, because they're dangerous. They're like John Cleese when he's doing one of his silly sketches. The British aren't renowned for their rhythm and movement, but I think even Peter Catillano was shocked by how badly these people danced. Nevertheless, we'd left the semi-royals at Stringfellow's and bumped into yet more aristocracy at the Hippodrome, and being Americans, the Catillanos loved anything connected with the royal family. I was hardly going to dampen their belief that London in general and my clubs in particular were full of partying aristocrats. I sent Roger Howe to get the names and addresses of all the hoorays in the Hippodrome so I could get them to become members. Among the group was a redhead called Sarah Ferguson. She was very much an 'OK, yah' type, but I liked her.

We used that list many times over the years when we sent out VIP invitations for important events at the club. On one occasion we sent out a standard letter inviting our members to buy a £25 ticket for the Hippodrome's birthday party. We were giving away free champagne all night and putting on a buffet, so it wasn't particularly expensive. A week later I received a letter on Buckingham Palace notepaper from the Duchess of York. I was totally unaware that the Sarah Ferguson on our membership list was the same Sarah Ferguson who had married the Duke of York earlier that year. Our invitation had gone to her old address, yet she was kind enough to reply. She declined the invitation to buy a ticket, but wished me luck with the club. Had I known she was the Duchess of York, I would have happily given her a complimentary ticket.

The Catillanos, Coral and I had a brilliant evening. Over dinner Peter explained his Sicilian connections, though he was at great pains to stress that he wasn't a member of the Mafia. It all meant very little to me. I knew nothing about the Mafia anyway. I was eventually to discover that they were very influential in New York, but that night, I was 'green' Peter from London, the naïve Brit who wanted to conquer America. Coral was on dazzling form, chatting to Peter, confiding in his wife, doing everything a perfect wife should do in such a situation. At the other end of the club, Frizzby was being the perfect mistress by keeping out of the way.

After the Hippodrome closed, we went to a Greek restaurant which sold drinks until 8a.m. Like the Sun Luck Chinese restaurant, it was one of those places with a mysterious invisible all-night drinking licence. The owner ushered us straight to a table. We'd only been in there about twenty minutes when a blonde girl at the next table waved at me. I swear that I'd never seen her before in my life. As we were all laughing and chatting, she leaned over and said something in my ear. I didn't hear what she said, and I carried on talking to Peter and his wife. A few minutes later she leaned over again and whispered to me again. At that moment Coral flew off her chair, grabbed the girl by her hair and yanked her to the floor. I couldn't believe this was happening in front of my prospective landlord and his lovely wife. I quickly dragged Coral off her, but it was too late, the damage was already done. The girl was already in floods of tears. 'I was only asking him for a job,' she wailed. Coral was unrepentant. She'd become very jealous and possessive, which was flattering in one way, but deeply embarrassing in others. The Catillanos loved it. Coral's fight had been the cherry on top of the icing on the cake. It made their trip. They'd been impressed by the duchesses at Stringfellow's, amused by the hoorays at the Hippodrome and now thoroughly entertained by my wife fighting on the floor of an illegal drinking den.

When Peter Catillano returned to New York, he decided to keep the $10,000 deposit as his 'fee' for changing deals midstream and as part-payment for the exorbitant rent he was going to charge me. It was the first of many times my fingers were burned doing business with Americans. By the time I'd finished with New York, or rather, New York had finished with me, I would have learned a lot more. For instance, I couldn't understand why no one person owned anything outright in New York. Every club, restaurant and bar had between five and thirty owners, who were the investors. The front man never put up the money himself, which was an alien concept to me. I've always wanted to be numero uno, the front man, the owner and in charge. But the Americans did it the clever way. I now know that New York is a city full of bankrupt bars, nightclubs and restaurants. I should have realised that no bugger survives there for any length of time. With the exception of Doubles, which was New York's answer to Annabel's, everywhere, I mean *everywhere*, went bankrupt. (OK, a slight exaggeration, but that's how it looked to me.) It never crossed my mind that Stringfellow's would go the same way. After all, I was successful Peter Stringfellow, owner of the best nightclubs in London. *Of course* Stringfellow's New York was going to be a massive success.

As usual, not everyone shared my view, particularly not Brian Smith. I decided the only way to get him on my side was to show him New York. His first words on seeing the place were, 'How much?'

'$400,000 to build it. I can't see me spending more than that.'

Brian looked at me, with that chain-smoker's look: eyes narrowed, head on one side. 'It'll take another zero to finish it.'

How right he was.

Before we left New York, I took him to Club A, which was the city's most sophisticated jacket-and-tie nightclub at the time. I'd heard that the South American owners had put $7 million into it, which seemed like an extraordinary amount of money. It was built on the same lines as Régines, with a small dance floor and lots of room in the restaurant to walk around. The entrance fee was $15, approximately £10 in 1985, and £3 more than we were charging to get into Stringfellow's. The drinks were $7 to $8 each, which wasn't so expensive considering that the measures were double the size of those in Britain. I made a quick mental calculation that Club A must be making profits of $2 million a year. Brian was impressed with the figure. He'd wrongly doubted my profit predictions on the Hippodrome, so this time he was prepared to believe me.

The next time we went to New York, Brian brought along an investment banker. He was one of the top risk-venture capitalists, who shall remain nameless for reasons that will become clear. Brian, the banker and myself all went out to the Chelsea Rendezvous on Tenth Avenue. The entrance to the club was through a curtain in the back of an antique shop. It led to a wonderful basement with a brilliant atmosphere. It had two rooms, jazz upstairs and rhythm and blues downstairs.

On previous occasions I'd taken a girlfriend with me, so I was quite impressed by all the female attention we were getting. I was even more surprised when the banker left early with one of the girls. I hadn't realised until that night that the basement was full of New York hookers. Thank God he'd agreed to a three-quarters-of-a-million loan before he realised he'd caught VD. He was absolutely devastated because he had to tell his wife.

The moment the lease was signed and the money to build the club was arranged, I put all my energy and effort into New York. Stringfellow's and the Hippodrome were both doing well in London, so for the first time I was starting a club from a position of financial security. The Hippodrome was doing phenomenal business in those days. Our average takings were £120,000 a week, sometimes £130,000, and Stringfellow's was grossing £70,000 a week. I sent Paul Roberts, the principal designer of the Hippodrome, to New York. He was a good-looking guy and a perfect ambassador for Stringfellow's New York. I rented an apartment for him to live in on the condition that he slept in the lounge and kept the only bedroom free for me when I was in town. Paul would check out the latest restaurants and clubs, chat up the girls, then I'd finish the job when I flew into New York – in other words, we'd get the girls. Paul never knew that I made love to two of his girlfriends out there. Unlike Roger Howe, Paul wasn't into sharing. He now lives with my daughter Karen and is the father of my grandchild, so I know he's not going to be too upset about the infidelities of his exes.

It took Paul and me quite a while to work out that in New York 'let's party' meant 'where's the cocaine?' To me it meant 'let's get a limousine, go out to dinner and a nightclub, then back to my place for more champagne'. During the year it took us to build Stringfellow's New York, Paul and I became known on the club scene as 'those weird guys with no drugs'.

Apart from being a friend for me to party with, Paul was primarily in New York to see that everything ran smoothly with the new club. I hadn't realised that New York was a unionised city. They had a union for the electricians, a union for the people who brought the fittings to the electricians, a union for the carpet fitters, for the builders, the architects, the plumbers – the list went on. Every few days someone would down tools and want me to negotiate with their union representative. By the time the club was finished, I was on speaking terms with every union representative in New York City, including the Teamsters.

I brought in Jonathan Park and Mark Fisher to do the lights. Of course, the other electricians immediately stopped work and demanded to know why non-union members were being allowed into the building. To get over that one we ended up paying a union representative $2,000 in cash and Fisher–Park started work. After the fiasco at the Hippodrome, I was adamant that I didn't want any prototypes. 'Do you hear? None,' was what I said.

Except I wanted a glass dance floor and a glass ceiling, and I wanted the lights to be concealed. Jon and Mark explained, very patiently, that they would have to build special lights in order to achieve the effect. They put thirty wonderful, mirror-reflecting spotlights behind the glass ceiling. Guess what? They didn't work. Well, to be fair, they did after a fashion – people would come up and ask, 'What's that flickering in the roof?' The 'fabulous' effect was about as dramatic as twelve people clicking their lighters in unison. I added the 'invisible' lights to my list of costly mistakes, along with the lilac carpets at Cinderella's and monogrammed plastic beakers for the Hippodrome.

From the day we started building, the money disappeared so fast that we didn't see it. Brian Smith virtually forced me to close Hippodrome Records. He thought thirteen flops and a £1 million loss was quite enough. He began finding money from everywhere for New York. We cashflowed Stringfellow's and the Hippodrome, and in spite of the unfortunate incident in New York the banker advised his bank to lend us more money.

By the time Stringfellow's New York was ready to open, it had cost in excess of $4 million – in fact, it was nearer $5 million, but I'd stopped counting. Three days before the launch we discovered that our attorney hadn't filed for the correct cabaret licence. My attorney had been a colonel in the US army. He was a delightful gentleman and the nicest American I'd ever met, but unfortunately, he wasn't hard enough for the New York business game I was about to play. In desperation I phoned up Steve Rubell, who had run Studio 54. He'd relaunched the Palladium, which was now the most exciting place to go in New York. He'd put in Vary lights, which were laser-type multi-directional spotlights. The effect was so fantastic that I immediately ordered some for the Hippodrome – I didn't want to lose my 'world's greatest disco' tag.

I was madly envious of Steve and his partner. When they opened the Palladium, the *New York* magazine had put them on the cover as the 'comeback kids'. I called the magazine and asked them to put me on the cover as 'the first-time kid'. Needless to say, they ignored my suggestion. A lot of Steve's so-called friends had deserted him since his prison sentence for drugs and tax evasion. I'd met him only a couple of times, but I liked the guy a lot. When the *New York Post* asked him what he thought of Peter Stringfellow's new club he said, 'I wish him well, but I don't think he understands the problems of running a club in New York.' How bloody right he was. I didn't get to speak to Steve personally, but his secretary gave me the name of his solicitors, Davidoff and Mallito. I phoned them and told one of their attorneys my problem: that I was three days away from opening and my cabaret licence was still being processed at City Hall. My attorney was Mr Nice Guy and had filed everything correctly, but I needed a Mr Nasty to pull some strings. The solicitor wanted $25,000 as an immediate payment, plus a payment for whatever time it took, plus his fees. I was in no position to argue. It sounded like a bargain: $25,000 for the licence as opposed to what it would cost not to open. I agreed to pay the money. The attorney told me to go ahead with the opening and he'd be there with the licence. Davidoff and Mallito were the best firm of attorneys in New York and it was worth paying extra for their expertise and influence – and I mean *influence*.

On Thursday 10 March 1986, Stringfellow's New York opened its doors. Ten minutes later the attorney arrived with the licence. He was followed by the fire brigade, who had been called by a 'well-wisher'. They blocked Twenty-first Street with their engines and threatened to empty the club. Roger and I had to convince them that no, we didn't have a fire; no, we weren't overcrowded, and yes, we did have a licence. The fire brigade set the tone for the rest of the evening, which careered from one disaster to the next.

I'd been determined not to make the same mistake with my London crowd as I'd made with the Manchester people. I didn't want them to think I'd lost interest in them. While New York was being built, I'd hit the microphone in London, play Frank Sinatra's 'New York, New York' and give the audience an update on the progress of Stringfellow's II. To make them feel even more a part of it all, I arranged a televised satellite link-up between the two clubs on New York's opening night. I hadn't expected it to cost $25,000, but what the hell, it was a great idea. I'd arranged for Bradley to host a celebrity party in London, which would be screened in the New York club, and vice versa. What I hadn't thought about was the time difference. Of course, 9p.m. in New York is 2a.m. in London. The London crowd has been partying since 9p.m. on free drinks. They were having a wild, riotous time.

Unfortunately, things weren't quite so good in New York. Instead of standing on the door to greet people, I was strapped to a microphone with a cameraman following me around. As I was saying, 'Hello, London, welcome to New York,' I could see water cascading from a ventilator to the left of me. While Roger and the busboys tried to stop the waterfall and rope off half the restaurant, I carried on smiling into the camera, pretending that we were all in a party mood. Eventually I took off the microphone and started greeting people at the door. Robin Leach, presenter of *Lifestyles of the Rich and Famous*, said, 'That'll teach you a lesson. It's not as easy as it looks, is it?' I had to agree.

What made the opening even more traumatic was not having Frizzby with me. Coral was still my wife, so it was only right she should take her place beside me. I knew it would have been too humiliating for Frizzby to have to watch it all from London, so I sent her and her mother to Tunisia for a holiday. She told me later that, apart from having her mother there, it was one of the most miserable weeks of her life.

Missing Frizzby that night didn't help matters. It was, without exaggeration, the nightclub opening from hell. I had to put my personality aside and let my doormen play the New York game of ignoring people. It is against the law there to refuse anyone entrance to a nightclub with a public licence, so the doormen couldn't say no. They just stood there in silence as hundreds of people pestered to come in. I found the whole thing incredibly rude. I never got the hang of staying silent and ended up being sued twice in Los Angeles by a nerdish-looking dog dentist I refused to let into the club.

I'd employed a 'picker' called Leslie to stand on the door in New York. He'd worked at the Limelight and knew the trendy crowd there. Unfortunately, when I told him that no one was allowed in without an invitation, he followed this to the letter and ignored Michael Musto, who was the top gossip-writer on the *Village Voice*. Michael was also the spokesman for the gay political set in New York. OK, so he was wearing a red, sparkly evening dress and wig at the time, but that's New York. If I'd been on the door I would have carried him in, drowned him in champagne and made him my best friend. Les's *faux pas* took eighteen months to put right. Michael Musto took umbrage and wrote in his column that Stringfellow's had refused him because of his dress. This was followed by a review in *Details* magazine which called the club the 'black hole of Calcutta'. I had to agree with them on that point. On the opening night the neon butterfly underneath the dance floor wasn't working and Fisher–Park's concealed ceiling lights were so concealed that no one saw them. Once again I made a mental note, *never* to buy another prototype.

Despite the calamities, one thing saved the evening for me totally. Christopher Reeve, a.k.a. Superman, turned up. Forget the host of other celebrities: no one could top my comic-book hero. He was followed by Pierce Brosnan, who later became James Bond, and a host of other celebrities.

After the star-studded opening, *Rolling Stone* magazine asked me if Stringfellow's was a 'yuppie' club. I'd never heard the word before, but I liked the sound of it, so I said, yeah, of course my club was 'yuppie'. Naturally, the interpretation *Rolling Stone* put on that was that the downtowners would never set foot in the place. However, the Wall Street crowd loved it as their own. It was different from anywhere else in New York. For a start, it had only one owner, and an Englishman at that. It was a novelty for them to see the owner talking on the microphone and walking around the club chatting to everyone, and on top of that, it was the most beautiful club in New York.

We employed a chef called Peter Hoffman who specialised in French and Thai dishes. The Japanese, Italians and French loved his food. The only people who didn't understand it were me and the rest of New York. His speciality was a clear fish broth with three silver, red and blue fishes floating on the top. Nearly everyone complained that the fish were too small, or wondered why they had tinfoil floating in their soup. Peter Hoffman was probably the finest chef we ever employed, but within months we'd driven him out with our constant menu changes. The final insult was asking him to cook fish and chips.

I'd decided we'd have a special English night. I arranged for copies of the *Sun* to be flown in so we could serve the fish and chips in authentic newspaper. It was a surprising success, and lots of people ordered the fish-and-chip special. After the seventh request we were told that the chef had run out of fish. I couldn't understand it – we'd bought a huge load of cod from the market that morning, which had been flown in specially from the North Sea. It transpired that Peter Hoffman thought the fish-and-chip special was a joke, so he'd given most of the cod to his kitchen staff for their lunch. I was speechless with anger. Peter left soon afterwards. His parting words were, 'You guys are fucking crazy.' We replaced him with a New York Italian called Joe Decarti and changed the menu to pasta.

New York attracted two very distinct crowds: those who came to eat in the restaurant, and those who came to dance. It was impossible to get the eaters to stay and dance, or to persuade the dancers to come early and eat first. It wasn't long before the restaurant reviewer's attitude to nightclub food reared its head in my career again. One night Gail Green, the restaurant reviewer from the *New York* magazine, turned up. Scott, my young head waiter, was totally in awe of her. 'Peter, whatever you do, don't go over and introduce yourself.'

'Don't be silly, Scott, I'm the owner. I know who she is, it's no secret.'

'No, no, you mustn't do that.'

Gail had arrived with a couple of young guys. She had a reputation for liking young, handsome waiters. It was all, 'Ciao, bella,' kissy-poo, kissy-poo, the moment she arrived anywhere. Scott was too panic-stricken so there were no kissy-poos from him. As the night progressed I could see that Gail was getting drunk. By the end of the night she'd literally fallen off her chair. When I went over to introduce myself, she was so smashed she didn't care who the hell I was. As for her review, it never appeared.

My New York PR, Colby Smith, was a friend of Robin Leach. She was an ex-stunt girl from LA and extremely smart. Coral immediately disliked her. She wasn't a dolly girl, so Coral felt threatened by her. Despite our disintegrating marriage, Coral wanted to be queen of the New York scene. Colby would come to the club and dine with top designers and people who were part of the New York social set. Personally, I don't like that kind of crowd. Sure, we chased the stars, but that particular set of so-called celebrities, the ones New York called 'Eurotrash', were never going to be good for the club.

Colby called one day to say she'd arranged for an interview with Andy Warhol, who was running a magazine called *Interview*. She even suggested he might like to put me on the cover. At the time I considered myself a big cheese. With hindsight it sounds stupid that I put myself on a par with Andy Warhol, and you might well think, 'How dare he.' But I was proud to be the first Englishman to open a club in New York, and to have done it without American investors.

Colby took me to Andy Warhol's office and left me there, saying that he'd be along shortly. One of the young receptionists took me into a room and gave me a glass of wine. After about ten minutes a few other people started arriving. Half an hour later there were six of us sitting there drinking glasses of wine. I wasn't in a sociable mood that day. I thought I'd been invited to see Andy Warhol, not have a general directors' meeting with a load of other people. An hour later they brought out a buffet and told everyone that Andy would be along later. It began to dawn on me that this was how Andy Warhol conducted his interviews. He invited half a dozen people along for wine and canapés, then didn't show up for over an hour. It was like being presented to the Queen. At the time I was full of my own self-importance and felt affronted by this. Out of bloodymindedness and anger, I started drinking too much. By the time Andy Warhol arrived I was pissed off and pissed up. I could see him from across the room, shaking people's hands and holding brief conversations. It was like watching Prince Charles working a room. After he'd talked to three people without getting round to me I went over and said, 'Excuse me, I'm Peter Stringfellow.'

'I'm very happy you could come,' said Andy Warhol with a smile.

'Well, I'm not happy. I waited one and a half hours, and I want you to know that I waited for you, but now I'm going.'

'Oh don't do that, I want to talk to you,' he said, very gently.

I refused to be mollified and flounced out of the room like a queen. It was a very silly thing to do. Now I'd not only alienated Michael Musto from the *Village Voice* and got *Details* magazine against me, I'd horrified Andy Warhol's team at *Interview* as well.

It took months to rebuild those fences. Coral and I went to the launch of Robin Leach's autobiography and literally bumped into Michael Musto in the elevator. The doors opened and there he was. The moment he realised who I was, he went a deathly shade of white. Coral said, 'Don't,' but it was too late. I grabbed hold of him and gave him a big hug and a kiss. 'You little shit,' I said. He started laughing, with relief more than anything else. By the end of the night Michael Musto and I were friends. For months he'd been rude about Stringfellow's New York, and as a result the name had become a byword for anything not good. Still, he gave me a lot of plugs, even if they were all negative, and from that night on he became a friend of mine and a fan of the club.

For every step I went forward in New York, I seemed to take two backwards. One night Roger went into the champagne room and found a well-known model agency boss chopping up lines of cocaine on one of our drinks tables. He was surrounded by six of the city's most beautiful models, all of whom were waiting to snort the stuff from his $100 bill. Roger very politely asked him to remove it because of our anti-drugs policy. The boss looked at him and said: 'Hey, what's your problem? You wanna line?'

Roger declined and brushed the whole lot off the table with his hand. The model agency guy went berserk.

'You will never, I mean *never*, see any of our models in here again.'

He left the club and never set foot in the place again, and neither did any of his models. I look back on that incident and think, 'Jesus, what was I doing in New York with a $5 million club and an anti-drugs policy?'

Before opening Stringfellow's New York I'd been to the Area Club and seen unisex toilets for the first time. To me this was a wild idea because you could go into the loo with a girl. I was probably the only man in New York who took a girl in there for sex; everyone else went in to snort cocaine. I know that if I'd been into drugs and allowed them in my club, I would truly have been the king of the New York scene. My club was sensational. I had a sliding wall that separated the restaurant from the dance floor. At 11p.m. each night we'd play Tchaikovsky's *1812 Overture* and slide back the wall to see the disco lights and the smoke. Then it would be party time. It was a crazy, crazy time for me, but I managed to have fun without touching cocaine or smoking marijuana. I'm not being pious – I believe each to his own. My stance on drugs was, and still is, personal, not moral. My drugs are vodka, champagne and sex, copious amounts of each in equal measures.

Like all nightclubs, Stringfellow's New York had its problems, but people taking drugs was not one of them. My bar staff taking money was. It came as a big shock to my New York barmen when we introduced stock control. In fact I couldn't find a stocktaker in the whole city and ended up having to fly in my own guys from London. I put a stop to free-pouring the drinks, which upset the barmen. One of them said to me, 'How much do you want from a bottle of vodka?' I told him $150. He said, 'That's great. Anything we get on top of that is ours.'

'Are you crazy?' I said. 'Any money you take in the club is mine.'

This was not what they wanted to hear. One night I walked into the club and saw two beautiful girls at the bar. I offered to buy them a drink and they both asked for champagne. They didn't know I owned the place, so it was nice to hear that they thought the club was wonderful. When I offered them more champagne they said, 'Oh, don't buy any more, we always get our champagne free in here.'

'Oh, really? Why is that?'

They took me into the bar in the disco area and asked the best-looking barman in the club for three glasses of champagne. He saw me standing behind them and very coolly asked them for $33. I was impressed. The girls went into shock.

'But George, we've *never* paid. We haven't got any money.'

I told George to put the champagne on my bill.

'OK, Mr Stringfellow.'

The girls, of course, stared at me in astonishment. After they left I asked one of my managers to tell George that he was costing me as much as $1,000 a night because of all the champagne he was giving away. I said, 'Tell him to give me back $100 and promise never to fiddle again, and he can keep his job.' The manager went over to George and passed on my message. I saw George take $100 out of his top pocket without hesitating and hand over the money. I told my manager to sack him immediately.

Why did I do that? Simple. He had $100 in his pocket and we'd only been open two hours. If he'd just been giving the girls free drinks I could have dealt with that, but he wasn't, he was fiddling a lot of money. Barmen only give free drinks for two reasons: in the hope of a bigger tip, or to get a girl's knickers off. If we caught our bar staff stealing, we sacked them on the spot, and that's still my policy today. It was much easier to sack staff in America; in Britain it usually involves a tribunal. Of the eight times we've been before tribunals Stringfellow's has won only twice, and believe me, I only sack staff after several warnings.

Although New York was a success, the money was going out faster than it was coming in. My expenses alone were colossal. Apart from all the travelling, I had my apartment, and everyone else's accommodation, to pay for. Paul Roberts was in a company flat, I'd flown in my executives from London and put them up in hotels, and I'd even found a small place for myself. Then there was Roger, who had come over to manage the club. Unbeknown to me, Roger had rented himself a palatial apartment on West Eleventh Street. I'd shown Roger my huge profit projections for New York and he was one of the few people who believed the figure. Not only did he have a fabulous two-bedroomed palace, he was having antiques shipped over from England. Roger was very quiet about his homestead, suspiciously quiet, considering that I was paying for it all. I got the shock of my life when I popped over to see him one day. I was living twenty-seven flights up in a one-bedroomed studio, while Roger had two bedrooms, a palatial lounge, kitchen and bathroom, all on expenses. My first words were: 'What the fuck have you got here?' I told him his spare room had to be used when staff flew in from England, except that by then all the staff were already in New York.

After a year I had to send Roger back to London. We both knew we had to curb expenses, so he agreed, albeit reluctantly, to return to Stringfellow's in London. He had his beautiful new girlfriend, Katy, waiting for him and an old Georgian house which he'd just bought on the Thames. Roger's London lifestyle was even more luxurious than his lifestyle in New York. He'd invested all his money in the house on the Thames, and like a lot of people, he ended up losing everything when the property market crashed.

I brought in Julian Russell to take over from Roger. Julian was the general manager of Stringfellow's in London and the Hippodrome and an old friend from the north. While I'd been away he'd somehow picked up the title of executive director. I hadn't given it to him, but I let him keep it. I've always been generous with titles. When my staff ask for a pay rise, I invariably give them a new title instead. I brought in John Neilson Jr as his assistant, and Julian, John and I moved into Roger's old apartment. John's father, you'll remember, had been my lawyer for many years. When he was dying of throat cancer in the early 1980s he asked me to take care of his son and give him a chance. After John died, I gave John Jr a job. Before he came to work for me I told him what I tell all my married male staff, that his marriage wouldn't last. I know from experience that it is virtually impossible to sustain a relationship working in the leisure industry. Long hours and access to beautiful girls are the two main factors. True to form, John's marriage did eventually collapse.

Whereas in England journalists would usually ask me about girls and drinking, in New York the first question was nearly always: 'How do you deal with the Mafia?' My reply was always the same: I hadn't borrowed any money in America, so there was no 'funny' money – Mafia money – in my club. The traditional way people get involved with the Mafia is by looking for investors. Without exception, I was the only club in New York with no American investors. No one could put the 'squeeze' on me, as they say over there, because they had nothing to threaten me with, except, of course, 'I'll tell your wife.' But I didn't need the Mafia to squeal about my infidelity, the girls themselves did a good enough job already.

I'd grown up with the black-and-white-film image of the Mafia-sponsored Chicago club boss. He was the guy who organised the booze runs during prohibition and ran a string of hookers. In my imagination, he was short, fat and bald and carried a couple of guns. Thank God I didn't fit that image. I was upfront and incredibly legal. I even had to have my fingerprints taken before the New York police would grant me a liquor licence.

In my naïveté I thought I was safe. I was about to discover that the Mafia don't need to invest in your nightclub to have a hold over you. I was happy for them to dine in my restaurant, but not so happy when they machine-gunned down the front doors. It seemed rather drastic action to take over something so trivial as the table napkins, but believe me, these guys didn't mess around.

19

MAD WORLD

New York is a violent, unpredictable city, yet there was never any fighting outside Stringfellow's. It had nothing to do with my club, and everything to do with the city's gun laws. You never knew who had a gun or when they might decide to use it. Only a lunatic would pick a fight with a stranger in New York.

My doorman once refused entry to a guy in a white suit. It had nothing to do with his suit, my doorman just sensed that there was something odd about him. This guy said, 'I'm coming in, one way or the other.'

'You're not coming in, period,' said the doorman.

With that the guy took out a gun and fired two shots into the ceiling of our reception. Then he coolly walked outside and hailed a cab. I immediately called the police. I was about to describe the guy when the cop said, 'Anybody hurt?'

'No, but he fired two shots.'

'If he comes back, call us.'

'Er – don't you want to know what he looks like so you can go and find him?'

'No one's hurt, buddy. What's your problem?'

My problem was being British. When someone once shot at the door of Stringfellow's in London, the Metropolitan Police virtually sealed off the area and had every available squad car looking for the perpetrator. I expected the same in New York, not a so-what-buddy-get-a-life kind of attitude.

One night I walked into the restaurant and there were no napkins. Julian, my manager/executive director, told me that we were having problems with the laundry company. I told him to get a new laundry. So Julian told the old laundry that they weren't getting our business any more and hired someone else. A day later someone from the old firm called Julian and offered him $8,000 to renew their contract. He refused.

Two nights later I got a phone call at 5a.m. Someone had machine-gunned the plate-glass doors at the front of the club. My night security guard said it had been like something from a 1930s gangster movie. A limousine had cruised past with a machine-gun sticking out of the window. The gunman had sprayed the front of the club and sped off into the night. Suffice to say the New York police weren't interested. Against all my principles I gave the old laundry their contract back. There are two things you don't mess with in New York: garbage collection and the laundry. There is still a bullet hole in the wall.

I wasn't daunted by the laundry incident, it merely added to the colour and drama of being in America. I had videos made of myself in New York and London. In New York I had the Statue of Liberty in the background with me saying, 'Good evening, London …' and in London I was in front of Big Ben saying, 'Good evening, New York.' I'd learned from experience that my clubs need me, and the videos were my way of saying, if I'm not with you personally, I'm with you in spirit. It worked. The Hippodrome, however, didn't need a video. From the day it opened it had its own identity and personality. It roared away, with or without me.

Sometimes I'd fly into New York with Frizzby, sometimes Coral, although Coral was happier holding court at String-fellow's in London. She let it be known that Frizzby wasn't welcome in there. Coral's contempt for poor Frizzby got so bad that she threatened to kill Frizzby on her birthday. I'd arranged for the royal box at the Hippodrome to be covered in roses for Frizzby, and she had dressed for the occasion in a stunning white ballgown. When Coral got wind of this she told me she would kill Frizzby if I went near her that night. Coral was capable of anything, so I didn't take the threat lightly. I asked my doormen if one of them would shadow Frizzby for the night. I had seven doormen at the Hippodrome, all incredibly tough guys, yet not one of them would volunteer. Coral was so formidable that I ended up having to give one guy £100 to take on the job. It was a sad night for Frizzby. She looked sensational and I couldn't go near her. We had to use some elaborate ruse to get Coral to the other end of the club so that Frizzby could leave. When she finally went, clutching dozens of red roses, she burst into tears. I was about to experience the full force of Coral's violence, but Coral and the plant-pot story comes a little later.

Frizzby's outrageous image was perfect for Stringfellow's New York. She touched base with the downtowners, who by and large stayed away, whereas Coral was more at home with the uptown crowd. Frizzby's American counterpart was a downtowner called Julie Jools who was the upfront leader of the trendy crowd. Julie came in with her posse one night while socialite Cornelia Guest was in the club with her uptown friends. It was like the trendies mixing with the Sloanes, except that such things didn't happen in New York. Different groups kept themselves separate. I'd seen voluntary racial segregation there. Black people were more than welcome at my club, but we only ever saw a handful, usually the sports stars. It was the same with the uptowners and the downtowners. On this particular night Julie Jools came up to me and said I'd ruined her night out because I'd let in 'those snotty people', clearly referring to Cornelia. Then Cornelia said, 'I've brought my friends to your club, and you've let in those smelly, dirty people,' clearly referring to Julie Jools. I thought it was a brilliant mix, the first time I'd ever seen New York looking like London. I liked everybody: uptown, downtown, black, white – who cared, as long as everyone was having fun? Robin Leach told me to give up on the idea. 'Why bother trying to mix them? You've got the best crowd. Why bother with the scummers? They'll never love you, they'll only take advantage.' Robin might have had the measure of New York, but that didn't make it right in my eyes. My philosophy has always been to mix crowds, it makes life more exciting.

Frizzby loved Stringfellow's New York, but she wasn't overly impressed with the rest of the nightlife. I once took her on a tour of the nightspots, starting at the Hard Rock Café and ending up at the Tribeca, which was a trendy one-nighter held at the

Heartbreak Club. The Heartbreak was like a truckers' café inside, not at all the glamorous New York she had imagined. She thought I was deliberately winding her up and stomped out into the street.

As we trudged along Fifth Avenue, a black and red limousine pulled up. A black guy wound down his window and said, 'You guys look like you need a ride.' Frizzby and I got in the back. The driver turned out to be Curtis Knight, a soul singer from the 1960s. I remembered playing his music at the Mojo Club. His claim to fame was that Jimi Hendrix had been discovered while playing in his band. Curtis had given up music to drive a limo for a living. From that night onwards Curtis became my personal driver, picking me up and running me around whenever I was in town.

One night I was watching Channel E, a horrible, disgusting cable channel that had nude chat-show hosts and adverts for hookers. Suddenly my red limo appeared on the screen and out stepped Curtis with two escort girls. I was in shock. I'd been using him for a year, and all the time he had been running hookers around New York. He was very open about it, and told me he did it for the extra money. Thank God Frizzby never knew, or she would never have set foot in his limo again. Despite her outrageous image, she was one of the straightest people I'd ever known.

One night a man brought a big frog into the club and sat it on the bar with a cigarette in its mouth. He was one of the 'connected' Italian boys with a warped sense of humour. He thought the whole thing was hilarious. Frizzby was heartbroken, of course. I didn't find it particularly funny either and so I asked him to take the cigarette out of its mouth. As he was leaving, Frizzby pleaded with me to take the frog away from him. The Italian was cool: 'Hey, you want the frog, you have it.' Frizzby and I were going out that night, so the last thing we needed was a bloody great frog. She wanted to release it in Central Park, but we didn't have time. Curtis wasn't around that night so I had to pay another limo driver $100 to take the frog into Central Park and put it into the pond. Frizzby insisted on taking the guy's phone number. Two hours later she called him on his mobile to check he'd taken the frog. 'Yes, ma'am, I took the frog. I parked the car and walked to the pond and let him go.' I'd been in New York a lot longer than Frizzby, and I didn't know one limo driver who would go to Central Park, walk to the pond and release a frog after taking a $100 cash advance. I thought it wise not to tell Frizzby just how far away the car park was from the pond.

Those early days of commuting to New York were heady ones. American Airlines would upgrade me to first class flying to America and British Airways would upgrade me to Concorde flying back from New York. I always found it bizarre that it was never the other way round: I was never upgraded to Concorde flying to America, only on my return. Concorde reminded me of my old E-type, incredibly sleek with just enough room, and you knew you were going fast. I was having dinner with stars on both sides of the Atlantic. I'll never forget Robert De Niro coming into the New York club one night and taking a shine to my daughter, Karen. He asked her to dance and wanted a date. She was so faithful to Mark she didn't give him a second look. I thought my daughter was lily-white until she told me she'd spent a weekend in Seattle with the singer Paul Young. When she found out Mark was seeing other girls, Karen started seeing my designer, Paul Roberts, behind his back. Mark and Karen had been running the New York club for about a year when I got a call from Mark.

'Peter, she's thrown me out.'

'What do you mean?'

'We're over. It's finished.'

'What happened?'

'One of her friends has told her about all the different girls I've slept with.'

'Is it true?'

'Some of it is.'

'Well, apologise to her.'

'I've tried that.'

'Take her some flowers.'

'I've tried that too. She won't talk to me. I'm out, and I don't know what to do.'

'Look, let me talk to Karen.'

I called Karen to see what was going on.

'Daddy, I love you. Please don't get involved. It's over. End of story.'

Karen has always been a soft, beautiful lady. I'd never seen this side to her. It had to be Coral's influence. Coral had put up with me, but Karen had witnessed it all. She'd seen all the arguments about my unfaithfulness and knew how unhappy it had made Coral. She could accept it in her daddy, but, by God, her own man could never be unfaithful. I knew that Mark was a womaniser, but I could hardly take the moral high ground with him. I didn't want to tell Karen because she loved him: they were engaged to be married. Rightly or wrongly, I thought it should be Karen's choice. He was a good-looking guy and she's a beautiful woman, and it was their lives.

I was fascinated by how strong she was. It really was over for her. Mark would never get another chance. In his own words, he had 'screwed up'. I knew he would have to leave New York. I mean no disrespect to Mark, but Karen was my daughter and it was her club. She had to come first. Mark came back to London. Despite what had happened I really liked him. He came back to work for me in promotions. He's told me since that he never recovered. He was in love with her, but he made the mistake of thinking that she would take from him what she'd grown to accept in me.

Within a year of splitting up with Mark, Karen came to see me about taking time off. She and Paul Roberts had planned to go backpacking around Asia. She was definitely my daughter. Her Asia was my Doncaster: she was looking for adventure. I sat her down to give her a piece of my wisdom. I told her the trip would be a big point in her life and that if she wasn't sure about Paul, the next guy who came along would be really pissed off that she'd done something so wonderful with her ex. Karen paused for a few seconds. 'Hard fucking cheese on him.'

Karen was much tougher than I thought. She was brilliant for the New York club. She could deal with everyone, even the weird and wonderful types. I remember two slick-looking Italians coming in one night with an older guy with white hair.

They looked an interesting trio so I went over and introduced myself. The older guy wasn't drinking, but the two good-looking Italians were downing champagne by the bottle. They insisted on buying it for anybody who came near the bar, which was fine by me. I liked them both enormously and suggested they joined me for dinner the following night.

One of them looked around the bar before replying: 'Another time we could all be friends, but we won't be able to have dinner with you for at least eight years.' I thought they were going into the army. It turned out that they were two mafiosi on their last night of freedom. They were up in court the following day for racketeering and already knew what their sentence would be. The white-haired man was their lawyer. He'd put up $1 million bail, which was why he wasn't letting them out of his sight. I never saw them again, which was a pity.

Another evening two elegant guys came in with a beautiful young woman. I invited them to join me in a glass of champagne, which they accepted. I started chatting to the older guy, while the younger one, who had thinning hair, went off to dance. He said they were all from Monaco. As quick as a flash I remembered that a week before Prince Albert had been to the club, although I hadn't been there myself at the time. I said to the older guy: 'Ah, Monaco. You may know a good friend of mine, Prince Albert.'

'Oh really? Does he come to the club?'

'Yes he does, he was here only a week ago.'

'How well do you know him?'

'Very well. He'll often join me for a glass of champagne.'

'That's funny, because he's just taken his girlfriend for a dance.'

The sweat hit me. I'd just been caught lying through my back teeth.

'I'm sorry. I'm trying to be a good host and keep people happy,' was my feeble excuse. When Prince Albert came off the dance floor we had a laugh about it. They carried on drinking champagne all night, which, I hasten to add, I paid for all night.

New York was a fantastic success. I loved the fame of owning nightclubs on both sides of the Atlantic. It was 1988, and all three clubs were doing brilliantly. I had a wonderful, albeit complicated, sex life, but I wasn't complaining. I could leave both Coral and Frizzby behind in London and fly into New York and play with girls there. I used them both as protection. I didn't lie to the American girls. I was straight. I told them I had a wife and a regular girlfriend, so no one could say, 'You never told me you were married.'

What more could a man want? Well, for a start I wanted a nightclub where the sun didn't stop shining. London was cold and New York was muggy. I still had my apartment in Marbella, so I decided to look there first. If Barclays of Spain had lent me £1 million I would probably have opened Stringfellow's Marbella. But they turned me down, which meant I had to look elsewhere.

I thought about Miami. The last time I'd been there was with Frizzby before we opened New York. We met up with a very old friend of mine from Leeds called John Hawkins, who eventually became manager of Stringfellow's New York. He took Frizzby and me to a small bar where the girls danced naked on stage. John gave one of the girls $5 and she came over to our table and began dancing and taking off her clothes. Frizzby was so horrified that she got up and walked out. The outrageous Frizzby the public thought they knew and the Frizzby I really knew were two different people. She was not only incredibly straight, she was so prudish she couldn't stand the idea of a girl dancing topless on a table. It was a foretaste of what would eventually break up our relationship.

I went back to Miami with Frizzby to look for my sunshine club. It was a beautiful sunny day. Had the weather been crappy, I might never have set my heart on the place. This time we went to look at a club called Cats. Cats was very Latin, full of older men in open-necked shirts and gold chains. Frizzby literally stopped the traffic when she walked out of there. Whereas New York was super-cool, Miami was crazy. Dozens of flashy sportscars circled her outside the Mayfair Centre: Ferraris, Porsches, Maseratis, all driven by handsome young Latin Americans flashing their lights and hooting their horns. I loved it: this was the Miami I wanted to see. It had all the glamour of

Miami Vice and, just like on the television, the sun was shining.

Within a matter of weeks I was back again. This time I chatted to the owner of Cats. He wanted out. His club had lost its kudos and he didn't have the enthusiasm to relaunch it. I saw its potential straight away. If I knocked into the boutique beside it, I knew I'd have enough space to build a fantastic club. To make it even more attractive, the landlord wanted to give me $1 million for tenant improvements. I'd never had a landlord *give* me money before: the offer was too good to refuse. A smart New Yorker would have taken the $1 million, spent $500,000 refurbishing the club, and kept the other half. Peter Stringfellow took the $1 million and then spent another $2.5 million on rebuilding.

I never got the chance to discuss the deal with Brian Smith. He hadn't ever liked the idea of me being in America in the first place. The last time I spoke to him he gave me his second piece of advice: 'Peter, sell New York. If you can't sell it, give it away.'

I didn't take his advice, although I know now that he was a very wise man. Brian went on holiday shortly afterwards and while he was away he died of a massive heart attack. He had directed me through all my financial problems and had become a good friend. His death was a great personal loss and a great loss to the company. Along with all the staff and all his friends, I went to Brian's funeral. I've always found funerals strangely sexy. I know this sounds weird, but there is something sexual about opening up your emotions. Also, everyone wears black, and it's easy to imagine the girls in black stockings and suspenders under their funeral clothes. I bumped into an ex-employee in the church and we ended up going back to the church in Highgate and making love. I'd never thought of this girl in a sexual way before that day. I knew Brian wouldn't have minded. He was a friend, not a close relative, so the grief was different. Some years later, when my mother died, the funeral was another matter altogether for me, and sex was the last thing on my mind. Then the grief was overwhelming.

Cliff Silver took over from Brian Smith and he has been with me ever since. Cliff is a brilliant accountant, totally straight and happily married. I don't always discuss things with Cliff, as I hadn't done with Brian. When I decided to go ahead with Miami, I didn't discuss the deal with anyone.

While the club was being rebuilt, I became friendly with a guy called Mark Packer. He owned a successful Italian restaurant in New York called Canistells. It was so popular you had to give the maitre d' at least $20 to stand a chance of getting a table. He'd just opened Canistells in Miami and made my friend John Hawkins the manager. Mark kept telling me how wonderfully successful his new restaurant was, but the place was never full. The food was good, but there was never anyone there to eat it. In the end Mark got so depressed that he stopped going in himself.

Before Stringfellow's Miami opened, Canistells Miami closed. It should have been a warning, but I didn't take any notice of the signals. As far as I was concerned, my new club was going to be a brilliant success. Every time I flew into Miami, I stayed at the best hotel and hired the same flashy sports car, an Excalibur, a 1930s reproduction of a Jaguar SS100. I hired the car so often that everyone thought it was mine.

The Mayor of Miami, Xavier Sourez, became a friend during the building of the club. When Xavier and his wife, Rita, came to London for a holiday I had arranged for them to meet the Mayor of Westminster at Stringfellow's. The evening went very well and did wonders for my friendship with Xavier. It helped me ask a favour of him before my club opened in his city. Every weekend about fifteen Miami policemen would direct traffic around Coconut Grove, the address of Stringfellow's Miami. I asked Xavier if he could dismiss the police for a weekend to see what would happen to the traffic. To everybody's surprise it worked wonders and Xavier gave me a certificate to say that I had the keys to the city.

Not long afterwards the Queen was visiting Miami, and Xavier insisted that I was present in the line-up of dignitaries. 'Peter, I know she'd feel more at home if you were there.' I had to go along with that because everybody in America thought I was a personal friend of the royal family. On the day she arrived I stood in line thinking, 'Oh my God.' To my astonishment, she came down the line-up and said, 'Oh Peter, that's where you are.'

Of course, Xavier had pointed me out long before she got to me and the Queen, being the super-nice person she is, carried it off wonderfully. I briefly spoke to her and though I say it myself, did a wonderful PR job for Miami. The incident gave me immense standing in the city, and Xavier and I became lifelong friends.

Just before Miami opened in spring 1989, I took Coral to Barbados for a make-or-break holiday. We had a fantastic time for ten days, but every day, twice a day, I'd leave the room and call Frizzby. I'd sent her to Tenerife to cheer her up, but she was having a miserable time. By the end of the holiday my phone bill was £1,400, and I paid it very quietly.

Coral thought we'd made it up in Barbados, but I knew the marriage was over. Yes, we did have a wonderful time, but the die was cast. Many years later I would take Frizzby to Barbados for a make-or-break holiday while I knew that my girlfriend Christine was on the next island having a similar holiday with her boyfriend. It was the last holiday I took with Frizzby. Even more recently, I took Christine to Barbados on holiday, and that, too, proved to be our last. I'm not saying that Barbados is jinxed, but the island has certainly marked the downfall of all my major relationships. I know the Barbados Tourist Board hate me telling this story, but it's the truth.

I knew it was only a matter of time before Coral and I divorced. Our final fight came shortly after the Barbados trip. Coral and I had been fighting since 1963. We'd loved a lot, played a lot and fought a lot, and by 1989 I was exhausted. I can't even remember what our last fight was about, only that it was our last. It started in the usual way, with accusations, then shouting, then Coral slapping me, then both of us wrestling on the floor. Then something inside me just snapped. I let go, and I said, 'That's it. We've stopped. We're finished. No more. It's over.' I opened my eyes to see Coral standing over my head with a very large plant pot in her arms. I remember looking up and thinking, 'So it's come to this.' In my bravado I said, 'Go on, throw it.' She did. With a lightning reflex, I brought up my leg and my arm just in time to protect my head. Coral claims that she never aimed at my head, but my face and hair were covered in bits of plant pot and aspidistra, so if she didn't, she was pretty damn close.

I knew that if we didn't part then, we'd end up killing each other. So I left that night and checked into the Waldorf Hotel. The following night I moved to the Savoy. I remember feeling sad, but wonderfully free. When I went back to pack my stuff, Coral wanted to talk things through. She was even prepared to forgive me over Frizzby. I loved Coral, but I was no longer in love with her. When you're in love, you can take the fights; when love goes and all you're left with is the fighting, it's time to say goodbye. I didn't leave Coral to live with Frizzby, I left to start a new life on my own. The feeling of freedom was exhilarating. I had Frizzby in London and America as my playground.

When Coral had stopped being sad and angry, she got legal. Within weeks I called into the solicitor's office to negotiate a settlement. I remember sitting opposite the lawyer at a big round table. He said, 'Well, Mr Stringfellow, your wife wants £2 million in cash, or half the company.' I looked at this man for a second before I realised he was *my* solicitor. I said, 'Excuse me, whose fucking side are you on?'

Coral wanted £250,000 straight away and for us to negotiate her share settlement. As the solicitor was explaining all this, I went into a reverie. I had a vision of Coral and me at company directors' meetings. No way; no way on earth could Coral be a major shareholder. I had to pay her off. But I didn't have any cash. On paper, I was a multi-multi-millionaire. If my company had gone plc I could have capitalised between £10 and £20 million, but it was out of the question. I knew I couldn't operate with a board of directors breathing down my neck. The only answer was to sell the Hippodrome.

I still needed another $1 million to finish Miami. I'd cash-flowed Stringfellow's and the Hippodrome to pay the contractors, and New York was still in debt. The Hippodrome was showing a pre-tax profit of £1.2 million, which was a staggering amount of money, considering the generous way I run my clubs.

Mecca were the first people to call me. I spoke to a Tony Marshall, who was working with Mike Guthrie, the managing director of Mecca. Mike was a good friend of mine, so he didn't want to negotiate with me himself. I told Tony I wanted £7 million for the Hippodrome. After a lengthy meeting Tony said, 'We'll pay £6.3 million, and no more.' I flew back to Miami to think about their offer. It wasn't enough.

Around this time I was approached by a real-estate agent called Peter Dunne. He flew to Miami from Los Angeles to talk to me about opening a club there. He said his company had watched my progress from London to New York and were interested in having a Stringfellow's in Beverly Hills. Despite my own disappointing experience of the place, the magic words 'Beverly Hills' were still the epitome of glamour. I flew to LA to look at the site. He showed me the plans for a magnificent shopping mall opposite the Beverly Wilshire Hotel. The architect had designed the mall in the style of a typical European street. In the middle was a beautiful patio, which was attached to the unit designated for a nightclub. Underneath the mall was the car park. It was pure LA, and it was perfect. Peter Dunne said the landlord would give me $1 million for tenant improvements. It sounded too good to be true. They were one year away from finishing the project, which I knew would give me ample time to get Miami up and running first. I flew back to Miami very happy.

It was only a matter of days before I got a telephone call from European Leisure wanting to know if I'd done a deal with Mecca for the Hippodrome. The voice on the end of the phone said, 'I believe you know our managing director, George Hendry.' I certainly did know George. He'd bought the Penthouse from me in 1970, and given me my first profit on a club. My message to George was this: 'I have only one price. It's £7 million. You've got twenty-four hours, or I'm selling to Mecca.'

An hour later I got a call from European Leisure. They wanted to do a deal with me. I flew back to London to meet George Hendry and his chairman, Michael Ward. I was impressed with Michael. He'd launched European Leisure to take on Mecca. Instead of building nightclubs, he'd raised £70 million from the City to buy up successful businesses from entrepreneurs like me. They wanted the Hippodrome as their flagship. They introduced me to Michael Quaglini, one of their satisfied customers. Michael had sold his Newcastle nightclubs to European Leisure and had taken part of his payment in shares. The company's shares were currently worth 90p and were expected to rise to £2, probably more, after they'd bought the Hippodrome. But shares didn't interest me: I wanted the cash. I couldn't see Coral taking shares, and neither did I want her to have any. Michael Ward said he'd heard enough. He shook my hand and agreed to pay me the £7 million. The last person to have shaken my hand on a deal was Eric Morley, when he bought Cinderella's–Rockafella's. Eric hadn't reneged, and I assumed that Michael Ward, too, would be a man of his word.

I went back to the Hippodrome to tidy up the office. News travels fast in the City, and I'd only been there a couple of hours when Tony Marshall from Mecca called. He said they'd heard I was doing a deal with European Leisure and told me that Michael Guthrie was on his way to see me. The first thing Michael said was, 'Have you signed?' I told him they'd agreed to pay £7 million.

'I thought we had a deal.'

'No, Michael. You passed me over to your financial guy, who was as hard as nails.'

'OK, what will it take? We don't want European Leisure to have the Hippodrome.'

'It's too late. The deal is done.'

'You must have a price, Peter. We'll go to £7.5 million.'

I'd expected him to top the price by £250,000. Half a million was an awful lot of money. I was tempted, but two things were holding me back: firstly, I'm not a greedy man, and secondly, I'd already shaken hands on the deal.

'You may have shaken hands, but it cannot mean the same to Michael Ward. You think you've done a deal, but Michael has to ask his shareholders.'

'We shook hands. That means the deal is done.'

'Don't be naïve, Peter.'

I rang Michael Ward and asked him: 'When we shook hands, was that a deal?'

'Absolutely.'

'So what's this I hear about needing the shareholders' agreement?'

'I checked with the shareholders before I made you the offer.'

A handshake is a handshake. Eric Morley could easily have gone back on his word, but he didn't, and I was not about to break my gentlemen's agreement with European Leisure. Ironically, the company did eventually crash spectacularly, but when they handed me their cheque for £7 million, there was no sign of a recession and they were one of the top leisure companies in Britain.

Out of the £7 million, I took £2 million, I gave Coral £1.1 million, the taxman took £800,000 and the rest went back into my company. I needed money to finish Miami and money to build LA, so it wasn't going to be in the bank for very long.

I never regretted giving Coral one penny of her settlement. The divorce hurt her deeply. She'd supported me every step of the way, and she deserved the money. Coral eventually went off to America and met a wonderful new husband. She is happily married and settled in her own ranch in South Carolina. We have remained friends to this day.

But I was in no hurry to marry again. I think it shocked Frizzby that I didn't move in with her when Coral and I divorced. I was enjoying the freedom too much. When I flew into London I stayed at my own apartment in the Savoy. Up until leaving Coral, I'd never washed a single dish or cooked a meal in my life. Now I had the entire staff of the Savoy looking after me.

When Miami finally opened, it was, as I'd hoped, a brilliant success. It gave me yet another playground. I had London, New York, Miami and as many women as I wanted. What more could one man possibly want – apart from a boat and a fabulous apartment?

I put $100,000 deposit on an apartment overlooking the Biscayne Bay. I bought myself a Jeep and a boat. I had everything any man could possibly wish for. I looked around one day and thought, 'How can it get better than this?' I believed it would go on getting better. I thought Stringfellow's LA would be the icing on top of my already delicious cake.

I'd spent my life looking for glamour, and Miami was pure glamour. I loved the Latin American people – their culture, their lifestyle, everything about them. My club was the toast of the town. I was too wrapped up in the success of it all to notice a very important omen. As I opened, the television programme *Miami Vice* was holding its wrap party to mark the end of the final series. Don Johnson came into the club one night to tell me about a new restaurant he was going to open in Miami. I said, 'I hope we're not going to be in competition.' Don and his wife Melanie Griffith were two lovely people, and I didn't want us to be rivals. 'Don't worry,' he said. I didn't worry for very long. The following week someone shot Don's chef. It was something to do with a waitress's husband who had slept with another waitress, and it was all very bizarre.

Miami was full of rich, glamorous, beautiful people and a smattering of racists. One day a non-Latin American asked me to swear that I would never let a Cuban into the club. Of course I ignored him. As usual, everyone was welcome.

I'd heard all sorts of stories about Miami, particularly tales about how the city had been built on drugs money. It did seem odd that there were so many banks in such a small place, but then there were an awful lot of rich people in Miami. I was probably the only person in the city who couldn't tell the difference between a kilo of cocaine and a packet of washing powder. It sounds ludicrous, I know, but if it hadn't been for a deserted island and a speedboat full of bullet holes, I'd still be none the wiser. I was about to star in *Miami Vice* myself, but this time the script was for real.

20

MOON OVER MIAMI

I lost count of how many times I grounded my boat. Suffice it to say I had three new propellers in the first month. Only a matter of days after I'd bought it, Frizzby and I decided to sail to Bimini Island in the Bahamas. I'd had one lesson in navigation and could just about read a map, but I knew nothing about the sea currents around the Bermuda Triangle. We set off with me at the helm and Frizzby down below packing away our provisions. I was doing about 20 knots, which was fine for the calm waters around Florida Keys. But I didn't know that the Florida current hits the Atlantic current just off the coast of Miami. Experienced sailors approach the Atlantic waters with caution. Brand-new Peter Stringfellow hit them at 20 knots. *Bang!* The boat hit a 6ft wave and our heavenly cruise turned into the boat trip from hell. We were pitching and tossing and rolling and listing. It took me twenty minutes to regain control. When the boat finally settled down, I remembered Frizzby. She emerged from the galley covered in orange juice and food. 'What the fuck are you doing?' she shouted. I was in shock. It was the first time I'd heard Frizzby swear.

The calm didn't last long. I could see a rain cloud in the distance. It was like a cartoon version of a rain cloud, and we were heading towards it. I was too inexperienced to change course, so Frizzby and I braced ourselves and prepared for the worst.

Two and a half hours later, Frizzby's pink tresses looked like a saggy bag of candy floss and I'd aged about twenty years. But we were both alive, which was the main thing. In the distance I could see an island, which I assumed was Bimini. In fact we'd missed the Bimini Islands by thirty miles, and the little speck in the distance was one of the Cat Key islands. Thank God we made it to Cat Key, because the next island was seventy miles away.

In my excitement, I approached Cat Key too fast and managed to damage the propeller. We limped into James Port and moored the boat. I put on my goggles and dived down to investigate. Both the propeller and the shaft were bent. I asked in the nearest bar if there was someone around who knew about boats.

'Man, you've come to the right place,' said the barman. 'My cousin knows everything about boats.' An hour later his cousin turned up. He said he had a Trojan like mine himself and could fix my boat in the morning.

The next day we waited at the bar for the cousin. When he finally showed up he had the crappiest pair of goggles I'd ever seen and an air tank that looked like a relic from the First World War. My heart sank when he asked for a hammer. He disappeared under the water with it and spent the next five minutes bashing the propeller shaft. He popped out the water with a smile on his face. 'Man, your boat's all straight.'

I shook his hand and gave him his $150 fee for fixing it. He'd fixed it all right – fixed it so that the damned thing wouldn't sail. However, I didn't realise this until the following morning, when Frizzby and I tried to sail back to Miami. The boat was making so much noise that I went back to the bar to look for the cousin. Of course, he'd left the island. I telephoned my boatman in Miami, who had to come out and tow us back to the mainland. The whole saga took five days.

The next time Frizzby and I went sailing, I made sure I had a gizmo on board that would plot the course. We set sail to Cat Key, but ended up stopping on a tiny little island halfway between there and Bimini. In fact it was more of a knoll than an island: it had no name and only one beach. We decided to have our lunch on the deserted sand, so we anchored the boat and took the dinghy ashore. It would have been idyllic, except that the beach was covered in plastic bottles and rubbish. I hate that.

There was no way I could eat my lunch amid all this crap. So while Frizzby organised the food, I went back to the boat for some black plastic bags. Frizzby wasn't surprised. She knew I hated litter – I'd already cleaned up half of Biscayne Bay. I started at the sea and worked my way up the beach towards a row of bushes. When I reached the top, I could see two packets of what looked like washing powder under the bushes. It was inside some heavy, see-through plastic which had been sealed at the ends. I put these bags with the rest of the rubbish and went back to Frizzby, feeling really proud of myself. I'd cleaned up the entire beach and filled three black binbags. I said, 'Frizzby, can you believe that someone would dump packets of washing powder on a beach?'

Frizzby got the packets out of the bag. 'Peter, this is cocaine.'

'Oh, my God.'

Frizzby wanted to know what we were going to do with it.

'Throw it away.'

'Throw it *away*? Do you know how much it must be *worth*?'

Each of the bags was very heavy and the size of a box of washing powder. They probably weighed about three kilos each. I've no idea what six kilos of cocaine is worth, but it had to be multi-thousands. I had two choices: either I handed it in to the police, or I threw it away. It wasn't a good idea to give it to the police, because I owned a nightclub in Miami. Whether I was innocent or not, the newspapers would certainly have concocted some story about a club boss and cocaine for the headlines. I decided to dump the bags in the marina rubbish bins at Cat Key.

After we'd got rid of the drugs, we sailed north of Cat Key and found a little cove called Silver Dollar Bay. I could see an upturned speedboat on the beach, so we decided we'd stop there and have our lunch in its shade. I thought the boat was an old wreck until we got closer – then we saw that the entire hull was riddled with bullet holes. I'd seen enough episodes of *Miami Vice* to know that the bags of cocaine and the bullet-riddled boat probably went together. Frizzby and I made a quick exit and finally ate lunch on the boat instead.

In spite of these alarming episodes, for the first time in my life I'd found a hobby other than nightclubs. Frizzby and I went everywhere together on the boat. If there was a time I seriously thought about marrying her, it was during our sailing days around Miami. The only problem was the timing. I knew LA was coming up and I didn't have time to think about marriage.

Like all American cities, Miami had its stars. By 1989 I'd met most of the big-name celebrities, but occasionally someone new would walk in and I'd get a kick out of seeing them. One night I was in the club with a good friend of mine, Carlos Kernoffler. He was the Dudley Moore of Miami: small and sexy. Carlos and I were having a drink when my manager came over and told us that John Travolta had just come in. At that time he wasn't a big name – he had not yet made his comeback – but to me he was fascinating. I brought him into the champagne bar and introduced myself. He congratulated me on the club and we started talking about his latest film. After we'd had a few drinks I asked him if he'd mind the club's photographer taking a picture of him on the dance floor. John went cold. 'I haven't danced in a disco for ten years.'

I was aghast. John Travolta was Mr Disco himself.

'Look, Peter, I want to forget *Saturday Night Fever* and *Grease* – in fact that whole period of my life.'

'I don't understand, John – it was a wonderful period.'

'Not for me. It ruined my life.'

For the next twenty minutes, I tried to explain to John the importance of that period. I told him he had created an industry, which he had. The seventies *were Saturday Night Fever* and *Grease*. How could I forget the impact on my crowd at the Millionaire? Those two films transformed the image of night-clubs throughout the world. He said he'd never realised that before. He'd spent the last ten years trying to forget those characters. I was amazed that he thought that way.

Robin Gibb from the Bee Gees felt exactly the same. I remember him coming into Stringfellow's one night and asking me if I would stop the DJ playing 'Stayin' Alive'. I said, 'Are you crazy? It's a classic record of all time.' We never hear Paul McCartney apologising for 'She Loves You' or 'Yesterday'. It is important to love your past and go forward.

John and I became friends after that. Later on he did take a girl on to the dance floor and he did his *Saturday Night Fever* number, finger in the air and everything. We had an absolute ball. I wasn't at all surprised when he became a massive star again in *Pulp Fiction*.

Stringfellow's Miami was a fantastic club. When I was there, I'd go sailing most days, then into the club at night. The boat was my escape from the world. It made a change from entertaining my friends in the nightclub. About six months after I opened Miami, I had a call from Jean Rook. Jean and I had become friends around the time of my divorce from Coral. I'd asked Jean if she would do a sympathetic piece with Coral to counteract the tiresome series of stories the *Sun* had been running, with headlines like 'MY MARRIAGE FROM HELL', and 'GO TO HELL, DARLING'. Jean did a brilliant article about Coral and me in the *Express*. It wasn't soft, but it was fair. From that day onwards, I had great respect for her as a journalist.

Jean had phoned to tell me that her son and his friend were on holiday from Eton and thinking of touring America. Could I give them a job? Sure, I said. I'd be able to find them something. I ended up employing them as busboys. I think they lasted two nights. I suggested that Jean should fly over with them and take a holiday. But she arrived in Miami very ill. She knew that she was dying of cancer, but she was very brave and kept it to herself. Everyone thought she had 'flu because she kept sneezing.

I threw a dinner party for Jean which coincided with a party I'd already organised for the officers of HMS *Ark Royal*. She was in her element, and queen for the night. I took them all sailing the next day. While the boys and I went diving for lobsters, Jean stayed on the boat and read. We anchored in Biscayne Bay and began diving down, no deeper than 10ft. After about an hour, we eventually found a lobster. All three of us were like a bunch of girls trying to get hold of this thing. When I finally got it in my hand, I turned round to get Jean's attention, but I couldn't see the boat. Suddenly I realised that my 33ft dream boat was a mere speck in the distance: Jean had dozed off, unaware that the boat was dragging its anchor out to sea. We had no choice but to set off, swimming with the tide. I can swim far enough to save my life, and I've proved it on a couple of occasions. This was one of them. Halfway towards the boat, we were all totally exhausted. All three of us were screaming for Jean's attention. Eventually she woke up, realised what had happened and managed to throw us a rope. We all climbed aboard. Jean never knew how close she came to being rescued by the coastguard – never mind us.

In a matter of two years, three of my friends died from cancer: Jean Rook, Bernie Winters and the television producer Alan Walsh. Bernie's death was a real shock. He was planning to throw a big sixtieth birthday party. When I got a message from his wife, Ziggy, to say that Bernie wasn't feeling too good and they'd have to cancel it, I knew immediately that it was serious. Within a matter of months he was dead. Bernie once gave me some advice which I didn't take. He told me not to leave Coral. He said he'd once nearly left Ziggy. He was halfway up the motorway with his suitcase when he thought, 'What the fuck am I doing?' He turned the car round, went back to her and they stayed together until he died. Bernie tried very hard to talk me out of splitting up with Coral, but in the end Bernie and I were very different people with different lifestyles.

I was totally peripatetic throughout the eighties. I was never in any one place for more than two weeks at a time. I would fly to New York from London, spend two days there, then fly to Miami for a fortnight before returning to London. In an attempt to curb my expenses, I moved out of the Savoy after nine months. I loved it, but it was costing a fortune. Karen was living in New York, so I moved into her flat in Highgate. It was a fantastic place in an old converted church. It gave me a wild freedom. I no longer had to play around in the back of cars, emergency exits and hotel rooms: I had my own apartment in London. Frizzby had her own flat, for which I was happy to pay the rent. I liked us having our own places.

I'd been at Highgate about a month when Frizzby called one day.

'Can I come over?'

'Sure.'

She turned up with two suitcases. Her roof had collapsed on

to her bed and she didn't have anywhere to live. We both knew what this meant. She stood on the doorstep of the church and said, 'Well, make your mind up.'

It wasn't what I wanted, but I thought we'd give it a try. Much to my surprise, I enjoyed it. Frizzby was a real home-maker. She redesigned the church and was incredibly easy to live with. Once again I thought about marrying her, but I didn't. Living with Frizzby meant I couldn't play in London any more. At the age of fifty I had to go back to playing in cars. I had a driver called Tony, my London Curtis – except that his car was an old stretch Ford, not a limousine. Things happened in his car that made the Kama Sutra look like a cartoon. Tony was incredibly loyal. He never sold any stories about me and girls, not even after he left.

With Frizzby in the flat I had to be careful about where I played. One day an executive from the *Sunday Mirror* came to see me. He said one of my girlfriends had given the paper a good story about me and they wanted my version. There was no way I was going to give them that: it would have hurt me, but I knew it would have hurt Frizzby even more. The *Sunday Mirror* wouldn't drop the story, but I asked them for a favour: instead of running it immediately, would they wait one week? The executive agreed to put it off until the following Sunday. I called Frizzby and told her we were going away. I rented a cottage on a remote island in the Carribean. It had no television, no telephone and no fax – a perfect hideaway.

A couple of days into the holiday Frizzby disappeared. I thought she'd gone off to feed some wild cats we'd found, but I discovered later that she'd been to the island's only restaurant and called her friend in London. No wonder she'd been gone such a long time: her friend had read her the whole story. From that moment onwards the holiday became difficult. My philosophy has always been to lie, lie and lie again. I always lied to Coral, even in the face of incriminating evidence, like the time she found the polaroid picture of my penis. My 'baby, it has nothing to do with me' line wasn't going to work this time: the kiss-and-tell girl had described the church flat in Highgate and said that I'd made her wear a tutu which was hanging at the bottom of the bed.

The pink tutu was one of my sexual fantasies. I made my

waitresses wear them when I opened Stringfellow's and have only recently changed the colour from pink to white. Frizzby would occasionally put on the tutu for me as part of our love-making. The tutu revelation hurt Frizzby more than any other part of the story. The first thing she did when we got back to London was to burn the bloody thing. I very nearly had to change the waitresses' uniforms altogether.

Frizzby and I got over that particular drama and once again I thought about marrying her. I didn't, because in truth, I didn't want to get married. Frizzby and I had a great time. We had a kind of marriage, but we didn't have the bits of paper. She was still in her twenties and didn't want to start a family, so there was no urgency. I could play around in London, albeit discreetly, and I had a free rein in New York and Miami. I knew my business was worth multi-millions on paper, even though it carried a debt factor, like all companies. I was paying myself £200,000 a year plus whatever I needed. While another company director would have to spend extravagantly on girls, I owned all the extravagances already and had as many girls as I wanted. And I had a boat. OK, it wasn't a 60ft yacht, but it was still impressive. I could jump on a plane and go anywhere in the world I wanted.

Knowing I can do that is still very important to me. I would be incredibly miserable if that option were taken away. Money does make you happy: financial security gives you confidence and adds greatly to your life. It's a load of bollocks that money can't buy happiness. Yes, if you are a miserable sod, money will never make you happy: it can't turn a miserable personality into a happy one.

I had every reason to be happy. Miami was hugely successful. Our Tuesday nights became legendary. People would travel fifty miles to have dinner and to drink at the club. The place was filled with more beautiful girls than I'd ever seen in a nightclub. It was just a pity I couldn't be there all the time. But wherever I was staying, my managers knew they could always contact me.

One Tuesday night I was asleep at the church flat in Highgate when John Hawkins called me. After Canistells had closed, I'd given him a job as my manager in Miami. It was 11p.m. in

Miami and 4a.m. in London. At 11p.m. on a Tuesday night in Miami there was always a queue outside and the place would be packed. We'd have to wait for people to come out before letting more in.

'Peter, I've got the FBI outside.'

'So? What do they want?'

'They want to arrest two drug dealers they've had under surveillance.'

'What's the problem?'

'There are six of them out there and they've all got guns.'

The guns were a problem. I'd been in America long enough to know how quickly people took their guns out. I asked John to put the senior FBI guy on the phone. He spoke just like an FBI agent. 'Yes, sir. It's very serious.'

'Can't you just wait until they come out?'

'No, sir. They're armed. They're dangerous and we want to apprehend them now.'

I knew they'd fly in there, scare the shit out of everybody and cause a scene.

'I'm sorry, I can't allow you in my club with your guns.'

'Sir, can I remind you that we are agents of the Federal Bureau of Investigation. We can close your club down tonight, with or without your permission.'

'OK. Why not put two guys inside to watch them, then make the arrests outside?'

I'd seen *Miami Vice*. I knew how to organise the FBI.

'Yes, sir, that's exactly what we intended to do.'

John got back on the phone.

'Peter, I don't feel good about this.'

He hung up and called me back ten minutes later. Apparently, all six FBI agents had run up the stairs into the disco. They'd walked into the champagne area, up to two of the best looking guys in the whole club, who were sitting with four gorgeous girls, and put guns to their heads. John knew these guys by reputation. They were both Colombian drug dealers who drank champagne by the bucketload. They turned over the table and started fighting the FBI, a shot was fired in the ceiling and the drug dealers were handcuffed and dragged downstairs. As John was describing the scene I thought, 'That's it, I'm ruined.'

'So what happened next, John?'

'Well, everyone started dancing again.'

It meant nothing to the Miami crowd. This was their kind of cabaret.

'Did they pay their bill?'

'Are you crazy?'

The bill came to $1,500, which we sent to the FBI. They never paid it, and I never saw the two Colombians again. If anything, the drama added to the club's reputation as a hip and happening place.

When I couldn't sort out a problem on the telephone I'd jump on a plane. My suitcase was always under my bed, half packed. I perfected the art of choosing and packing six outfits in ten minutes. The airlines knew me, so there was never a problem getting on a flight. The jet-lag was something I learned to live with. I was constantly jet-lagged for eight years, because I was never anywhere for longer than two weeks. When I think back to all those years spent at airports, on planes and in limousines I wonder why I did it. Anyone who travels for a living will know the feeling. I remember being happy at the time, but there is no way on earth I would do it now. I don't deny that I had a fantastic time. I loved the rush of warm air every time I stepped off the plane in Miami. It was a very sexual experience. Swimming pools, palm trees, champagne, beautiful girls, status – I had it all. It was better than being a rock star. I'd started in a church hall, so everything came gradually to me – I didn't wake up one day and think, 'Wow!' I've grown with my success. I took it one step at a time. I've never needed drugs to handle the pressure, because I grew with it.

A rock star has to deal with screaming fans. If he's successful he can't sit in a restaurant or go shopping without being mobbed. If he's not being mobbed, he doesn't feel successful. I've never had to cope with that Catch 22. Only a handful of rock stars can manage their fame. Rod Stewart and Cliff Richard both handle their stardom in their different ways, and it works for them. I've never felt the need to be self-deprecating about my success. I didn't win the lottery or wake up to find I had a hit record: it's been hard work. I've given my whole life to my work, because I love what I do.

Not everyone would like my life. On the outside it looks fun, and it is, but there is a price to be paid. The people I've brought in along the way have had to pay it, too, but I don't think any of them would say that it was a bad day when they met Peter Stringfellow. I've changed a lot of people's lives. I know that I enriched Frizzby's life, and I took Coral on a wonderful journey for twenty years. I love the adventure of life. I got the same buzz in my youth from jumping on my rickety old bicycle and cycling to Doncaster railway station as I did later from jumping on a plane to Miami. I loved the journey and the glamour of seeing the trains with names. I've been hung up on glamour all my life. As a kid I always wanted the Queen to wear her crown. I would be really disappointed if I saw a picture of her in a two-piece suit and headscarf. Even now, I get a real thrill from seeing her dressed up for state occasions. Then, damn it, she goes and puts her glasses on.

Miami was the epitome of glamour and the pinnacle of my success. I didn't sit back and think, 'I've made it.' I sat back and thought, 'How can I make it better?' It's only with hindsight that I know that the glamour peaked in Miami. Even when I had everything any man could ever want, I still wanted LA.

Nothing could be more glamorous than Beverly Hills. It was Hollywood, home of the stars and the centre of the movie universe. Peter Dunne called me at a perfect time. Miami had been open one year, and I was ready to move on. If he had suggested Chicago, I would have shaken my head; if he'd said Dallas, I would have felt the same; maybe if he'd just said Los Angeles, I wouldn't have been swayed, but he used the magic words: Beverly Hills.

I remember taking Peter Dunne on the boat in Miami. He was negotiating on behalf of his landlord and we were about to do the deal. I'd seen all the plans. The disco was going to be above the restaurant; the restaurant would overlook Wilshire Boulevard and seat one hundred and fifty diners. We'd even have car parking underneath the club, with a guy to park the customers' cars. To top all that, we'd have the magic address 2 Rodeo Drive,

Beverly Hills. It was a world away from 24 Marshall Street, Pitsmoor. The rent was $750,000, which was an astronomical sum of money, but I thought I was going to make millions so it didn't seem that bad at the time. The landlord would put in $1 million for tenant improvements, and I would put in $2 million to build it. For $3 million I knew I could create the best nightclub LA had ever seen.

I was tremendously excited that day on the boat. We anchored in No Name Bay, which was a little place off Biscayne Bay, and opened a bottle of champagne. We couldn't have picked a more idyllic setting, surrounded by yachts and clear blue water. But Peter Dunne was in pensive mood.

'Are you sure you want to do this?'

His question surprised me.

'Are you sure you want to put all this at risk, Peter?' I knew what he meant.

To take on the lease for Beverly Hills meant not only New York and Miami on the line, but getting a guarantee from the parent company in London, which would put Stringfellow Enterprises on the line as well. But once again, it was simply a question of 'where do I sign?'. Only this time the consequences would be very different.

'I don't understand what you're saying,' I replied.

'What I'm saying, Peter, is something I shouldn't be saying. We've spent some time together and I like you. No club has ever lasted for any length of time in LA. It's beginning to get tough. I would hate it all to go wrong for you.'

Jesus Christ couldn't have talked me out of signing. I was determined to have Stringfellow's LA. But just before I signed I had a gut feeling that maybe, just maybe, it wasn't a good idea. The moment I put my signature on that contract, it was as if somebody had started switching off the lights, one by one.

Within days I had a message from New York. 'Peter, you're spending too much time in Miami. The club is beginning to suffer.' I didn't take it seriously. I thought I'd fly into New York, throw a few parties and everything would be OK. I'd just spent a fantastic New Year's Eve, 1989, in New York. We'd taken a fortune that night. I couldn't see the problem. I didn't realise that 1989 had been the last year of the eighties in more ways than one. In my experience, a new decade is always marked by a shift in attitudes. I saw it from the sixties to the seventies, the seventies to the eighties, and I was now about to experience the new mood of the nineties. After the crazy New Year's Eve, New York started to go flat. People began to talk about the recession, which was a word that belonged to the 1930s as far as I was concerned. Until 1990 I'd never heard it used outside an historical context.

While I was poring over my designs for LA, I had a nagging feeling about New York in the back of my mind. It wasn't recovering. I asked around and everyone said they were doing fantastic business. I wasn't spending much time in New York going to clubs and restaurants, so how was I to know they were all lying? It finally hit home when Marino, the maitre d' from Canistells, told me that the Four Seasons restaurant was in trouble.

'How's your business?'

'Terrible. I don't understand why.'

'It's terrible for me, too.'

If it was bad for Canistells and bad for the Four Seasons, something was seriously wrong. I phoned the other clubs and admitted my business was crap. They were all relieved. Business was bad everywhere. But I convinced myself that everything would soon be fine. After all, London and Miami were doing well, and I was halfway through building LA. There was no recession in LA. But the recession was like a disease.

I decided to hang on until 4 September, when Labor Day would herald the end of the summer and the beginning of party time. Labor Day came and went and didn't make the slightest difference to business. New York was heading for disaster. Then came the news I didn't need: Miami had caught the disease. People were no longer fighting to get into the champagne room and my legendary Tuesday nights were suffering.

It all seemed to happen in the blink of an eye. Suddenly I had a sick New York losing money and a sick Miami losing money. Thank God London was still thriving. Money was flowing from London into America, not only to support New York and

Miami, but to finish building LA. I convinced myself that LA would be wonderful. Beverly Hills was incredibly famous. Of course the club would make money.

I was about to learn one of the biggest lessons of my life. The Americans have a saying: people go to New York to work and LA to dream. By the time I'd made my dream come true, it was too late. I thought LA was where the stars went to party. If I'd known they partied on lettuce leaves and water, I could have saved myself $3.6 million and an awful lot of misery.

21

PRIVATE DANCER

The best news I had in 1990 was the birth of my grandson, on 7 June. Karen was due to have him by Caesarean, so she knew almost to the hour what time he would arrive. I flew into New York especially for the birth. As Karen and Paul Roberts weren't married they gave him the name Stringfellow, which pleased me enormously. What pleased me even more was Karen taking Taylor Stringfellow Roberts to the nightclub when he was just eleven days old.

Apart from the arrival of Taylor, 1990 was doomed from the start. By the autumn I knew I was in deep shit. London couldn't give me money to support New York and build LA at the same time. With a very heavy heart, I decided to go Chapter 11. Chapter 11 is an American regulation which protects against bankruptcy for a period of six months. It is designed to give a business time to sort out its debts and to stop anyone suing it.

I threw one last party before I closed the club. All the stars came in, along with Harry and Leona Helmsley. I'd read her story and admired the lady. She'd come from nowhere, fallen madly in love with Harry, and the pair of them owned Helmsley Palace, one of the biggest hotels in New York. Unfortunately, Leona was about to go to prison for evading $1 million in tax. I couldn't believe it. Multi-millions were being made from insider trading on Wall Street, and the authorities picked on her for a measly $1 million. When the couple arrived at the club, I saw for the first time the cruelty of New York. Stringfellow's was packed, but no one would go near the Helmsleys. They sat there alone, in abject misery, shunned by society. I went to sit with them and opened a bottle of champagne. I was making a statement. I'd never spoken to the Helmsleys before that night and I've never spoken to them since, but I knew how they were feeling. I was in the shit with New York myself and beginning to despise the place.

The fact that Americans speak the same language as the British doesn't make them any less foreign. It's always baffled me that we consider France, only twenty-odd miles away, to be more foreign than America, which is 3,000 miles away. If Americans spoke another language we might be more aware of their difference and understand them better. I've always been pro-America. The country fascinates me. It's not the strongest nation on earth for nothing: the majority of its citizens come from tough, immigrant stock, people who arrived with no money and had no welfare system to support them. Their toughness is genetic. They are hard people. Most of the New Yorkers at my last party had probably stayed at the Helmsleys' hotel and accepted their generosity, but now the couple were social outcasts. The society set would rather have sat with the head of the Mafia than with somebody accused of tax evasion, yet these same people will make heroes out of sports stars accused of murder and politicians accused of rape.

I was glad that it was my last party in New York. I was getting tired of it all. The problems, the jet-lag, the uncertainty – it was all getting too much. So New York had closed and Miami was on crutches. Geoffrey had moved to Miami to try to hold it all together. We were putting money into the club, but we couldn't pay the bills. I could have carried on supporting New York, but I chose Miami instead. It was still my playground, and I still had my toys there. I also had a lot of friends, like Baron Joseph de Bronski, known as Seppy. He'd produced the last film Errol Flynn made and lent his house for the filming of *Deep Throat* with Linda Lovelace. He used to throw parties swarming with beautiful models and always made me welcome. When I wasn't partying in Miami and LA, I was flying backwards and forwards to New York to try to salvage something from the mess.

I started to hate New York. From being its walking PR, I became its number one enemy. New York was like the girlfriend who'd asked me to leave. It had turned from a beautiful woman into a downmarket hooker. Not only that, my super, super friends had gone with it. I wrote a letter to Peter Catillano, my landlord, explaining the situation. I told him I would sell the club and pay him the rent I owed, but in the meantime I'd gone Chapter 11. Peter and I had become good friends, and we are still friends today, but by return of post he issued a writ. The recession had hit him, too. He subsequently went Chapter 11 himself on one of his companies, the one that owned the Stringfellow's building. I was his anchor tenant: without my rent, his firm was in jeopardy. Peter was a proud man, and he didn't tell me this until much later. At the time he was playing his own game with the real-estate agents. They were all in denial.

I gave up my apartment in New York and went back to staying in hotels when I flew into town. I turned on the television in a hotel room one night and saw the news that even Donald Trump was in big trouble. He was about to lose the biggest casino ever built, in Atlantic City. The interviewer asked Donald for his advice to the business world.

'Cash is king.'

I thought, fucking great, Donald. Who's going to give me cash for New York? I'd already dropped the price from $2 million to $600,000 and I still couldn't find a buyer. As I said before, businessmen can smell desperation like animals smell fear. Not only was I desperate, I was also fearful of the media. I didn't want the news about New York to come out before I'd opened LA.

Donald Trump was big news in America and there was no way he could hide his problems. Every time I turned on the television, he was on some channel or other, talking about his business troubles. I'd met him only once, in my club very briefly. We didn't have a chance to talk, and Donald and I never became friends. As his empire collapsed around him, Donald gave the waiting media his new dictum: 'Survive until 1995.'

His words were prophetic.

I decided to hang in there until the recession was over, convinced that LA would save me. One night I was sitting in my

Miami club feeling very depressed. Hardly anyone was in the place and I knew it couldn't survive for much longer. My friend Carlos asked if I wanted to go out for the night. I needed a very good reason to leave. A girl was a good reason, but not a guy.

'I'm depressed, Carlos. I don't want to go out.'

'I'll take you out.'

'No, Carlos.'

'Come on.'

'I can't.'

'You'll like it.'

'No, I won't.'

'Believe me.'

'OK, OK.'

Carlos had his limousine waiting outside. It was the longest limousine in Miami. Anywhere else in the world it would have damaged rather than enhanced his reputation, but not in Miami. Carlos was an American importer of Colombian coffee who'd spent the first three months of our friendship convincing me that he wasn't a drug dealer. He was in his thirties and still a child, so we got on like a house on fire. He said he was taking me to Solid Gold, a nightclub where the girls took their clothes off. I was embarrassed. I couldn't believe I was on my way to a strip joint. Things were going downhill fast. We jumped into the limo and he opened a bottle of champagne. Most people carry a map in their car; Carlos carried champagne.

We were greeted by the management at the door of the club.

'Welcome to Solid Gold, gentlemen.'

I peered inside, expecting to see a typical strip club. It was nothing like I'd imagined. It was more like an upmarket disco with a stage instead of a dance floor. On stage were two beautiful girls, one of them a stunning blonde, dancing in a very erotic way. You can tell more about a girl by watching her dance than you can by talking to her. By the time the girls had taken off their clothes and were dancing in their white panties, I'd fallen in love. Carlos was amused by my expression. I was definitely transfixed.

'I knew you'd like it, Peter.'

'Like it? I love it.'

The club was full of respectable-looking guys. After my experiences at the Penthouse I never let stag parties into any of my clubs. More than six guys together without women was always a recipe for trouble. But here were over two hundred guys without partners, and yet there wasn't a hint of rowdiness.

When the blonde girl came off stage I gave her my 'Hi, would you like to marry me?' look. It's a Stringfellow special I've perfected over the years. As she came closer she got more beautiful.

'Hi, you're Peter Stringfellow. I've been to your club on a Tuesday night.'

I don't know how she'd managed to get in without me seeing her. Well, I do I suppose – out of 700 girls in Miami, 500 would be drop-dead gorgeous. It was one of the reasons I liked the place so much.

'It's my first time here. Would you like to dance for me?'

'I'd love to dance for you. That will be $10.'

She could have said $500 and I wouldn't have flinched. Ten dollars was a bargain. She started dancing and taking off her clothes two feet away from me. It completely blew my mind. Being a typical English gentleman, I didn't want to take my eyes off her eyes, yet I was trying to take in her breasts, body and legs at the same time, which is very hard. One hour and many dances later, I'd given her $300. She kept asking me if I wanted her to dance and I kept forgetting what she looked like without her clothes on, so on and on it went.

I'd been told by Carlos that none of the dancers were allowed to give out their telephone numbers or go home with the clients. It didn't stop me asking, though.

'No, I'm sorry. That won't be possible.'

'Maybe I could have your telephone number.'

'I'm sorry, I can't give you that.'

'Maybe I can give you mine.'

She said she had a great memory and that she'd call me in the morning. It's now 1996 and I still haven't heard from her.

I've added that to the list of promises never to believe: 'The cheque's in the post,' 'I won't come in your mouth,' and when a topless dancer tells you she'll remember your phone number, you're more likely to find that the cheque's in the post.

But what I saw that night took my breath away. I'd also seen the answer to my problems in New York. I wanted to find out who owned Solid Gold, but the only name I could get was Michael.

Two days later I had a call from David de Falcom, who said he was interested in buying New York. David owned School Dinners in London, a restaurant that treated its diners like naughty schoolboys. It became notorious after Prince Andrew was photographed leaving the place. Everyone ate at long tables, served by waitresses in gymslips. Occasionally someone would be brought to the front of the restaurant and caned for talking.

'Surely you're not thinking of turning my club into a School Dinners?'

'No. Have you ever been to any of Michael J. Peters' topless clubs?'

I immediately made the connection. 'That's funny, I was in one two days ago.'

David made contact with Michael and we decided to take the idea to Peter Catillano. It was too hard to describe the concept exactly, so David and I presented Peter with a picture of a raunchy cabaret that might involve girls taking their clothes off. I knew Peter had political aspirations and wouldn't be sold on anything to do with nudity.

'How many girls will it involve?' he asked.

'Just one or two,' I said. In Miami I'd counted forty-five, and that was on a quiet night. David said he had a backer from Ecuador who was willing to buy the club. I had LA coming up and needed to free myself of New York, so I had no intention of getting involved. I was more than happy to sell it to him.

A week later David called to say his fabulous backer was going to give him $600,000 with a further $400,000 over two years. It sounded like a deal. The next day he called to say that the backer's sister had been kidnapped and he'd left for Ecuador. Twenty-four hours later, the backer himself had been kidnapped as well and there was no money and no deal.

I decided to approach Michael J. Peters myself. He'd heard about me and read in the papers that I was a friend of the Prince and Princess of Wales. That was an exaggeration, but what the hell, this was America. I'd taken along John Neilson Jr, who was now helping run Miami and was good with figures. The idea was for me to license the name Pure Platinum from Michael. In return he would supply the girls and take a percentage of the gross. My plan was to get New York open as a topless bar and then sell it. There was one small problem: I had no money.

I flew back to London to be told by my British bank that they didn't want another penny going to America. I could feel the net closing in. A couple of days later I received a letter from Ronnie Riley, who'd created a chain of fashion boutiques in Ireland for Next and had just sold it back to them for a substantial profit. He was interested in opening a Stringfellow's in Dublin. The letter intrigued me, first because it was well written and secondly because the timing was perfect. Ronnie flew over to meet me. He had a quiet seriousness about him, but a lovely Irish twinkle in his eyes. He sensed straight away that I was in trouble. 'You're coming over slightly apologetic. It sounds like you've got problems.'

I told Ronnie the truth. I needed a big investment. He said he knew a company that worked for the group U2. I wasn't a big fan of their music, but I knew they were one of the richest bands in the world. He arranged for me to fly to Dublin to meet his friends.

From the moment I stepped off the plane, I was treated like a superstar. I've always been reluctant to describe myself as a celebrity, but in Dublin that is exactly how they saw me. Ronnie and his friends showed me the premises they had chosen for the club. They wanted to franchise the name Stringfellow's and pay me a licensing fee and a percentage of the profits. My only involvement would be to fly over to Dublin occasionally. It sounded brilliant.

They took me out that night and introduced me to Dublin's nightlife. We were sitting in one club at 1.20a.m. when suddenly the manager shouted, 'Drinks down,' and switched all the lights on. Three policemen walked in, looked round the club, had a few words with the manager, then left.

'What was all that about?'

'That's a raid.'

'A raid?'

'Yeah. The licence stops at 1a.m.'

'What do we do now?'

'We carry on drinking.'

We moved on from there to Leeson Street. Every hotel in the street had a basement bar-cum-nightclub. They all served drinks until 6a.m., even though they only had wine-bar licences, which finished at 11p.m. We went into one of the basements and ordered drinks. After a couple of hours the music suddenly stopped, the lights went up and in walked the police. It was exactly the same routine. Everyone put down their glasses, the police had a look around and then they left. To a licensee from England, it looked just like a scene in a sitcom. I was so baffled by it all that I went over to chat to the barman about it. 'I don't understand these raids. The police can see that you're drinking.'

'Ah no. They don't actually *see* us drinking, sir.'

'They can see the glasses on the tables.'

'Yes, sir, but if there is no music, no dancing and no one is actually drinking when they walk down the steps, we're not open.'

'But they can *see* you're open.'

'No, sir. What they see is a bunch of us friends here having a chat.'

There was no answer to that one. I asked the barman if I could have a vodka because I didn't like the wine.

'We can't sell vodka, sir.'

'Why not?'

'It's against the rules, sir.'

'What rule says you can't drink vodka?'

'Well, it's like this, sir. Our licence is for a wine bar. So we can only drink wine.'

'Yes, but your licence stopped at 11p.m., so we're drinking illegally anyway.'

'I know, sir, but if we served anything stronger, it'd be a lot more illegal.'

It was now 5a.m., and I couldn't take any more.

There was no way a Stringfellow's in Dublin could compete

with all these illegal clubs. I told Ronnie this, but I didn't completely dismiss the idea. I invited him and his friends to Miami and took them to Solid Gold to see the topless dancing girls. They were three happily married Irish Catholic men who had never seen anything like it. They didn't need to be told about the 'no touching' rules: they were so stiff, I thought they'd died on me. The following day I took them out on my boat and anchored in No Name Bay. We were eating lunch when a huge yacht drew up alongside us. It was so impressive that it made my pride and joy look like a rowing boat. On the lower deck was an old man sitting in a wheelchair with a tartan blanket over his legs. Either side of him were two uniformed crew members. 'Look, Ronnie. That man left it too late.'

Ronnie looked up and saw the old man in his wheelchair. That one remark was to change Ronnie Riley's whole life.

The next day we flew to LA, where the builders were feverishly trying to finish the club. I showed the Irish guys the LA nightlife, which of course was non-existent. They saw what I saw: a city in need of a super nightclub. What I should have seen was a city that didn't want a nightclub because everyone goes to bed at 10p.m.

Lastly, I took them to New York, to a rather sad, closed Stringfellow's. The maintenance guy put the lights on so that they could see it was still a fabulous club. From there we flew to London and parted company.

Two days later, Ronnie called me to say that U2's property company wouldn't be investing. I was disappointed, but there were no hard feelings. A few days later, he rang again. 'Peter, are you serious about the girl club in New York?'

'Very serious.'

'Well, I'm thinking about putting my own money in.'

'What's made you change your mind?'

'I can't get that little old man out of my mind.'

'What man?'

'The one on the yacht. I don't want to leave it too late like him.'

So Ronnie became a 25 per cent partner in New York and we started making plans to relaunch the club as a girl bar. At the same time I had to go Chapter 11 in Miami. The bills were mounting and I didn't have a choice if I wanted to finish LA. All my money and effort was going into the new club. Not only was America in the throes of a deep depression, but the Gulf War had started as well.

As the LA opening approached, I began to get a cold feeling in the pit of my stomach. It was November 1990, the sun was still shining and I was staying at the Beverly Wilshire Hotel, opposite the club. I wasn't happy. I couldn't quite put my finger on the trouble. There was problem after problem at the club and it was eating up money until there was nothing left. The final count was $3.6 million.

Just before we opened I had a piece of luck. Rod Stewart had decided to marry his girlfriend, the New Zealand model Rachel Hunter, and his PR told me he wanted to hold a stag party in the club. In spite of my views on all-male groups, private parties were different, and I was hardly going to refuse Rod Stewart. Unfortunately, in the end Rod didn't make it to the club for his stag party. He started drinking with his crazy football friends and I didn't see him all night. A few days later, Frizzby and I went to the wedding, which was fabulous. As the pair of them were saying 'I do' Rachel slipped her hand on Rod's bum and gave it a squeeze. Everyone clapped and laughed, which completely threw the priest – he couldn't see what she was doing. Rod and Rachel came to my opening night, as did one of Rod's ex-girlfriends, Kelly Le Brock. As usual Rod took this in his stride. I have to admit that I was hoping his ex-wife, Alana Hamilton, would turn up as well, but the publicity generated by the presence of Rachel and Kelly was good enough.

Two days before the opening night, I'd had a call from Paul Roberts, who was once again designing the club.

'Peter, we've got a problem.'

'Tell me something new.'

'It's serious. I've got the new fire marshal here. He says they've made a mistake with our numbers.'

American fire inspectors are like the licensing inspectors in England. Before any building work starts on a club, they look at the plans and give it an assembly number (a capacity number).

'Tell him we've already had our assembly number agreed for 740.'

'I have. He says he's just checked the plans, and the number should be 285.'

'*What?*'

I raced over to meet Mike Smollen, the new fire marshal. His looks were like his attitude, small and weaselly. I hated him on sight. Paul explained that Smollen was new to the area and that he'd brought along another inspector.

'Hi, gentlemen. I'm Peter Stringfellow. What's the problem?'

Smollen rustled around with a copy of the plans and repeated what Paul had told me. I explained that I didn't build nightclubs without permission and without an agreed assembly number. I showed him my certificate from the previous fire marshal, which was stamped with the figure 740.

'As far as I'm concerned, that's the number I've built it for and that's the number I will be letting in.'

'As far as we're concerned, you may have built it for that number, but only 285 will be coming in. Our marshals will be counting on the night.'

According to Mike Smollen, our emergency exits weren't far enough apart. In his view that constituted a fire hazard, so they'd more than halved the numbers to be on the safe side. That put me into the jaws of bankruptcy. I'd taken the precaution of employing an ex-mayor of Beverly Hills as my licensing solicitor. I told him I wanted to sue the Beverly Hills authorities for $10 million, because it was their mistake. Unfortunately, I discovered that, in the country where litigation rules supreme, you can't sue the local authorities. I couldn't shout, I couldn't sue and I couldn't arse-lick – I'd tried that with the mayor's office and got nowhere.

I went to see the head of the fire brigade with my solicitor and pleaded with the guy. I told him how much I loved LA, how this would spell the end of my company and that everyone would lose their jobs. I must have touched a chord somewhere, because he said he'd look into it personally.

The chief managed to increase the figure to 380, which was a marginal improvement, but still not economically viable. If I'd been given that figure in the first place there is no way on earth I would have built the club. But now it was too late. On the opening night, in December 1990, the fire marshals were waiting to count everyone in. They were joined by three television crews, half a dozen radio journalists and a huge queue of people waiting to get into Stringfellow's.

Anyone who throws high-profile parties will know that the B-list people always turn up first. They have to, otherwise they won't always get in. The A list are the last to arrive. Mike Smollen stood and counted everyone in. He was like the ghost of Sergeant Monday, the policeman who had done exactly the same thing at the Penthouse twenty years earlier. By the time the B list were all in we'd reached our capacity. When the real celebrities turned up the marshals said the club was full. It was probably the first time Sylvester Stallone had ever stood in a queue. He was joined by Eddie Murphy, Charlie Sheen and a host of starlets. In fact it was more interesting standing outside the club than being inside it.

I put on a brave face for the cameras and said how wonderful it was to be opening in LA. I was diplomatic in the extreme: I talked about the problems with the fire marshals, but didn't call them a bunch of shits, which is what I felt like saying. Anyone looking in the club could see it was half empty. There was so much space, I could have fired a gun in there and not hit anyone. As the night progressed we started asking the B list to leave. Fortunately most of them were local dignitaries like bankers and councillors who only stayed an hour anyway.

By the end of the night we had a wonderful crowd. Everyone was safe. I knew I'd constructed the club properly and that the emergency exits were in the right place. If somebody had deliberately set about sabotaging the club, they couldn't have done a better job.

Although my liquor licence ran to 2a.m., the Beverly Hills fire marshals used their influence to amend this to 1.45a.m. All drinks had to be finished by 2a.m. It made the British licensing laws look liberal. My bar staff had to go on a special course to learn how to deal with drunken customers. In LA the barman is held responsible if a customer leaves the club drunk and kills

294 / PETER STRINGFELLOW

someone on the road. Because of this none of my bar staff would help me by serving drinks after hours. LA's drinking laws explain a great deal about the city. No wonder cocaine was king: nobody could get a bloody drink after 1.45a.m. As if that wasn't bad enough, the minimum drinking age is twenty-one. The authorities insisted that we checked girls' identity cards before admitting them to the club. If they'd insisted they were virgins as well it wouldn't have made things much more difficult.

During the following year I met just about every film star and bedded scores of beautiful young starlets. I consoled myself with sex because I wasn't getting anything else out of the club. I quickly learned that the stars don't pay, though to be fair I've never made them pay in any of my clubs anyway. Within months we were falling short of the $30,000 a week profit projections. The main problem was lunches. I've no idea why we bothered with lunch at all. Beverly Hills ladies ate only leaves, and not very expensive ones at that. I became obsessed with lettuce and water. We had to provide iced water free on every table. No one seemed to drink alcohol.

I also learned that when the stars play in LA, they do it behind closed doors, not in nightclubs. Charlie Sheen was in one night, drinking water while I drank vodka. By now I considered him a friend. I had found that there were two Charlies, the London Charlie and the LA Charlie. I couldn't understand why he wouldn't join me for a drink. He was very straight with me. 'When I'm in LA, I can't be seen to be doing *anything* in public. If I want to drink and chase women, I have to do it in private.' His words chilled me. The LA I'd imagined and the LA I was experiencing were not the same place at all.

In anticipation of the Hollywood spending power, in the realms of my imagination, I'd stocked the cellar with the finest clarets and champagne money could buy. It was three weeks before I saw a decent bottle of wine being drunk in the restaurant. My wine waiter called me over excitedly. He was about to open the third $150 bottle of claret that night. I asked him to introduce me to the people at the table. I was expecting to meet some big Hollywood name.

'Mr Stringfellow, I don't think there will be any point. They're from Spain and don't speak English.'

I began to wish I'd opened in Madrid instead. I started having fantasies about selling the club at a bargain price. I've always been an optimist, but even I could see that Stringfellow's LA was never going to work.

Roger Howe, who had come over to manage the place, had a brilliant idea. 'Why don't we open for Sunday lunch?'

'Sunday lunch? These people don't eat during the week. What makes you think they'll eat on a Sunday?'

'It'll be packed, you'll see.'

To my astonishment, Roger was right. Even more astounding, they were all drinking Bloody Marys. It cheered me up enormously. Obviously LA only drank on Sundays. But that was too much to expect. 'Er, no, Peter, there's no vodka in the tomato juice, and the juice is on the house.' That was the last time I had lunch in my own restaurant.

After the Sunday lunches ended, Roger had another idea: 'black' nights. We tried it. The black people who came into the club were always gorgeous looking and brilliantly dressed. They were also drinkers. Eddie Murphy, O.J. Simpson, Magic Johnson and Mike Tyson all became regulars.

Mike Tyson had certainly changed since I'd met him in London. I remember him as an excitable and impressionable young man, but the Mike Tyson I saw in LA was a cool superstar, complete with entourage. The girls would line up to meet him; they'd be squealing and flirting and almost fighting to get the boxer's attention. Most of them would have died to have their asses pinched by the hands of a champ, and by the time Desiree Washington appeared on the scene, Tyson must have thought he could have any woman he wanted. Sadly for him, he was wrong, and he ended up going to prison.

In contrast to Mike Tyson, O.J. Simpson was a quiet, calm, normal kind of guy. I was amazed when he was arrested for the murder of his wife, Nicole. The O.J. Simpson I met and chatted with was certainly very different from the O.J. portrayed in the media during his trial. As for Magic Johnson, I wasn't at all surprised by his HIV revelation. There were a lot of rumours around LA about Magic and young men, but he always vehemently denied being homosexual.

The 'black nights' looked set for success, except that it turned out that Roger and I were the only two non-racists in the whole of LA. I could deal with customer complaints from my white regulars, but I couldn't deal with the attitude of the LA police. Every 'black night' the club would be surrounded by them: they'd wait in the car park and search people. One night they frisked everyone – and found over a hundred guns. After three months I decided to close the black nights. It was a great shame, because despite the police harassment they'd been a success and the bar profits were up considerably. But it seemed everything we tried in LA was eventually doomed to failure.

Frizzby could see I was getting depressed. She decided to rent a house in Beverly Hills to make me more comfortable. The house was fabulous. It had sliding doors dividing the bedroom from the jacuzzi, and a beautiful garden full of orange and lemon trees. In the middle of the garden was a wonderful cactus that only flowered at night. I added the $4,000-a-month rent to my list of other expenses, like Roger's apartment, our hire cars and travel. Although Roger's LA apartment was not as palatial as his NY pad, good old Rog still insisted on living in Beverly Hills.

Without doubt, the club was the most beautiful I'd ever built. It had the sharpness of New York in its decor and an English music policy. Maybe it was just too damned good for LA. I'd spent my life courting celebrities and searching for glamour. To me the two things were inextricably linked. But it wasn't long before LA showed me the faces behind those glamorous masks, and believe me, they weren't a pretty sight.

22

HOLLYWOOD NIGHTS

To the outside world Stringfellow's LA was a stunning success. To my team on the inside it was a stunning failure. If the success can be measured by the number of stars who came through the door, then we were a success, but unfortunately, accountants need more than that.

One night Charlie Sheen came in with one of my all-time idols, Clint Eastwood. He only sipped at a beer, but it was an improvement on water nonetheless. I took the microphone to announce the start of the disco. This was something new to LA, so the crowd always gave me a round of applause. As I was talking I saw Clint Eastwood get up to leave. I just couldn't resist remarking on it. 'Ladies and gentlemen, I'd just like to say goodnight to my new friend, Mr Clintwood.'

It was actually a genuine mistake, but it raised a laugh. Later on, the comedian Rodney Dangerfield came over and congratulated me on my stage presence and wit. For every fun evening like that, there were dozens that were difficult. After a couple of months in LA I started to loathe celebrities. It was a bit unfair, considering that LA was their home and they were what I'd come there for. But I'd also come to make my fortune, which was impossible in a city where everyone drinks water and goes to bed in the middle of the evening. Still, the fact that I wasn't making any money wasn't their fault. I made numerous mistakes, the biggest one being opening the club in the first place. The second biggest was banning Eddie Murphy.

I'd always considered Eddie a friend. He'd been to the Hippodrome and Stringfellow's in London many times in the past. In England he had a reputation for chasing girls and ended up appearing in a cartoon in one of the papers. It showed two waitresses wearing tutus and chastity belts, talking to Frizzby and me. The caption read: 'Can we take these off now Mr Murphy has gone?'

Eddie came into the New York club one night and bumped into Ricky James and his entourage. Ricky was a fantastic guy who was never any trouble. He was one of the few stars who embarrassed me by asking for cocaine, although I remember Simon le Bon coming into the Hippodrome one night with a beautiful girlfriend and asking me if he could use my office for a while. I was happy to oblige. I could only think of two reasons why Simon would want to use my office: either he wanted sex, or he was arguing with his girlfriend. Later I went into the office and found a line of cocaine on my desk. I'm not saying Simon left it there, but somebody did. I did the only thing I could do: I brushed it into the bin.

Up until the night Eddie Murphy saw Ricky James's entourage, I only ever saw him with one friend at a time. But lo and behold, the next time Eddie came into the New York club, he brought a whole load of people with him. These guys became a permanent fixture. Wherever Eddie went, they followed.

One night I was sitting with Connie Stevens, of *Hawaiian Eye* fame, in the LA club. She was one of my favourite stars and a really lovely person. We were drinking and talking when one of my managers came up. 'Peter, Eddie Murphy's upstairs and he's got a problem.'

'What's the matter?'

'He wants to sit in the champagne room but there isn't any room.'

'Let me talk to him.'

I went upstairs and sure enough the place was packed. Standing in the corner were eight black guys all wearing sunglasses. They all looked the same – I'd no idea which one was Eddie. I didn't want to address the wrong guy, but neither did I want to offend him by having to ask. I thought I'd avoided an embarrassing situation when one of the guys spoke.

'Peter, we want to sit down.'

'Look, Eddie—'

Suddenly a voice to the right said: 'You better tell me. I'm Eddie.'

That got things off on the wrong foot. 'I can take you guys into another VIP area,' I went on, 'but the champagne room is full.'

'We want to sit in here.'

'I know, but I can't throw these people out.'

'We want to sit down now.'

'For God's sake, it isn't possible to sit up here.'

'Yeah, but you let this white disco trash sit here.'

I was shocked. 'Eddie, everyone is looking at us. Why don't you keep smiling, come downstairs and I'll give you my table?'

I was prepared to move Connie and my guests to keep Eddie happy, but that wasn't good enough for him.

'We want to sit up here, now.'

'I've had it with you,' I said, and I walked downstairs, smiling, and gave Eddie a wave. He was a monster star who had swallowed his own publicity.

As Eddie and his entourage marched out of the club, one of my managers came over and said, 'You shouldn't have done that to Eddie.'

'Shouldn't I? Well, you can go and tell him he's banned.'

Nobody was impressed that I'd banned Eddie Murphy. One friend said: 'Are you crazy? That guy's got so much status he could empty your club.'

I knew I'd made a huge mistake, which meant doing some big-time arse-licking. I passed the word on to Eddie that I was sorry and he was welcome in my club any time.

A week later he came back. Neither of us apologised but we let the matter drop. You cannot ban film stars in Hollywood. They can ban each other, but an outsider can't do it.

For every nightmare star there were plenty who were wonderful. Jack Palance came in one night and behaved like a real gentleman. I started talking to him about one of his films, which I'd seen many years ago. I couldn't remember the title, but I described how he'd played twin brothers. Jack gave me a blank expression. He was in his seventies when we met, so he'd made an awful lot of films by then. Meeting him still made my day.

One night my restaurant manager told me some guy having dinner wanted to ask about membership. I went over and he introduced himself as Ahmet Ertegun. When I explained the cost of the membership he looked astonished.

'I never pay for membership.'

Well, you'll have to pay in my club.'

'I don't pay in any nightclub.'

'And I don't give membership to people who ask.'

'If you don't make me a member I'll never set foot in this club again and neither will any of my artists.'

As he was getting up to leave he said, 'You obviously don't know who I am.'

It was true, I didn't know who he was, and neither did I care. When he'd left the club Richard Johnson came over and asked me what Ahmet had said. Richard was, and still is, a very influential journalist on the *New York Post*.

'You mean the little fat guy in the restaurant?'

Richard couldn't believe what I'd just said.

'Peter, Ahmet Ertegun owns Atlantic Records. He could empty this club if he wanted.'

I knew Atlantic Records had some of the biggest artists in the world, including Aretha Franklin, AC/DC, the Rolling Stones, Sister Sledge and Foreigner. I also knew I had some apologising to do. The following day I sent a letter to Ahmet's office and the $60 he'd paid to get into the club. When he came back two days later, I sent him a pink celebrity membership card and told him his guests would be welcome for free. From that night onwards Ahmet and I became friends, although it didn't stop him turning down Frizzby's record, which was eventually taken up by CBS and flopped.

Around the same time Joan Luther, my PR in LA, said she'd secured the premiere party for Kevin Costner's film *Robin Hood: Prince of Thieves*. Joan was an absolute battleaxe, but a lovely battleaxe. I'd taken her on out of fear more than anything else. She was the doyenne of the Beverly Hills circuit and one of those people you'd rather have with you than against you. Her news brought a smile to my face.

'You've got the Kevin Costner party? Do you want to take a bet on that?'

Joan looked baffled. 'Yeah, I've spoken to all the right people and they've got a budget of $75,000.'

Joan might have secured the party, but I knew we wouldn't be hosting it. 'It won't happen, Joan.'

'I promise you, Peter, I've got the word of the film company's top PR.'

'Maybe you have, but does Mrs Costner know this?'

I knew something Joan didn't know for once. A year earlier I'd met Kevin Costner in Stringfellow's in London. Sherry Stewart, my PR at the time, brought him into the club and introduced us. He was an absolute gentleman. 'You won't have heard of me,' he said modestly, 'but I've got a film coming out and I've just finished making my second one.'

Dances With Wolves was about to be released and he'd just finished filming *Robin Hood*. During the making of *Robin Hood*, Sherry and Kevin had an affair. He told Sherry he wanted to divorce his wife and take her back to LA to live with him. My advice to any man is never to promise love or marriage unless you mean it. Dinner, flowers and jewellery, fine – but never love and marriage if you can't deliver. Without fail it backfires on you. If you don't believe me, ask Kevin Costner.

Kevin flew back to LA and never contacted Sherry again. She was heartbroken and sold her story to one of the newspapers. It's impossible to hide a kiss-and-tell from a partner. As I've recounted, I'd tried it with Frizzby. I took her to the remotest cottage on the remotest island I could find, out of communication with the outside world, and she still found out. Of *course* Mrs Costner would have known about her husband's fling with the PR from Stringfellow's.

Nevertheless I let Joan go ahead with her plans for the party. Within hours of the announcement appearing in the *LA Times*, Joan telephoned me. 'My God, Peter, they've cancelled.'

'Surprise, surprise.'

'Aren't you upset?'

'No, Joan. Forget it.'

What you gain on the roundabout, you lose on the swings. I'd enjoyed the publicity from the kiss-and-tell and now I was paying the price.

One party that did go ahead gave us one of the most memorable evenings at Stringfellow's LA. It was the Oscars party hosted by Ginger Rogers and James Stewart. They were the king and queen of Hollywood. I'd seen them at the Sheffield Coliseum as a child and now they were playing hosts at my club and calling me by my first name. There are times when I can be impressed, and this was definitely one of them. It was a wonderful party, but at the end of the night nothing had changed. It didn't matter how many movie legends came to my club: I couldn't make enough money to survive.

The last six months of LA were like the last days of the Roman empire, including the orgies – except that I was the only guy. That's how it was, and how it's always been. When Frizzby was in town I was very good. The moment she flew back to London I'd have parties in my jacuzzi. I was like a crazed Caesar waiting to be stabbed in the back by Brutus.

We had a reputation for being one of the hardest clubs to get into. This was largely due to the fire marshals rather than to any policy of exclusivity. I couldn't compensate for the reduced number of customers by putting the prices up because LA was one of the cheapest cities in America. No one would pay $20 to get in: they wouldn't even pay $15, which is what I charged in Miami. Ten dollars was the maximum price for LA. We had to bring down the price of champagne from $8 to $6 a glass and vodka from $6 to $4. I was losing money on the door and at the bar. The stars made no difference; if anything they added to my problems, because they didn't drink and neither did they pay. The rest of LA was full of would-be movie stars who didn't have any money. I had the best-looking waitresses and barmen ever – they were all out-of-work actors desperate to get into the movies. The rich guys I'd seen in New York and Miami didn't exist in LA. One night an English couple came and asked me why LA was cheaper than Stringfellow's in London. I felt like grabbing them by their throats and shouting, '*Because they're so fucking tight, that's why!*'

Once the recession finally hit LA, I knew it would be only a matter of time before I closed. The debts piled up and I couldn't pay the astronomical rent. Doug Stitzel, who owned the building, had told me we could always work something out if I had problems with the rent, but unfortunately, he died shortly after I opened the club. The final bombshell came when the Japanese bought the complex for $200 million. I was informed by letter that I had three weeks to pay the back rent or I would have to close the club.

I had no choice but to fly to Japan to meet my new landlords. Roger, my attorney and I booked first-class tickets to Tokyo. They were a huge extravagance, but I didn't care. If I was on a ride to ruin, it might as well be a comfortable one. I sat in front of the managing director and tried to explain that LA was in the middle of a recession and that they would have to suspend my rent for the foreseeable future. The MD sat and nodded. I thought I'd convinced him until the door opened and in walked his lawyer. He had a pointy head, thick glasses and was wearing a black coat over a very neat collar and tie. He looked like some evil character from a Japanese war film. Terrifying. He spoke in Japanese to the MD, then turned to my attorney and told him that they wanted all the back rent immediately and the future rent to be paid on time. I'd been calm and polite until that moment. How dare this rude bastard come and dismiss everything! I stood up and banged the table.

'That's it! I'm going Chapter 11, and I'm going to make the front-page news in LA. You won't see another cent for months!'

For twenty minutes I shouted and ranted at the Japanese MD and his lawyer. I'd been storing up all this anger and frustration for six months, and now these guys were getting the full force of it. I think I even mentioned Eddie Murphy, with a lot of 'fucks' thrown in. At the end of my tirade the two Japanese chatted to each other. We then spent two hours working out a deal. I'd pay my back rent at a reduced price over a period, then they'd increase the rent to cover the reductions. I never understood what we agreed – I didn't care. When we left the meeting the Japanese were smiling, and I didn't have to pay my rent for a few more weeks.

It gave me a breather, but it didn't solve my problems.

Stringfellow's LA was doomed. Its failure was a stark contrast to the success of the all-girl cabaret club. Exactly one week after LA opened, Stringfellow Presents Pure Platinum had opened in New York. Michael J. Peters fulfilled his part of the contract and brought ninety-five beautiful girls from Florida. My part of the bargain was to pay flights and hotel bills and all Michael's expenses, and to give him a hefty share of the club's profits.

Although Ronnie Riley had put in $400,000 to refurbish and relaunch the club, it was nowhere near enough money after we added on expenses. Ronnie came to the opening along with Peter Dunne. Peter was too much of a gentleman to remind me of his warning about LA. He knew the club was already a disaster and saw little point in rubbing salt into my wounds.

My very good friend Robert Windsor also turned up, even though he thought it was a bit of a yawn. He'd dated Koo Stark, so I assumed he didn't think the girls were beautiful enough for him. The following week he invited me to lunch in LA with two girls he'd been chatting up. Knowing how bored he'd been in New York, I was expecting to find Julia Roberts and Kim Basinger at least. When I saw them I couldn't believe it. These girls were sisters, but the only thing they had in common was their ugliness. It wasn't as if he didn't know what a beautiful woman was: after all, he'd been married to the singer Grace Kennedy and now lived with a very beautiful blonde Spanish girl called Mia. I occasionally stay with him at his house in Majorca, and now know that everything in Robert's life, including women, takes second place to golf.

Robert was definitely on his own in thinking the New York club was a yawn. From the opening night Pure Platinum was a phenomenal success. The champagne came out, the best whisky, the finest wines. I couldn't believe that New York and Los Angeles were in the same country. We charged $20 admission at Pure Platinum and sold our drinks at a premium, but no one moaned about the prices there. America was still in recession, but it didn't seem to affect our club. We were grossing $150,000 a week, which was unbelievable when the rest of New York's nightclubs were teetering on the verge of bankruptcy. The only other exception was a club called Scores, which had opened shortly before Pure Platinum. It was a combination of a sports bar and a topless dancing bar. Michael and I went in one night to check out the competition. I didn't think the concept would work, because the girls had to compete with football matches which were shown on huge television screens around the club. We were sitting at one of the tables when one of the managers came over and said, 'Mr Peters, I've got to ask you to leave.' I was surprised that Michael wasn't welcome. As we were being escorted from the club Michael turned to the doorman and said, 'You know why we're being thrown out? Your manager's a fink.'

This was the last thing I wanted to hear from my newest partner. I'd been in Miami long enough to know that a 'fink' was an FBI informer. There were a lot of rumours flying around about Michael J. Peters, which I'd rather not repeat. I have nothing horrible to say about the guy: clearly, we just weren't made for each other. We were opposites in every sense. He had a penchant for sparkly leather jackets and cowboy boots, whereas I wore Jean-Paul Gaultier and didn't possess a pair of boots. We even had opposing views of the business. He was absolutely appalled when he saw me giving girls money to dance. He simply couldn't understand it. I explained that I wanted to set a precedent. If the customers saw me giving them money, they would do the same.

Whereas I was upfront and happy to appear on television, Michael stayed behind the scenes and was not great in front of a camera. I hired a very straight PR guy called Steve Agins, who was brilliant for the club. I didn't want a crazy, showy, typical New York PR, because someone like that would have presented the wrong image. Steve was a quiet, inoffensive, happily married man. He'd never done nightclub PR, but he managed to get me on the *Larry King Show*.

When I arrived at the television studios, I met another guest on the show, a big fat guy in glasses. He was the leader of the moral majority in America, and seemed a nice enough chap. Before the cameras started rolling we had a pleasant conversation about travel. He was perfectly affable until the green light came on. From that moment onwards he turned into a raving lunatic. He accused me of being involved in child pornography, of being a slimeball, of corrupting America. I sat there open-mouthed with shock. When he started salivating about how I encouraged children to take their clothes off, I turned to the camera and said: 'I can't believe I'm in the same company as this horrible creep.' Then I turned to the ranting monster and said, 'How dare you accuse me of these things on national television? You don't know anything about me.'

'Yes I do. You're the kind of man who carries photographs of naked little boys in your pocket.'

'Larry, where did you get this pervert from?'

Larry was on my side. This guy had totally lost control. It wouldn't be the last time I would have to listen to such a tirade. A few years later the Bishop of Aston accused me of being the son of the Devil for wanting to open a topless bar in Birmingham.

After the *Larry King Show*, I was invited on to all the major American television shows, including Joan Rivers' programme. Michael couldn't hide his jealousy. One afternoon we were trying to hold a civil conversation when he turned on me: 'My friends are telling me I've created a monster in you.'

He hated the fact that I was getting all the media attention. It was obvious to us both that we were never going to get along. I didn't feel comfortable running the club with him. It was *my* club, but it was *his* concept and they were his girls. After our first major row I told him he could buy the club for $1 million. It was still in Chapter 11 with huge debts, so $1 million seemed a fair price. I wanted to take the concept to Britain and forget about New York completely.

I'd tried to persuade the landlord in Miami to turn the closed-down Stringfellow's there into an all-girl club but he turned me down flat. Since the club had gone Chapter 11 he'd become a born-again Christian so there was no chance of changing his mind. At this point, I thought LA might survive the recession. I decided I'd be happy with a Stringfellow's in London and a Stringfellow's LA, and would fly into Miami just to play with my boat. Of course I was deluding myself.

Michael said he would organise a meeting with some invest-ors to discuss buying me out of the club. They turned out to be a weird and wonderful collection of guys: cigars, dark glasses, gold chains, brandy. They were straight out of central casting. But instead of Humphrey Bogart they had Peter Stringfellow, and instead of Edward G. Robinson they had Michael J. Peters. I knew I would have to be tough with these guys. 'Gentlemen, I have nothing to lose, I want $1 million, or the deal's off.' Their idea of $1 million was to give me $340,000 paid over one year, starting in six weeks' time. They said they'd pay Ronnie Riley's $400,000 after a year and pick up the substantial debts from Chapter 11. I felt responsible for Ronnie. He'd put his own money into the club and I didn't want him to lose it. I called him in Dublin to ask what he thought about their offer. He said later it was one of the strangest telephone calls he'd ever taken. 'By the way, you're not a partner any more, and you'll get your money back in a year's time.' But Ronnie was happy to leave the deal up to me. I told the guys that they would have to pay Ronnie's money in six weeks, not a year, then we'd have a deal. I signed a piece of paper and thought I'd got rid of the place for good.

Six weeks later they hadn't come up with one dollar. I went back to Michael and we tried to work out a 'partnership' that would make us both happy. We agreed that Michael would run the girls, that his manager would work with my manager, and that I would continue to have total control of the club. For a while we tried to make it work, but our personalities continually clashed. We both had huge egos and we both wanted control, which was impossible.

By June 1992, LA was in serious trouble and Miami had gone from Chapter 11 to Chapter 7, which meant bankruptcy.

In August, Michael had started demanding money. He said he'd paid to get the girls to New York and wanted $40,000 immediately. When I told him I wouldn't pay him he decided to have a strike. He snapped his fingers one Sunday and sixty girls left. I snapped my fingers and five stayed. At least two of them were my girlfriends. Michael had the power because he owned all the girl clubs in Florida. The girls were upset, but they didn't have a choice if they wanted to continue working in the business.

The next day I opened the club with just eight dancers, one of whom was a girl called Christine whom I was yet to meet. She'd been working at Scores and had heard that Michael had called a strike. She got two friends and came over straight away. Christine was very wonderful and very calculating. With only eight girls on a shift instead of the usual sixty, there would be a lot more money. At the end of the night the girls sat on the carpet and counted their earnings. One of my girlfriends, Amy, had made $3,600 and the other, Cathy, had made $4,000. All eight girls were very happy that the others had left. The only unhappy person was me.

After a couple of days two of my regular customers complained. I knew it couldn't go on. Thursday, one of our busiest nights, was coming up. The only way to resolve the problem was for Michael and me to go before a judge and let him decide. We were both staying at the Hilton so we could hardly avoid each other. I'd press the elevator button and the door would open to reveal Michael. We didn't hate each other; we'd simply had a business disagreement that was costing us both money. We travelled to the court together and discussed our problems on the way. On the steps of the courthouse we were on the point of cutting a deal when Michael said he would agree only if I sacked the girls who had stayed on. I said, 'No way.' Michael waited until we were one second from going into court before he agreed to let the eight girls stay.

A couple of nights later, back in business once again, I was sitting quietly in one of the booths. It was the end of the night and I was rather smashed. Suddenly, from nowhere, a girl with long, long hair came up to me. She leaned over and said, 'You know what I like about you, Peter?'

'What?'

'You're a slut.'

She kissed me and walked away. I know it sounds ridiculous, but that kiss stuck in my mind. It worked. It wasn't the fact that she called me a slut, because I'd heard that many times before. I *am* a male slut – I've never denied it. The following day I couldn't get this girl's face out of my mind. She looked like another girl called Frankie, and I'd assumed it was her.

When Frankie denied kissing me I was baffled. She then suggested it might have been a girl who danced under the name of Jennifer.

Jennifer was Christine, a stunning brunette with hair down to her waist. The next night I saw her sitting with a customer. I went over and introduced myself. 'You are the girl who kissed me the other night.'

Christine didn't answer, she just smiled one of her silly little smiles.

The next evening I took her back to the Hilton. We played that night but didn't have proper sex – she told me she was living with her boyfriend and wouldn't have intercourse without a condom. I don't use condoms. I know it sounds irresponsible, but I never have.

The following night Christine joined me and my girlfriend, Amy, for dinner. I'd tried unsuccessfully to get Amy to sleep with other girls before, so I didn't hold out much hope of Christine and Amy getting together, but by the end of the night Christine had seduced Amy and we all went back to the hotel. I left them in the lounge and the next minute they were both in bed. Suffice to say we all had a wonderful time.

The very next night I wanted both girls to come out to play again. Amy had another boyfriend and said she couldn't come out. Christine and I went back to the hotel and ended up making wild, passionate love. Christine suggested that we called Amy and told her that we were in bed together, thinking about her. Amy's answering machine was on so I left the following message: 'Hi, Amy, it's Peter. I'm here with Christine and we're missing you. Give us a ring at the Hilton.'

Then I put the phone down.

Christine carried on talking about Amy's huge boobs and what she'd like to do with them. I then told Christine what it was like making love to Amy. Suddenly a voice said: 'If you want to leave a further message, please hang up and dial again.'

I hadn't put the receiver back properly. For ten minutes the phone had been off the hook, recording every word of our conversation. I rang the operator and told her it was a life-or-death situation: how could I erase a message from someone's machine? I couldn't. It was impossible.

The next day a very upset Amy called me. 'How do you think I felt listening to you two discussing my body and how I make love? What would have happened if my boyfriend had heard the message? I never want to speak to you again. Never ever ring me again.'

From then on it was just Christine and me. When I flew into New York she'd stay at my hotel. We'd set the clock for 4a.m., and she'd get up and go back to her boyfriend. For a whole year she was my New York girlfriend. I had one in Miami, one in LA and Frizzby in London.

The affair with Christine took my mind off more pressing issues. Sex was and is my release, my recreation and my drug. It's the one constant in my life, and possibly the thing that's kept me sane. Not long after meeting Christine I heard the news I'd been dreading. London had caught the disease. I would be forced to make a choice: America or England; Frizzby or Christine. My life was about to change dramatically yet again.

23

MONEY'S TOO TIGHT (TO MENTION)

The recession had crept into London. Stringfellow's was in desperate need of an overhaul and in desperate need of me. The banks wouldn't let me take any more money to America and neither would they give me any to refurbish London. I knew I should have closed LA sooner, but I had over 120 people relying on me for their jobs. I left Geoffrey and John Neilson in New York, Roger in LA and flew back to London, where Mary Dawes had been holding the fort, to try to sort it all out.

My insomnia started the moment I got back. I began waking up at 5a.m. in a cold sweat. At that time in the morning everything is starkly real, it's dark, it's cold and it's silent. There was no hiding from reality. I was in deep, deep shit. I was no longer controlling my business, it was now controlling me. I couldn't see a way out of LA, except to close the club. New York was doing great business, but I still had debts from Chapter 11; I had problems with Michael J. Peters, and he had problems with me. And now, on top of all that, my London Stringfellow's was suffering as well. I didn't need to read about tough times in the newspapers, I could see it for myself. No one was spending money in the club.

I hate failure. It's a horrible, hateful thing, especially when it's not your fault. I hadn't created the failure in America, it was America's failure, not mine. Sure, I'd been caught short, building too fast, opening too soon, but I'd done it in the heady, glorious days of the eighties, when anything had been possible and the word recession belonged to the past, not to the future.

In those dark, early-morning hours I began to look at myself.

How had I got myself this far? I'd got there alone. No one had handed me anything on a plate. I'd spent my lifetime knocking down doors. I'd built a mini-empire from a church hall in Sheffield. I'd enjoyed my success. I liked being autocratic in the good times, so I had to be autocratic in the bad times, too, and start making some decisions.

Michael didn't have the money to buy the New York club from me so I would have to find another buyer. LA was a disaster, and to have a chance of turning it round I would have to sit in the middle of the club every night and be visible. I couldn't hold the stars' loyalties by flying in and out of town every few weeks. It would mean moving to LA permanently. If London hadn't been suffering with the recession I would have gone to LA, but between a dying London and a struggling LA there was no contest. I still loved America, but Britain was my home.

With a very heavy heart I closed LA. I told the staff I was going Chapter 11 in the hope of raising some money to clear my debts. They weren't convinced. Within days they started to hand in their notices, and within a matter of weeks I jumped from Chapter 11 to Chapter 7. I threw one last celebrity party before I left. Frizzby stayed in London and I invited all the girls I'd made love to in LA. The chef put on a buffet and I gave my guests free champagne all night. It would be boastful to claim that the club was full that night. Let's just say the fire marshals would have been worried about the numbers! Frizzby flew in a couple of days later to close up the house in Beverly Hills. It was the most peculiar afternoon. All the neighbours came out and were super-friendly. By then it was too bloody late.

I went back to London to salvage what was left of my business. I needed nothing short of a miracle. I thought the miracle had happened when the telephone rang one day and a man with a Birmingham accent said he'd heard I had problems and needed some money. It's just as well for him that I've forgotten his name. He started telling me things I wanted to hear, like, 'Here's £10 million – don't worry about paying me back.' At any other time in my life I would have laughed him off the phone, but I was desperate. He had a wonderful idea that involved filling in some forms which had something to do with green petrol dollars from Europe. Then, hey presto, I'd get £10 million. He wanted £250,000 up front for introducing me to the scheme.

'Any chance I won't get the £10 million?'

'Well, er . . . yes . . . er, a slight chance.'

'Then what?'

'Then we pay you back the £250,000 over five years.'

Needless to say, I put the phone down on that one.

A few days later this guy called back. He said he'd like to introduce me to a contact of his who had money to invest. I had nothing to lose, so I invited them to London. The contact was from Manchester. He was wearing an open-necked shirt and a ten-year-old suit. The guy didn't look right.

That afternoon Michael had suggested I bought him out of New York for $2 million. I had $5 million in debts from the club and a further $4 million debts from Miami and LA, plus all the other debts. I told the Manchester guy I needed about £10 million to save my company.

'No problem.'

A few days later the guy from Birmingham introduced me to a man called George. That wasn't his real name, but you'll see why I've changed it. He was a small, sharp Londoner who, like his friends, didn't possess a decent suit. At one point I looked at these three stooges and couldn't believe I was discussing my business with them. On top of the £10 million they were going to lend me, they wanted to open a chain of Stringfellow Hotels. I'd only had three glasses of wine so it wasn't something I'd drunk.

I actually ended up in Miami with these guys. I introduced George to the managing director of one of the top hotels there and began negotiating a deal to buy it. George said he was about to get $100 million from LA: in fact, the bank draft was on its way that very afternoon.

I was sitting in my hotel room when George knocked on the door. He said he wanted to talk to me privately.

'So-and-so has been shot in LA.'

'Well, what's that got to do with me?'

'He's the head of the Mafia.'

'So?'

'Well, I've been asked to take over.'

'Are you telling me you're connected?'

'Yes. I'm So-and-so's best friend.'

'Is the money Mafia money?'

'No, it's the pension money from the Teamsters.'

I knew then that I was in the company of an idiot. I wrote a letter to the hotel manager and apologised for wasting his time. This guy was more than a con man – he was outrageously deluded. I was a bloody idiot myself. I was like a drowning man grabbing hold of a twig in a last desperate attempt to save himself. I flew back to London and prepared for the worst.

Stringfellow Enterprises, my parent company, had loaned out so much money that it was now in big trouble. New York, Miami and LA were bankrupt, but Stringfellow's in London was still financially viable, even though it was struggling. In a strange way I was almost grateful for the recession. I wasn't the only club in London suffering, which meant I had a chance of saving Stringfellow's. By law, the liquidator had to offer Stringfellow's for sale. My bank offered to lend me enough money to buy it back, but warned me that if another leisure company outbid me, I would lose it.

I let it be known that I would walk away from Stringfellow's if anyone put in a bid for the club. They wouldn't have my name, so the club would be worthless. Naturally no one bid. With the help of my financial director, Cliff Silver, and Barclays Bank I bought the club back. The liquidator took everything else. I lost my apartments in Marbella and Miami, my boat and my jeep. I didn't need them any more. I was left with what I'd started with: one nightclub in London. Barclays wanted to take my passport as well. They were worried I would fly off to America. I had unfinished business in New York which would take a further six months to sort out. I promised that once New York was finalised, my affair with America would be over for good.

There was no hiding from the media. My bankruptcy made front-page news. I knew the guys who had made me could now break me. With the exception of one journalist, they were all fair and no one ripped at me personally. The exception was Chris Hutchins, a reporter for *Today*. We'd done a few stories together over the years and I considered him a friend. After my company folded he wrote a piece saying it was all over for me. He then described how he was sitting at the bar in Stringfellow's looking at the cigarette burns in the armrest of the chair. It was hurtful and unnecessary. I'd been called a slimeball and the son of the Devil, but nothing hurt as much as Chris's article. I didn't want to read what I already knew. I had no money to refurbish Stringfellow's and I didn't need my face rubbing in it.

A weird kind of peace came over me after the bankruptcy. I'd faced the wall and I'd faced the media. I no longer lay awake at night wondering what to do. The decision had been taken from me. I did interview after interview, and appeared on every TV news bulletin. The notoriety helped in a strange way. My old crowd came back into the club to offer their sympathies and I did my best to hide my sadness. Geoffrey and Roger had both been financially hurt by the collapse and all three of us had to start again. Geoffrey stayed in New York for a further year to wrap up the American disaster, while Roger came back and rented a cottage in London.

There was more sadness to come when my mum died, on 19 June 1993. She'd been ill for some time. At first we thought she had premature dementia, but we eventually discovered she had lung cancer. When Mum got too sick for Dad to take care of her, she went into the best nursing home in Hove. I'd bought them a flat near the seafront, so Dad could visit her in the home every day. I knew she was dying when she called me to tell me she'd stopped smoking. Her cigarettes, television and a cup of tea were Mum's life. I spoke to her just before she went into a coma. Dad and the Stringfellow sons can never thank the nursing staff enough for the wonderful way they cared for Mum in her final days. She died very peacefully at the age of seventy-two. I know in my heart that she would have lived at least another ten years if she hadn't been a smoker.

That year was one of the most difficult periods of my life. I had to come to terms with the loss of my mum, the loss of my business and accept that my relationship with Frizzby was over.

I set myself two goals to see me through 1993: the first was to get London back on the road and the second to sell New York and bring the all-girl cabaret to England.

If the recession had ripped the heart out of my business, it had also ripped the fashion industry apart. Grunge came in, big-time. Everywhere I looked, I saw beautiful girls in leggings and boots. Even gorgeous, glamorous Frizzby started dressing down. I hated it. One day I ripped a cap I hated off her head, which was a big mistake: she'd fixed it on with fifty hairclips, so I nearly took her head off.

Frizzby's grunge period had nothing to do with the fashion trend and everything to do with the topless bar in New York. She was making a statement. She hated the idea, and she didn't want to compete with topless dancers. When Frizzby stopped dressing up for me, our sex life took a nose-dive. I couldn't find anything sexy in leggings and boots. In stark contrast to London, Pure Platinum still had glamour. New York was no longer a bitch, she was now a glamorous temptress. It was like stepping into a male fantasy land. I couldn't deal with grunge. I'm not a grunge man. Sure, I've got a leather jacket, but it cost $1,000 for God's sake, and it's clean.

If I hated grunge, I hated bottled beer even more. I didn't like the working-class image of beer and after the Penthouse I made it a rule that pints were not to be sold in any of my clubs. Roger insisted that we started selling beer in bottles. He said we'd lose the young crowd if we didn't, because every other club was selling it. I let him go ahead with bottled beer on the condition that we would get rid of it the moment the recession was over.

I was surrounded by scruffy girls, beer-drinking men and a club that needed decorating. If that wasn't bad enough, I had a girlfriend who refused to discuss the girl cabaret club.

'Frizzby, this is going to be a major part of my life.'

'It's not going to be a part of my life.'

'But I'm bringing it to London.'

'If it comes to London, we're finished.'

'Frizzby, listen . . .'

'*No*. No way on earth are you going to be surrounded by

ninety-five semi-naked American girls and not make a move on them.'

I tried to convince her that it wouldn't happen. Of course, Frizzby was right. There was no way on earth I could ignore ninety-five beautiful semi-naked dancing girls. If anybody came into Stringfellow's and asked me about the New York club, Frizzby would turn to ice.

'Oh, haven't you seen it, Frizzby?'

'No. I don't want to see it, and I don't want to talk about it.'

I couldn't deal with Frizzby's attitude or her grunge. Across the Atlantic I had a very glamorous girlfriend in Christine. I didn't want to get involved with her seriously. I just wanted to have some fun. That's how affairs start. One girlfriend puts on the pressure, so you turn to the other one for fun.

It was around this time I decided to take Frizzby on holiday to Barbados. On the next island Christine was on vacation with her boyfriend. It was a major case of déjà vu. I'd been there in another life with Coral. Just like my holiday with Coral, the one with Frizzby was a success and we had a fantastic time, yet I knew in the back of my mind that we didn't have a future.

When we returned from Barbados Frizzby gave me an ultimatum. She wanted commitment and a baby. I flew to New York to think about it. While I was there my PA Pat Jay called to say that Frizzby was looking for another apartment. She was sick of the church in Highgate and wanted to start again. I didn't mind. It meant I had more freedom. I could stay with Frizzby for two nights at her flat, then spend the rest of the week playing with other girls in the flat in the church.

As much as I liked being in New York with Christine, I wanted to get rid of the club. Michael J. Peters' own empire was deteriorating fast and he had problems with the FBI. I didn't want to know about his racketeering charges, I just wanted to get out of there as quickly as possible. I put the word out that I would sell for $1 million but would only look at letters from attorneys. I'd had my fill of idiots pretending to have money.

I received two letters. My attorney urged me to look seriously at one of them.

'Anthony, have you seen the heading on this letter?'

'Yeah, what's the problem?'

'It says Davidoff and Mallito.'

'But it's from a Brian Travis.'

'I don't care. He's got the toughest lawyers in New York. They have connections with the authorities. These guys got me my licence for the club in twenty-four hours. Something isn't right here.'

The other letter was from a Larry La Spina, who mentioned that one of his associates had worked for Michael J. Peters. Neither approach was ideal, but I didn't have time to look for any other buyers. The clock had started ticking. I was on the verge of a hostile takeover and I knew that I could lose the club altogether.

Larry La Spina was a heavy-looking man from Florida, deep tan, casual clothes. He didn't look as if he could raise $1 million, but he had charm. He browsed through the figures and agreed a price, but didn't want to get involved with Michael. He had an idea. He wanted me to put New York into Chapter 7 – bankrupt the club – and then he would buy it back from the landlord and cut out Peters. It was a typical fucking New York deal. Nothing is straight in America. Why couldn't someone say, 'Here's $1 million, $250,000 per annum for the name, it's a deal'? Larry's suggestion was dodgy. I knew Peter Catillano wouldn't want to get involved, and I certainly didn't want to start doing complicated deals at this stage.

This story began with me in prison. I have a fear of police and imprisonment, and I made a vow to myself in 1962 that as long as I lived I would never again do anything to jeopardise my freedom. I'd just had three clubs go Chapter 11 on me and not one of them happened to catch fire. I'm always suspicious when a nightclub burns down. I've had fourteen nightclubs and the only fire we ever had was a tiny one at Stringfellow's in London, which the chef put out in three minutes flat.

I turned down Larry's offer gently and very diplomatically. There were no bad feelings. That night he came to the club and paid the dancers in $100 bills, which was most impressive. I didn't hear from him for a while. I moved on to Brian Travis, and arranged to meet him at his lawyers' offices. I left Geoffrey and John Neilson at the Hilton, having discussed with them the possibility of dropping the price because I was running out of time. Geoffrey knew I didn't have a choice. I wanted to leave New York with something rather than nothing.

I took Ronnie Riley and my attorney with me. There was a cold, unfriendly atmosphere at Davidoff and Mallito. Brian Travis was a weighty guy with a boy's face. I immediately knew he was play-acting the tough guy – his eyes gave him away. They weren't the eyes of a tough guy. His attorney sat down and told me their deal. They would pay me $500,000 over three years and pay Ronnie his $400,000 in one year's time. Two things struck me: how did they know I was willing to drop my price when I'd stipulated $1 million? And how did they know Ronnie's debt was important to me?

Ronnie Riley went white. We excused ourselves from the room.

'Ronnie, something's wrong here,' I said.

'I know. What can we do?'

'We can call their bluff.'

We went back into the office and I very confidently told their attorney it was $1 million or no deal.

'Peter, you're days from going before the Chapter 11 judge. We can put in a business plan and cut you out. You haven't got any money.'

These guys had information they shouldn't have known. I didn't say anything, I simply thanked them for their time and we left. Ronnie couldn't believe what I was doing. I knew I'd rather go bankrupt and lose everything than take their offer. I called Geoffrey from a callbox outside the office.

'Geoffrey, have you spoken to anyone about our financial arrangements?'

'Of course not.'

'OK, put John Neilson on the phone.'

'He's not here. When you went to your meeting he left the hotel.'

It was obvious that John had been leaking the information. He gave away my secrets in return for the job of president of the club. He came to see me a few days later and said he hadn't known they were going to try to cut my price. Two days later the deal changed to a cash deal and they offered to pay 100 per cent of Ronnie's money up front.

On the night we signed, I showed Brian Travis around the club and decided to have dinner with Christine for the last time. When Christine went off to the loo, I peed under the restaurant table on the carpet. No one saw me. It was a pathetic final act. Brian came over at the end of the night, squelching slightly, and said, 'No hard feelings, Peter?'

'No, Brian. No hard feelings.'

At last the nightmare was over. I left New York with no intention of returning. Christine left me a goodbye note saying that our relationship couldn't go on if I went back to London. In her words, it was 'too hurtful'. She ended with 'I love you.' My feelings on New York were therefore an odd mixture of elation and depression. The moment I got to London I called Christine and told her to come over for a holiday. I told her she would have to stay in a hotel because of Frizzby.

The moment I picked Christine up at the airport my feelings changed. I didn't take her to a hotel, I took her to Highgate. On reflection it was a calculated move. I knew it was over with Frizzby. She wanted commitment and a baby and I couldn't give her either of those things. I'd even been to see a fertility doctor to have my sperm count checked. The doctor had looked very grave when I went back for the results. 'Mr Stringfellow, you have an abnormally low sperm count for your age.'

I think he expected me to break down and cry. Instead I smiled and shook his hand. I couldn't give Frizzby what she wanted because I didn't have a choice. Nature had intervened.

Now I had to make a choice between Christine and Frizzby. She rang while I was in bed with Christine. I told her over the phone that I had my New York girlfriend with me and that I wanted to finish. Frizzby came to Highgate in tears. I felt wretched, but I'd made up my mind. We'd been together for twelve years and had had some wonderful times, but now it was time to move on. I made a financial arrangement with her that shall remain private. Frizzby now has a baby with her new boyfriend, David De Ville, and her own design company, and we remain friends to this day.

I didn't leave Coral for Frizzby, and I didn't leave Frizzby for Christine. On both occasions I wanted a clean break, the freedom to start a new chapter in my life. Things began to look up for about a month, until I got a call from my New York attorney telling me Brian Travis had reneged on his deal and none of the debts were being paid. Once again I was back on the merry-go-round. Larry La Spina stepped in with a deal to buy the club from Brian Travis, and after several sittings before the Chapter 11 judge in New York, they eventually cut a deal.

Larry agreed to give Brian $1 million in cash and to pay off $2 million of the club's $3.5 million debt. He also agreed to lease the name Stringfellow's for a period of ten years and wanted me to remain involved. When all the papers were signed I went back to the club. I told John Neilson to get the fuck out of the place. His tenure as president was short-lived. His dying father had asked me to give him a chance. I'd given him more than a chance, and he'd stabbed me in the back on numerous occasions. I never wanted to see the guy again.

Once again I thought I'd resolved my problems with New York. Larry told me he was happy to take a back seat and let me run the club, even though my only interest in the place was the name over the door. The first night he came in for dinner I went over to his table and told him I would introduce him to all the staff. He slowly took out a cigarette and lit it.

'That's great, Peter, but first I'd like a glass of champagne.'

'I'll get a waiter for you.'

'No. You get me the champagne.'

I couldn't believe it. It was as if Father Christmas had suddenly turned into the Devil. I ignored his remark and sent for a waiter. Later that night I took him to meet the chef. When he left the kitchen, the chef came up to me. 'Who is that man? He's told me I can't give the staff free food.'

I said I'd have a word with Larry after he'd finished talking to the head waiter. When Larry went to see the DJ, the head waiter came flying over. 'That guy has told me none of the dancers can sit in the restaurant!'

Twenty minutes later the DJ wanted to see me. 'Peter, the new owner has just told me I can't play dance music any more. He only wants to hear disco music, and that's going to make the girls unhappy.'

By now Larry was talking to the doormen. He'd seen a rock star in the club in a bomber jacket and jeans and was telling them never to let anyone in unless they were dressed in a suit.

I'd just got rid of one arsehole and now I'd picked up another. Larry had transformed himself from Mr Background into Mr Megalomania in one evening. At the end of the night he put his arm round me. 'Look, Peter, there are some things I don't like.'

'Fair enough, but we have managers to organise the staff. You can't make snap decisions like that, it upsets everyone.'

'Peter, trust me, it'll be fine.'

But I knew it wouldn't be fine. Within weeks Larry had reneged on our deal. It had been agreed, albeit verbally, that he would pay the remainder of my original asking price, which was by now $500,000 as Brian Travis had already paid the rest. He refused to pay because the books were in a complete mess and the company had acquired even more debt. Although Larry picked up $10,000 of my expenses and paid Geoffrey a salary for a while, he refused to pay for the name. It took eighteen months for him to change the name of the club. Even after he renamed it Tens he kept the name Stringfellow's underneath on the canopy. To my irritation it's still there today and, even more annoying, I've now been banned from the place.

None of my clubs could match New York for problems. I spent as many years trying to open there as I did trying to extricate myself from it. New York was more than a spurned mistress; she was the wife who refused to divorce me and then took me to the cleaners anyway. By taking Christine away from New York I was taking a piece of New York with me. On reflection she personified everything I couldn't deal with in New York. She was tough, emotionally undemonstrative, yet at the same time she was fascinating and sexy.

On the surface she was wonderful. She immediately made friends with all my old girlfriends and looked perfect in the club. During the week she stayed with me in London she called her boyfriend every night. She'd told him she was staying with friends. For that week I played at being in love. I asked her to live with me, even though I knew she had a boyfriend. I wanted to take my time with her. I suggested we waited until Christmas 1994 before making any decisions.

When she flew back to America I was a free agent once again. Two days later I was lying in the bath watching television when she called from New York.

'I've told him.'

'Told who?'

'I've told my boyfriend that I'm in love with you and I'm going to come and live with you in London.'

'What did he say?'

'He went crazy and put his fist through a window.'

'But I thought we were going to wait until Christmas.'

'But Peter, you asked me to live with you. Are you telling me now you don't want me to come?'

'It's not that I don't want you to come, darling. I just wanted us to take our time.'

'Oh, my God. You don't want me to come.'

Christine put the phone down. I thought, 'Shit,' and went back to watching the news. That night I went to the club and brought a wonderful girl back to bed with me. But I couldn't get Christine off my mind. The next night I got very drunk and called her.

'OK, Christine, get on the plane tomorrow.'

'Oh, my God. I can't.'

'Why not?'

'I've told my boyfriend it was all a lie and that I was testing him.'

'Well, tell him the truth.'

'I can't do that.'

'Go and tell him the truth, and come over tomorrow.'

I put the phone down and rang back ten minutes later. Her boyfriend answered this time.

'Hello, my name's Peter Stringfellow. I'm in love with Christine and I want her to come and live with me.'

Not surprisingly, he slammed the phone down on me.

Two days later Christine arrived. I know it sounds silly, but the moment I saw her I fell in love. I'd been in love before, but not like this. It was like a disease. My personality changed beyond all recognition. I became mentally unstable – ridiculously possessive and jealous, to the point where all my friends said I changed when Christine was around me. It was like acute paranoia.

I gave Christine 100 per cent fidelity all the time I was with her. I put all my sexual energy and passion into this one girl, and she simply couldn't deal with it. I thought my faithfulness was a wonderful gift. Christine couldn't understand this – it was no more than she expected from a relationship.

'Damn it, Peter. Fidelity is only what I expect from my boyfriend.'

I'd never given my fidelity to anyone else before. To me it was like giving the Crown Jewels. During the whole period I was with Christine I felt mentally unstable. It was like opening the Hippodrome all over again. All the power and energy I put into my nightclubs was now being directed at her. Amidst all this intensity, we had very different ideas about how our relationship would work. I wanted her beside me in the club, playing hostess and being Peter Stringfellow's super girlfriend, whereas Christine thought she was coming over to be my business partner. She wanted to change the menu in the club to include Americanised dishes. Don't get me wrong, I've always been open to suggestions, but it just wasn't right for Stringfellow's. I couldn't let her dictate to my staff, some of whom had been with me for fifteen years, because it wouldn't have been fair.

Whereas Frizzby had made a career out of being my girlfriend, Christine hated my fame. She was twenty-two years old and she didn't like living in my shadow, but at the same time she was happy to appear in newspapers and magazines as my girlfriend. On one hand she was wonderful, bisexual and an awful lot of fun, but on the other, she was difficult and independent and she couldn't settle in London. In some ways it was like being with Coral all over again, particularly in the way we would fight and make up. When Coral flew into London she arranged to have dinner, alone, with Christine. They got on brilliantly, although I never got to the bottom of their discussion.

I do know that Coral gave Christine our wedding ring, and that Christine was never the same after she met Coral.

By Christmas 1994, Christine had become homesick and flew back to America. It was clear that things were never going to work out between us. The relationship limped on into 1995, and eventually it petered out. After Christine had lived with me, she never went back to dancing. She is now a successful model and dances with Fem 2 Fem, an American group I introduced her to in London. To get Christine out of my mind I buried myself in work. I was still determined to bring the all-girl cabaret club to Britain. I'd seen the future of nightclubs in America, in the same way as I'd seen it many years before with the music at Studio 54. Back then no one wanted to believe that continuous music was the way forward. To survive you have to change and evolve with the times. I learned with Rockafella's not to give the people what they think they want, but to give them what they really want.

Once again I was about to encounter two old friends: hypocrisy and the Church. The former I've learned to live with; the latter I've chosen to ignore.

24

HERE I GO AGAIN

When business started picking up again in 1994, Frizzby helped me to redesign Stringfellow's. We stripped away the old decor and filled the place with angels and red drapes. We replaced the old chrome spotlights with chandeliers and had the furniture re-upholstered. It was like walking into a brand-new Stringfellow's. By the time the club was finished, we'd completely changed the look and put in a new sound system and lights. Then I took over the centre table in the restaurant and filled it with interesting people and, of course, lots and lots of girls. I gave up my right to privacy longer ago than I can remember. I live at the centre of my nightclub and I sleep next door in my apartment. Stringfellow's circulates around me: it's like my sitting room, except that people pay to come in.

The moment we upgraded the sound system, my regular customers started complaining about the thumping house music. I've been moving with musical trends since 1962, so I had no objections to techno, acid jazz or house music. I like being at the cutting edge. It's exciting, it's different, it's what living is all about. I like nostalgia, but I don't wallow in it. The only way forward is to look to the future.

When I asked the authorities for permission to have topless girls in Stringfellow's three nights a week, they immediately opposed it, with the backing of the police and local residents. It was like 1979, when I was fighting everybody to open Stringfellow's, all over again. When I found new premises for the topless club in Westminster and managed to get the police to lift their objections, the local planners turned me down. It simply meant I would have to go back and fight to have my topless nights at Stringfellow's. While my wrangles with Westminster were going on, I managed to get the same licence granted in Birmingham for a club called Tramps.

After Tramps, I was granted a topless licence for the Wriggly Worm Club in Manchester. History has repeated itself many times in my life, so I wasn't surprised to find myself back in Manchester, thirty years after I'd left the city, in the same club that had once been the Millionaire.

On 1 April 1996, I was finally granted the first table-side dancing licence in London. It was my third attempt at the licence and my second attempt for Stringfellow's. Although I'd hoped to build a new Cabaret of Angels I was happy to put the club within Stringfellow's for three nights a week. After the lady magistrate granted me the licence the local vicar, who had been in opposition, came over and said: 'Peter, where on earth is it going?'

'It's going beside the tables.'

'No, I mean where is it all going?'

'What, the business?'

'No, I mean everything.'

The vicar was a lovely man. We sat down and had a chat. I gave him a bit of my philosophy, which he seemed to appreciate. I told him that the prophets were the rock stars in Biblical times; people flocked to watch them as they do with pop stars today. The vicar seemed distressed that the young of today know too much too young. I told him that you can't stop everything; once the genie is out of the bottle you can't put it back.

I'm always amazed by people's opposition to change. The all-girl dancing club is the future. It's sexy and exciting. I'm looking forward to spending the rest of my life looking at gorgeous girls taking their clothes off. It's like 'here we go again'. One minute I've got the headlines for having the first topless club; the next, I'm on a centre spread in the *Sun* for seeing Helen Benoist, my sixteen-year-old girlfriend. Once again I'm on the merry-go-round of love, only this time I'm enjoying it.

People are always asking me why I continually take business risks. I do it because I enjoy it. It's not just about expanding my business, it's about expanding my lifestyle. I get a kick from going forward. I've spent my whole life pushing, pushing, pushing and moving on. I want to see this new concept accepted in Britain, then I want to relax.

As for retiring, what am I going to retire to? When I'm seventy I assume I'll still be in the club. My age-bracket peers, like Rod Stewart and Mick Jagger, just keep on going. I plan to do the same. A professional golfer doesn't retire. Maybe he retires from competitions, but he never retires from golf. I feel the same way about my nightclub.

As for the all-girl clubs, I've heard the criticisms: that it's morally bankrupt; that it exploits women. If I genuinely believed the girls were being exploited I wouldn't be involved. Women aren't the frightened creatures of the past century, waiting for their orders from men – they are powerful, independent people. The pill revolutionised women's lives. There was no going back after the 1960s. I've seen women's strength grow with every passing decade. Young girls no longer have to hide their sexuality. Feminists are forever telling me that I'm turning women into sex objects because I want a club where the girls dance topless. Their arguments are ridiculous. A woman's sexuality is her power and her strength. She can use it to the full and still be respected. Young girls in the nineties know the sexual power they have over men. I see it every night in my club. If a guy has to ask me how to get women, I know he doesn't stand a chance. My cologne helps, but I refuse to give a free plug to the company, so it'll have to stay a secret.

The majority of men aren't surrounded by beautiful girls every night of the week. I mentioned earlier that power is one of the greatest aphrodisiacs – sexual power, physical power, political power, financial power, mental power – any kind can obliterate physical shortcomings. It's a turn-on. I haven't got physical power or political power, but I know I've got mental power, which is knowledge, and financial power. Money makes me comfortable, warm and happy. Without it I'm cold, miserable and unhappy, which goes back to my childhood in Marshall Street when we didn't have any coal. It's not how much you've got in the bank, it's about how comfortable your life is. I've never been one to count the pennies. I still have difficulty counting the pounds. Cliff Silver, my financial director, tries to keep me in check, but at the end of the day it's my signature on the cheques. He came into my office recently and showed me a figure on top of a pile of restaurant chits: £5,000.

'What the fuck is this, Cliff?'

'It's your entertainment bill for last week.'

I wasn't surprised. Entertaining is my life. It's also my job. Sure, I eat caviar, drink champagne and chase girls, but it's hard work when you do it six nights a week. The only thing I'm less extravagant with these days is my poker games. I had my fingers burned at the Penthouse in Sheffield, but by the time I'd moved to Leeds my game had improved. My friend, Tunsh, would regularly play poker with me at Cinderella's–Rockafella's. At the Millionaire I'd play poker with my friend Asga. When I moved to London I never had any trouble getting a game, although the stakes were much higher – usually £2,000 a game. We'd play with four or five players and someone would walk away with £10,000 at the end of the night. My favourite is five-card stud, one card down, four up. It's a fierce game designed only for those who want to win money fast.

In New York I could never find anyone to play poker. One night my friend Hameed walked into Stringfellow's New York. Hameed was a big spender. His favourite drinks were Chivas Regal whisky and Crystal champagne. On this particular night he was looking for a poker game. Unfortunately, we couldn't find anyone else to play, so we ended up devising a game for two players. We went back to his suite at the Carlyle Hotel where John Neilson joined us as the dealer. He dealt four hands, but two were kept face down, so it was just Hameed and me playing against each other. Our cut-off time was 10a.m. the following morning.

The next day I walked out of the hotel with $10,000. The win was well timed as I needed to refurbish the cloakroom in New York and my winnings paid for the work. I didn't see Hameed for a while, but sure enough, the next time he walked into the club he was looking for a game. I always thought America was full of poker players, just like I'd seen in the old Chicago gangster movies. I had this image of a darkened room with glasses of whisky and plumes of cigar smoke. Unfortunately, I never found such a scene. Once again it was just Hameed and me, this time at the Hilton Hotel. We agreed on a $5,000 limit. Six hours later I walked out with $16,000. Yet again the win was timely. I'd wanted to upgrade the lighting in the club and my winnings paid for the work. I didn't see Hameed for a long, long time after that. To my surprise, he turned up at Stringfellow's London. I never had any trouble finding players in London in the eighties. After the club had closed that night, Hameed and I sat down with two other players, Alexander and Berak. Roberto, my restaurant manager, stayed behind to deal for us. The rule that night was either we all drank or nobody drank. I will not play poker with a non-drinker if I'm drinking, so we all decided to drink. The other rule was no women. I wanted the freedom to swear, to get angry and generally behave like men behave in an all-male environment. This was no hardship to Frizzby as she hated gambling.

By 9a.m. the next morning, only Hameed and I were left in the game. We'd started off with a stake of £1,000, but apart from the cash on the table we now had an awful lot of IOUs. The table was a blizzard with bits of paper. I was drunk, Hameed was drunk, but Roberto was sober. At 10a.m., Roberto insisted we play our last game. That's like a woman saying, 'OK, you can make love to me, but never, ever again.' Within minutes of starting the last game I had two eights, and must have thought I had another eight in my face-down cards. My other two face-up cards were a nine and a ten. Hameed was showing a jack, queen, king and an ace. I knew that if he had a ten in his face-down cards he'd have a run which would beat my three eights. I was sure he was bluffing, so I called pot. Hameed followed suit, and on and on it went until I eventually called his bluff. Sure enough he turned over a jack, which meant he had a pair of jacks and not a run. I triumphantly turned over my card and, fuck me, it wasn't an eight. I'd gambled all my money on nothing more than two eights. Hameed took away £8,000 plus the pile of IOUs. We both left the club staggering drunk, but happy. The following day Roberto rang me.

'How much do I owe, Roberto?'

'Are you still in bed?'

'No.'

'Maybe you should be.'

'Tell me. How much?'

'You owe Hameed £47,000.'

I phoned Hameed, hoping he would say, 'Forget it, we were both drunk.' I'd forgotten that I'd been happy to take his $10,000, then a further $16,000 from him in New York. That night I met him at Langan's and gave him a cheque for £47,000. I've never played poker since that night. It was a once-in-a-lifetime experience and too expensive to repeat.

I've spent my lifetime talking to different people. I'm immensely knowledgeable when it comes to human nature. One of the things I tell my girlfriends is, 'Tell me your problems and I can solve them.' And I usually can – it's mine I have difficulty solving. I'm brilliant at sorting out other people's love lives, but rubbish when it comes to my own.

I know that people see me in the papers and make judgements about me because I'm a nightclub owner. They see me surrounded by girls and make assumptions about my personality. I pride myself on being a gentleman; I'm certainly not vulgar or tacky. Like everyone else I can laugh at *Men Behaving Badly*, but in real life I hate that kind of laddishness. I'm always mortified if a guy tells a dirty joke in front of a girl at my table. In my club, if a guy ever points out a girl he's slept with, it's the last time he joins my table. In fact I've had guys thrown out for that. I'm fundamentally a ladies' man: I always give them the benefit of the doubt. If there is an argument between a boy and a girl, the boy goes out first.

I remember one night a girl coming over to me in floods of tears. 'Oh, Peter, he's horrible, he's over there.' She pointed to a guy at the bar.

'What's he said to you?'

'I can't tell you, it's too awful.'

'Don't worry, I'll get him out.'

I called over one of my staff and told him to remove the guy at the bar because he'd upset a young lady. I watched the guy being escorted outside and told the girl to sit down and tell me what the problem was. 'What exactly did he say to you?'

'He didn't say anything.'

'Well, what did he do to you?'

'He didn't do anything.'

'So what's the problem?'

'He brought his new girlfriend to the club.'

I quickly sent word to the doorman to get the guy back.

Sitting in the restaurant means I'm always on hand to make decisions. Nothing happens in my club without me seeing it at first hand, or at least hearing about it quickly. I very rarely ban people, only those who are totally obnoxious.

Not all of the stars behave well. One night I went to see Chuck Berry at the Hammersmith Odeon. After the concert I told his PR that I'd be delighted if he joined me later at the club. While I was waiting for Chuck a couple of the *EastEnders* stars came in and had a drink with me. I was so excited about Chuck Berry coming that I announced his impending arrival over the microphone, which, as I've said, is something I don't normally do. As I put the mike down Chuck walked in with his girlfriend. He ignored me totally and went to find a table in the restaurant. I went over and asked him what he'd like to drink and eat. He didn't answer me. The PR told me he was edgy because the music was too loud. I couldn't believe it. I'd just been blasted out of my seat at his concert. The PR said, 'Can you turn the music off? Chuck doesn't want to hear music.'

'But we're in the middle of a nightclub! Of course I can't turn it off.'

As I went over to talk to Chuck, he got up to leave. The PR said he would be going unless I did something about the music. I said goodbye to him and he walked out. Everybody in the club was watching. It served me right for announcing his arrival.

Later on that night, I was escorting one of the *EastEnders* stars to the door, when a group of four guys elbowed in past me. I asked my doorman why he'd just let in a bunch of thugs.

'Peter, you said Blur could come in any time they wanted.'

So that was Blur, the hot new band I'd been reading about for the last six months. They were yelling and shouting and causing such a scene that I told the doorman to ask them to leave.

The next week the *Melody Maker* ran a piece saying I'd spent the evening fawning over Blur. I wrote a letter back saying that Blur were a bunch of obnoxious little shits and that they were shouting for substances which we didn't sell in Stringfellow's, so they had best stay out of my club. I sent the letter, then remembered the Eddie Murphy incident and wondered whether I'd gone too far. Their manager called me a few days later and said the boys wanted to make it up. A couple of them came back and Damon Albarn and I ended up having a brilliant evening. He was annoyed that the letter implied he was asking for drugs: he is very anti-drugs, as I am, so we got along fine.

Even after they've read this book there will still be people who won't believe my stance on illegal drugs. It doesn't matter how many times I say it, people still, albeit only occasionally, ask me for coke, or whether I'd mind if they rolled a joint.

One night Nirj Deva, the Conservative MP for Brentford and Isleworth, came in with a group of his Asian friends. He told me before they sat down that his friends were in fact a group of dignitaries he was treating to dinner. After the first course, Nirj called me over. 'Peter, can you do me a favour? My friend says he wants a joint.'

I was horrified. Before he could say another word I launched into my monologue about drugs. 'I'm surprised at you, Nirj. First, I don't take drugs, and secondly, I don't supply them. How could a man in your position ask me for such a thing so publicly?'

Nirj listened in wide-eyed shock. 'Peter, what the hell are you talking about?'

'Nirj, you just asked me for a joint.'

'Are you crazy? I simply asked if my friend could join your club.'

Nirj and I still laugh about that incident.

Drink, of course, is another matter. One night Courtney Love came into the club and challenged me to a drinking contest. I knew that her husband, Kurt Cobain, had recently committed suicide but I didn't know anything about his band, Nirvana, or Courtney's band, Hole. I told her straight away that there was no way she could drink me under the table because she was a girl. There was another very good reason for my certainty, which was that she was half cut before we even sat down.

Forty-five minutes later, a couple of Courtney's aides and I gently helped her into a taxi. The next night she came back to the club. This time she was determined to really drink me under the table. We drank all night until the lights came up. I invited her to my apartment next door and she agreed to join me. One of her aides told me they were worried about Courtney getting back to the hotel. I asked her if she wanted a cab.

'No. Can I stay at your place?'

'Well, yes, but I've only got one bed.'

'That's OK.'

That was a problem. I liked the girl, but I certainly didn't fancy her.

We went up to my apartment anyway. She was a lovely kid. I remember her showing me pictures of her small child before we went to bed. We didn't have sex. We took a jacuzzi together, then went to bed to sleep.

The following day I kept getting calls from people saying it wasn't Courtney who had been in the club. Andy Coulson from the *Sun* was adamant that it wasn't her. 'Peter, she was a lookalike.'

'Andy, it was Courtney.'

'I bet you £400 it wasn't her.'

'It's a deal. You prove it wasn't her.'

We eventually upped the bet to £1,000, which both of us agreed would go to charity. On Hallowe'en night in 1995 Courtney turned up again, this time wearing a long black witch's wig. Someone rang the buzzer of my apartment and a voice said, 'Hello, Peter, I'm here with Courtney Love.'

'Put her on the phone.'

'Hi, Peter.'

'Hi, Courtney. Will you say the word "OK"?'

'Okaaay.'

'Fine, you can come up.'

One of the things I remembered about Courtney was the way she said, 'OK,' in a slightly sing-song way. It was very distinctive.

'So what's all this crap about it not being you in the club that night?'

'Being caught in Peter Stringfellow's jacuzzi is not the kind of image I want to portray, and anyway, you called the *Sun*.'

'I didn't call the *Sun*. One of the photographers called the *Sun*.'

Courtney had a drink with me, then left, and I was satisfied that it was her. Andy Coulson was still adamant she was a lookalike. The matter was resolved in January 1996. He ran a piece in his 'Bizarre' column asking the readers to identify the girl in the picture with me, the girl I was *convinced* was Courtney Love. To my amazement, someone identified her as a girl called Siobhan who worked at a hostess bar. I'm always happy to admit when I'm wrong. I gave £1,000 to the appointed charity and invited Siobhan to dinner. The girl certainly had chutzpah, although not enough to take up my offer.

No club in Britain, or the world, receives as much publicity as Stringfellow's. People are often asking me who my PR company is. I don't have one. People are fascinated by the club and my lifestyle. Only once has the media's attention got wildly out of control. I now describe it as my fat fiasco. It happened during the heatwave of 1995 when the club's air-conditioning was at full stretch. On one very hot night I went into the club early, around 11 o'clock. I was standing at the bar talking to a businessman. He'd been to my clubs in America and was telling me how wonderful he thought Stringfellow's was. As we were chatting I looked over his shoulder for a second and saw what can only be described as a shuffling tent. The apparition shuffled past me wearing a big black dress, a black shawl and black slippers. On top of that she was carrying a green plastic bag – not from Harrods, I hasten to add. The whole image was horrible. A nightclub's success is based on the quality of its crowd. People get refused from Stringfellow's and other clubs for a variety of reasons: too small, too tall, too ugly, too drunk, too loud and, yes, too fat. People judge the club on the people that they see. A shuffling tent is not our image. I immediately called the doorman over.

'What the hell are you doing, letting in someone looking like that?'

'Like what?'

I looked around. The woman had gone. I described her slobby appearance and sent him off to look for her. I called over my brother Paul. I told him the story and he joined in the search. Neither Paul nor the doorman could find her. The doorman reassured me she'd left. He explained that she'd arrived with three other girls who were all pretty and slim.

'I don't care who she came with, when a woman's as fat as that and slobbing it in terrible clothes, don't let her in.'

After Paul had gone back to the restaurant and the doorman back to the door, a guy at the bar asked me if I was banning fat girls. I didn't question who he was, I simply told him the story. I went into my whole door philosophy and the image of Stringfellow's. With that he introduced himself as Peter Willis from the *Sun*. I laughed, thinking it might get into the pages of the 'Bizarre' column. I never in my wildest imagination thought it would make front-page news, neither did I imagine it would start a furore around the world.

The story made every television news bulletin. I had journalists phoning me from radio stations as far away as Tokyo and Australia. The further away the inquiries, the more outrageous I became, yet at home I was desperately trying to back-pedal.

'Hi, this is Sydney radio, I hear you've banned fat girls.'

'Yes, that's right. No fat guy, or girl, is allowed in my club. Stringfellow's is full of beautiful people and celebrities and that's the way I want it to stay.'

'Hi, this is Essex radio, I hear you've banned fat girls.'

'Well, not really.'

'Do you mean that only fat celebrities can get in?'

'Well, yes, and ordinary people if they're not too fat and badly dressed.'

'Can you explain a bit more, Peter?'

'Well, I've only banned fat people if they're slobby.'

The more I said, the worse it got. Within days I had women with placards standing outside the club, and lots and lots of fat people. I went into Mr Nice Guy mode and tried to play the whole thing down. Slowly but surely, the affair died down, but it never went away completely. At least once a week, my PA, Pat

Jay, gets a call from someone wanting to make a booking for a group of girls.

'We're all size 10, except one of us is a size 16. Will that be all right?' Or, 'Can you tell me what the maximum dress size is for Stringfellow's?' Pat diplomatically deals with the calls. Of course, there is no size limit; it's how a person is dressed. It's sod's law that if the door lets someone in they shouldn't have, that person will stand in front of me at some stage in the evening.

Stringfellow's is like a soap opera. The setting is always the same, but the plot and the characters change on a nightly basis. People look at my lifestyle and think one of two things: either that I'm the luckiest man on earth, or that I'm the Devil incarnate. To some people it would be hell on earth, to others it would be heaven. To me it's simply my life. I've often wondered where my talent lies, if indeed I have a talent. I can't sing; I can't play a musical instrument; I'm not a sportsman or a statesman. The only thing I'm good at is being Peter Stringfellow.

Just that.

INDEX